THE GRIZZLY BEAR: *Portraits from Life*

THE GRIZZLY BEAR

Portraits from Life

Edited and with an Introduction by
BESSIE DOAK HAYNES and EDGAR HAYNES

with drawings by Mary Baker

UNIVERSITY OF OKLAHOMA PRESS : NORMAN

LIBRARY OF CONGRESS CATALOG CARD NUMBER: 66–10290

Copyright © 1966 by the University of Oklahoma Press, Norman, Publishing Division of the University of Oklahoma. Manufactured in the U.S.A. First edition, 1966; second printing, 1967; third printing, 1979; fourth printing, 1981.

ACKNOWLEDGMENTS

THANKS ARE DUE many people who helped us assemble the stories published in this book. Almost all of these kind people have left the positions they held when the book first appeared in 1966. We still wish to give them the credit they deserve: our sincere thanks are again extended to the staff of the Yakima Valley Regional Library, especially to Geneva Rand and Loretta Barringer, former interlibrary loan clerks at that library; to Alan Baldridge, formerly of the Portland Library Association; and to Priscilla Knuth, still working as research associate at the Oregon Historical Society. We regretfully note that Arthur McAnally, former director of the University of Oklahoma Library, is no longer with us. He and Mrs. Glenda Guilinger, administrative secretary of that library, are well remembered for their assistance, as is Arrell M. Gibson, George Lynn Cross Professor of History, University of Oklahoma. Cecil Lee Chase, no longer with the Bancroft Library at the University of California at Berkeley, was a great help to us, as were research librarians at the University of California Library, Southern Methodist University Library, University of Arizona Library, and the El Paso and Phoenix public libraries. We also would like to thank the Washington State Library and all the other libraries who loaned us books through the interlibrary loan system.

We should like to express our gratitude to the Fish and Game Departments of Alaska, Arizona, California, Colorado, Idaho, Montana, New Mexico, North Dakota, Oregon, Utah, Washington and Wyoming and particularly to Albert W. Erickson, formerly of the Alaska Department of Fish and Game, and to Jack W. Lentfer, present regional supervisor of the division of game for that state, who has kindly furnished us information on new methods of handling grizzly bears. We also wish to remember the help given us by R. J. Smith, former director of the Arizona Game and Fish Department, for permission to use portions of *Arizona State Bulletin, Bear No. 13-58*. Mr. Smith is now with the United States Fish and Wildlife Service. We wish to thank Ladd S. Gordon, former director of New Mexico Department of Fish and Game, along with Levon Lee, former chief of game management of the above department. Both Mr. Gordon and Mr. Lee have retired from the New Mexico Department of Game and Fish. P. W. Schneider, former director, and Mr. Cal Giesler, formerly with the information and education division, Oregon State Game Commission, granted permission for publication of "Bugle and Trailer in a Battle Royal." Thanks are due the National Wildlife Federation for permission to use excerpts from "Wilderness Monarch," by Robert F. Cooney, as well as to the late Harold S. Crane, former director, and James H. Hardman, former information specialist, Utah Division of Wildlife Resources, for sending us Frank Clark's story of the killing of Old Ephraim and for granting permission to reprint it. We also wish to thank Elliott S. Barker for permission to use his informative letter on grizzly depredations in New Mexico. Most especially we wish to thank Frank Craighead, Jr., and his brother John Craighead for data on the Yellowstone Park grizzly-bear project they researched from 1959 to 1971. Excerpts from Frank Craighead's articles, "Trailing Yellowstone Grizzlies by Radio," in the August, 1966, *National Geographic*, and "They're Killing Yellowstone's Grizzlies," in the October, 1973, *Natural Wildlife*, and John Craighead's article, "Studying Grizzly Habitat by Satellite," from the July, 1976, *National Geographic*, are acknowledged here, as is Christopher Cauble's article, "The Great Grizzly Grabble," from *Natural History*, August, 1977. We also wish to thank Maurice Hornocker, formerly with the Montana Cooperative Wildlife Research Unit, now with the Idaho Cooperative Wildlife Research Unit, for sending us information. Countless others helped us in many different ways, and to them we are also grateful.

BESSIE DOAK HAYNES AND EDGAR HAYNES

vi

INTRODUCTION

It is difficult to believe that grizzly bears, of monstrous size and ferocity, were once as common in California as they still are in Alaska. That the big brutes were a constant menace to the early explorers, fur trappers, and cattlemen is common knowledge; that one of the famous Sublette brothers died of wounds given him by a grizzly he met in a canyon back of Santa Monica seems utterly fantastic now that these canyons are close-built with the mansions of millionaires and motion-picture queens.

There is no record of a living bear of the grizzly species in California—the state whose emblem is the Great Golden Bear—since 1922. What happened to the bears which inhabited the coastal thickets and the wilderness of the Sierras?

The California Department of Fish and Game tells the story succinctly: "The grizzly was not afforded protection and as the land developed, if there was a conflict [with the settlers], the grizzly was killed. It was primarily a valley and low foothill country animal and would not, or could not, recede from the encroachment of civilization."

Legend and fact are inseparably intermingled in the history of this great bear. Vague references about bear are encountered in records of the Spanish conquest of the southwestern United States and Mexico. Journals of the Hudson's Bay Company agents contain accounts, laced with incredulity, of the bear's great size and fury. The agents wrote of him as "the white bear," "Yellow Bear," "coloured Bear," and the "grey" or "grisled" bear, but by the size, claw length, and the fineness of his fur the varicolored bear is readily recognizable as of the grizzly species.

Lewis and Clark provided some of the earliest scientific reports on grizzly bears within the present boundaries of the western states. From the Indians they learned of the invulnerability of the brutes and of their ferociousness. The explorers soon found their muzzle-loaders scarcely more effective against grizzly bears than the Indians' stone-tipped spears and arrows. Journals of the fur trappers who followed Lewis and Clark over the Rockies and down the Columbia during the early part of the nineteenth century contain vivid references to encounters with the big bears. The big-game hunters came in the mid-1880's, along with cattlemen, sheepmen, and gold seekers. On their heels came the men and women who settled the Far West. To all of them the grizzly bear was a fair target, either for sport or economic reasons, or for personal safety. Some slew bears for their hides and tallow; others ate bear meat or sold it for food; the cattle- and sheepmen considered the grizzly a predator and exterminated him. The wilderness diminished in size, and the grizzly vanished from alder thicket and mountaintop.

He was once found throughout western North America, from Mexico to the Arctic Circle. His former habitat extended westward from the Mississippi River through what is now Kansas, Nebraska, Texas, and the Dakotas, to the coast of California and the Cascade Mountains of Washington and Oregon; over the Canadian provinces of Saskatchewan and British Columbia and the territories of the Yukon and MacKenzie. Now the grizzly bear is found in few places. Montana still has a considerable number in the primitive areas in and around Yellowstone and Glacier national parks, the Bob Marshall Wilderness Area, and the Bitterroot, Cabinet, and Mission mountains. There are probably fifty grizzlies within the borders of Idaho, with half a dozen supposedly spilling over into adjoining northeastern Washington State. There may be a few of the big bears left in Colorado, and Wyoming still has about fifty.

In Alaska the picture is brighter. The grizzly range in Canada has retreated westward, but there is still an abundance of wilderness habitat in the Selkirk Mountains and along coastal streams where the salmon spawn. Civilization has not yet crowded the

Yukon and MacKenzie territory domains of the big bears. The Alaska Department of Fish and Game provides an encouraging report:

> The numbers of brown-grizzly bears in Alaska are known only generally. However, it would appear on the basis of legal harvests ... and our surveys of bears that a population in excess of 10,000 bears exist within the State. The population on Kodiak Island alone is estimated to number at least 1,600 bears on the basis of a fifteen-year sustained average annual kill by sport hunters of about 175 bears. The adjacent Alaska Peninsula, containing seven times the area of Kodiak Island, appears to sustain a similar population density. Elsewhere in the state substantial populations are known to exist on Admiralty, Chicagof and Baranof Islands and at least sparse populations exist over practically the entire Alaska Mainland.

Regional Supervisor Jack W. Lentfer, State of Alaska Department of Fish and Game, provides the following encouraging information on Alaska grizzlies:

> Our population estimate for Admiralty, Baranof, and Chicagof Islands in Southeast Alaska is 2,000 to 2,500. [Density estimates for the Alaska Peninsula and Kodiak Island were not available when Lentfer wrote in November, 1978.]
>
> Since 1966 many new developments in handling grizzly and brown bears have occurred. Different immobilizing drugs are more positive, consistent, and safer for the bears. Animals are immobilized from helicopters. This is more efficient than using traps and snares and allows biologists to be selective for the animals they want. Radio tracking is a highly developed art and provides better and more complete data than was previously obtained by mark and recapture only.

The rest of the West presents a different picture. Complete extinction of the grizzly has taken place throughout most of its historic range. The situation in Arizona is dismal:

> In the early days of Arizona's history the grizzly bear was an important member of the wildlife community. His habits were not compatible with the advance of civilization in Arizona,

however, and he has, during the last few decades, been considered extinct in this state. Occasionally reports are heard of individuals having seen a "grizzly," but none of these reports have been verified for many years.[1]

New Mexico game officials paint a similar picture:

The last grizzlies known to have occurred in New Mexico were killed in the mid–1930's. This was in the Gila country in southwestern New Mexico. One of them was killed at the head of Diamond Creek in the Black Range some forty or fifty miles to the east. None others have been reported in the state since then. Occasionally, reports are received in this office of grizzly bear occurrences, but we doubt their validity.

The only grizzlies left close to New Mexico are those very few found in southwestern Colorado with a few still found in Mexico. From tales we have heard, the grizzly bear of the southwestern mountains of New Mexico was a particularly fierce one. It is the subspecies known as the Mogollon (Mogey-own) grizzly and there are many tales of hunters and prospectors being attacked and seriously mauled if not killed by these animals.

Grizzlies definitely caused trouble with the cattlemen in this state, both in the Sangre de Cristo Mountains of Northern New Mexico and the Gila Mountains of southwestern New Mexico.[2]

Mr. Elliott Barker, professional trapper and hunter, forest ranger and supervisor, director of the New Mexico Game and Fish Department from 1931 to 1953, and himself reared on a mountain ranch, presents a strong case for the cattlemen:

I feel very strongly that the assumption that grizzly bears originally fed on carrion and rarely attacked or killed cattle themselves is entirely wrong. My personal experience and the experience of others in New Mexico will not bear out any such theory.

I will give you a number of specific cases of serious depredations of which I have personal knowledge, but first I want to give you my personal theory, which I think has some backing, as to

[1] *Arizona Game Bulletin, Bear No. 13–58*, Arizona Game and Fish Department.
[2] Letter to author from New Mexico Department of Game and Fish, October 15, 1963.

x

just what happened in New Mexico and perhaps in other states as well. I believe that the grizzlies originally killed elk as their natural prey. They could catch an elk all right whereas they might not so readily be able to catch a deer as a mountain lion can. Then when the Whiteman came he killed off all the elk, and . . . by about 1890 in New Mexico all of our elk had been exterminated. In their place the Whiteman put cattle and sheep back in the mountain country which was a natural grizzly range. However, by that time grizzlies had also been reduced in New Mexico by hunters and trappers. By being deprived of its natural prey the grizzly readily took to the killing of cattle and sheep. That seems to me to be a very natural assumption.

Now as to specific instances that I know of—in 1907 or 1908 some of the cattlemen up in the Chacon–Black Lake area sent for me to come up there to get rid of some bears that were killing their stock very regularly. I went up and looked the situation over and found that it was grizzlies that were doing the damage. However, just about the time I got up there a local stockman had killed a couple of grizzlies which no doubt were the ones doing the damage, and I did not remain to kill any more.

In the spring of 1908 a grizzly bear with two cubs killed three head of cattle that I know of in the Mora Flats area. I took that bear and the cubs and also a large male grizzly.

In 1913 while I was Forest Ranger on the Carson National Forest, my father was running cattle on the Beaver Creek area of the Santa Fe National Forest. A grizzly came into that area and in a period of fifteen days killed fourteen head of grown cattle, that is, yearlings or over, including a four-year-old Hereford bull, and a number of calves. This hurt pretty badly because I was half owner of the cattle that he killed. The same bear was periodically going over into the Pecos country and killing stock. I cannot recall now just who killed this particular bear but he was taken.

By 1923 grizzlies had become scarce in that particular area but one went on a rampage in what is now known as the Pecos Wilderness area and killed several head of cattle of George Viles, then owner of the Mountainview Ranch. Then he came across the mountain into the Beaver Creek Country where I was then running cattle out of my ranch on the Sapello Creek. He killed a two-year-old steer and a cow and a calf for me in one night and ate only a comparatively small amount off of the cow and did not eat any of either the steer or calf but the evidence of his killing them was conclusive. I rode back to the ranch and phoned George Viles that the grizzly was headed back his way and to be on the lookout. Viles advised me that he had fortunately killed the bear that very morning. The Game Department, as you know, now has that bear skin in a case on exhibit there.

In 1911 I was Forest Ranger on the Pecos with headquarters at Panchuela Ranger Station. Two grizzlies killed several head of cattle in the . . . area. There were some guests at the Mountainview Ranch from Kansas who were very anxious to kill a grizzly and I went with them and set traps at one of the kills and in a period of two days we took the two grizzlies plus a cub.

The grizzly taken in 1923 was the last one in the Pecos area, and one taken in the Gila National Forest by George W. Evans in 1930 or 1931 was the last resident grizzly in that area, although I saw a track near Eagle Peak in 1932. The grizzly that George W. Evans took was a regular stock killer.

. . . . In 1915 or 1916, I am not sure of the year, some grizzlies went on the rampage in the Pot Creek country and killed quite a number of sheep and cattle. M. E. Musgrave, who was then with the U.S. Geological Survey, came up there to try to relieve that damage and he was successful in taking an old grizzly in a trap and captured two cubs which I believe were sent to the national zoo. At any rate, I helped him crate the cubs there at Taos. I know of all of these killings of my own personal information and I have reports of many other killings that took place in the Pecos and Taos country in earlier years when grizzlies were plentiful, but I have listed only those of which I have personal knowledge.

It is certainly too bad that the grizzly is just not compatible with livestock back in the mountain country. He might be more so in an area which had been restocked with elk, which I firmly believe was his natural prey. I personally regret very much that the grizzly had to be exterminated from New Mexico but there just seems to be no possibility for coexistence of grizzlies in areas used by livestock. . . . [3]

[3] Letter, November 27, 1963, Elliott Barker to Levon Lee, chief of game management, New Mexico.

Game officials of other range-land states tell a similar story. From the Utah Department of Fish and Game comes this report:

> The grizzly bear never has been abundant in Utah and from research I find that the last recorded one in this State was in 1923. . . .
>
> Bears have never been classed as game animals, thus allowing, at the insistence of the livestock people, that they be hunted with no restrictions. Usually, all bear in this State are killed upon sight, despite the requests from our Department that they be spared. There is some hope and optimism among Department officials and biologists now that the livestock people have come to realize the folly of their blanket vengeance upon the species and that soon, perhaps, these animals will be able to take their rightful place among the elite "game" class.
>
> While the grizzly is to our knowledge extinct in Utah, there are enough black bear around for a good population nucleus, and we are looking forward to the day when we can do some management work with them.[4]

A Washington Game Department official, by letter of October 23, 1963, gives that state's grizzly picture as follows:

> We presently calculate that there are approximately eight to ten grizzly bears in the state of Washington. As far as we have been able to determine, this number has remained relatively stable for the past twenty-five or thirty years.
>
> This small nucleus persists in the northeastern section of the state. Some old records indicate that grizzlies at one time were found in parts of north-central Washington. It is our opinion that the grizzly did not exist in any great numbers in the past.
>
> We have one or two cases where the grizzly was taken in northeastern Washington in the period between 1945 and 1950. As you probably are aware, there was a case in the Okanogan country during the fifties when a grizzly was supposed to have been killing cattle. Although the local community organized hunts to eliminate this marauder, to our knowledge it was never taken. We have never known of an attack on humans in this state.
> [In 1883 William H. Wright, who in later years was a noted guide

[4] Letter to author from James M. Hardman, information specialist, Utah Department of Fish and Game, November 8, 1963.

and big-game hunter, reportedly saw eleven grizzlies on his first weekend hunting trip in the vicinity of Spokane, Washington!]

Because of the inability of most people to determine the difference between the grizzly and the black bear, they have never been protected in Washington, and even though open hunting has been allowed, the numbers present have not been affected by hunting.

At the eastern extremity of the grizzly's former range, the silvertip bear vanished at an even earlier date, as reported by the North Dakota Game and Fish Department:

> The grizzly bear has been extinct in North Dakota since around the turn of the century. The last authentic report we have of one being killed dates back to 1897 when an individual named Dave Warren accompanied by a boy killed two grizzlies near the small community of Oakdale on the eastern edges of the Killdeer Mountains.
>
> The grizzly apparently was quite numerous in North Dakota until the 1870's and 1880's when stockmen and eastern hunters moved into the state in considerable numbers.[5]

In Oregon, another livestock state, there has never been a closed season on grizzly bear, nor have they been treated as a game animal. The last recorded grizzly was killed September 14, 1931, by a government trapper in Wallowa County in the northeastern part of the state.[6]

In those areas where the grizzly bear still has a claw-hold on his wilderness domain, his rights are being given some consideration and his way of life is being studied to determine how best to perpetuate the species. The state of Alaska is conducting a detailed study to determine numbers, age composition, characteristics of harvest, and population trends of brown and grizzly bears, which recent taxonomic studies classify as being of the same species, and of the polar bears, in order to formulate future management procedures. Hunters are allowed to take one bear, with the killing of cubs or females accompanied by cubs prohibited.

[5] Letter to author from Pershing Y. Carlson, chief, Public Relations Division, North Dakota Game and Fish Department, October 15, 1963.
[6] Letter from Oregon State Game Commission, October 28, 1963.

Aircraft may no longer be legally used to drive, herd, or molest game and are allowed only as transportation to a pre-existing camp on the Alaska Peninsula. Skins of bears, as well as those of beavers and sea otters, must be presented to an authorized representative of the Game Department for inspection and sealing before being transported elsewhere. This procedure has permitted the collection of exact data on the number, population composition, distribution and chronology of kill, hunter success, etc. The 1963 brown-grizzly bear kill in Alaska totaled 211 for the spring season and 305 for the fall season, according to a letter from Albert W. Erickson, project leader of the bear investigations jointly financed by the state of Alaska and the federal government through funds available under the Federal Aid in Wildlife Restoration Act.

A project with a similar purpose was conducted in Yellowstone National Park through the co-operation of the National Park Service, Yellowstone Park Company, the Montana Cooperative Wildlife Research Unit, United States Fish and Wildlife Service, Montana State Fish and Game Department, Montana State University, and the Wildlife Management Institute. Initiated in 1959, the project was supported by a five-year grant from the National Science Foundation and from annual grants from the Research and Exploration Committee of the National Geographic Society, Boone and Crockett Club, and the National Park Service. Radio tracking of Yellowstone grizzlies was financed by a three-year grant from the National Science Foundation and Philco Corporation.[7] This intensive study of grizzly bears has provided a great deal of information on the species.

From 1959 to 1971 Frank Craighead, Jr., and his brother John Craighead conducted an intensive study of the Yellowstone Park grizzlies under the grants previously mentioned. They captured, measured, and physically examined 391 grizzlies. Two hundred of these animals were tagged, color-marked, and equipped with tiny radios that enabled the researchers to trace their movements. Many of these animals were captured more than once, either to move them away from campgrounds or to re-examine them.

[7] See Frank and John Craighead, "Knocking Out Grizzly Bears for Their Own Good," *National Geographic Magazine*, Vol. 118, No. 2 (August, 1960).

Using radio tracking and visual sighting of the tagged bears, the Craigheads ascertained that there were from 175 to 250 grizzlies in Yellowstone Park. They discovered that both sexes are promiscuous; that male cubs outnumber females two to one at birth, but at age four the sexes are equally numerous; and that adult females are more numerous than adult males. They also found that the grizzly bear's average life span is only five to six years and that killing of problem bears by park personnel within the park accounted for eighteen percent of grizzly mortalities. Hunters caused another forty percent of the deaths when the bears roamed outside the park boundaries. Disease, senility, mortal combat, and starvation further decimated the species.[8]

In an article published in 1973, Frank Craighead wrote:

> The grizzly population was moving from the back country of Yellowstone and adjacent forest lands into the open meadows and sagebrush areas of Yellowstone. They came into these areas because earth-fill garbage dumps were located nearby . . . [the dumps] are part of the ecology and the situation could not be suddenly altered without affecting their [the bears'] behavior, their movements, their reproductive success, and the mortality rate of the grizzly bear population.[9]

Because of the infiltration of backwoods bears into areas where tourist movements are most dense and because the animals congregated at the garbage dumps, a great controversy developed in 1967. The National Park Service decided to close all the dumps as quickly as possible, while the Craigheads recommended that this project should be phased out slowly and that supplemental rations, such as elk carcasses, should be made available to the bears during the transition period. Rather than agree with the scientists' proposals the park superintendent banned further marking of grizzlies. When the bears were captured in campgrounds or other areas where visitors came in contact with them, ear tags were removed and radiotelemetry equipment stripped off and confiscated by park

[8] Frank and John Craighead, "Trailing Yellowstone's Grizzlies by Radio," *National Geographic Magazine*, Vol. 130, No. 2 (August, 1966), 255.
[9] Craighead, Frank, Jr., "They're Killing Yellowstone's Grizzlies," *National Wildlife*, Vol. 11 (October, 1973), 4.

personnel. In 1971 the Craigheads were barred from further research in the park.[10]

Since 1971 the National Park Service has not permitted an independent census of Yellowstone's grizzlies but has relied upon haphazard "sightings" by park personnel and other observers who have questionable qualifications. Between 319 and 364 grizzlies were sighted in 1974 by those observers within the entire Yellowstone ecosystem. On the basis of their computer model, the Craigheads projected a 1974 population of between 82 and 233 grizzlies, with 136 being the most probable number.[11]

On September 12, 1976, a man was killed and devoured by a grizzly in Glacier Bay National Monument in Alaska. Shortly afterward two young women were killed and three other persons were mauled in Montana's Glacier National Park (only three other persons had been killed by bears in Glacier since 1913, while outdoor accidents had accounted for 69 deaths). One man was killed in Yellowstone, and others were mauled. There were 1,662,678 tourists visiting Yellowstone Park that summer, an increase of 5.8 percent over the previous year. Glacier Park was equally crowded. It was obvious that the great influx of people was a major cause of grizzly-bear incidents, caused particularly by tourists who ignored park personnel's admonitions against feeding or petting bears.

Tourists were up in arms when they learned that garbage dumps were attracting bears, and they demanded that the grizzlies should be isolated. Secretary of Interior Rogers C. B. Morton asked the National Academy of Sciences to enter the debate between the National Park Service and the conservationists. The academy issued a report in 1974 which vindicated neither the Craigheads nor the National Park Service. The NPS was criticized for excluding the Craighead brothers from Yellowstone Park and for shabby data collection methods. The Craigheads were rebuked for relying on computers to compile grizzly population figures. The academy scientists agreed that there was a grizzly bear conflict![12]

[10] Ibid, 5.
[11] Christopher Cauble, "The Great Grizzly Grabble," *Natural History*, Vol. 86 (August, 1977), 79.
[12] Ibid, 29.

As a result of the Craigheads' work in Yellowstone Park and the untiring work of local and national conservationists, the Endangered Species Act of 1973 was amended to include *Ursus horribilis* as a threatened animal.[13] At about the same time Montana conservationists proposed the creation of a 282,600-acre wilderness area in the Flathead National Forest and 136,000-acre area in Lewis and Clark National Forest in order to protect both the forest and the bears' environment.[14] In the fall of 1978 the Department of Agriculture proposed that Glacier National Park should be closed, making it a wilderness area. Neither of these plans have yet been implemented.

In 1973 John Craighead, aided by Steve Ford, son of President Ford, and others, began working on satellite computer maps in Montana's Scapegoat Wilderness, where they felt the maps could point out grizzly habitat in barely accessible wilderness. When the project actually got under way, the satellite maps showed "activity centers" where grizzlies congregated to feed. It was found that the grizzlies' favorite foraging grounds lie in the rocky vegetation at about 8,500 feet.[15] If the pesky bears could only be persuaded to remain at this altitude, far away from humans, perhaps the great grizzly controversy might subside, but this is not probable.

A bear-management program in Colorado failed for lack of subjects. A. D. Coleman, assistant game manager, State of Colorado Department of Game, Fish and Parks, reported on the attempted conservation project as follows:

> Several years ago we set up a grizzly-bear management area in the San Juan Mountains. This was for the purpose of protecting the grizzly and we have had meager information that there were a few of these animals in this area.
>
> A close check has been maintained, and so far no grizzly has been seen. Outside this refuge, we have seasons on bear (which includes the grizzly) and we have no authentic report on any of this species having been killed for game in twenty years.

[13] John Craighead, "Studying Grizzly Habitat by Satellite," *National Geographic*, Vol. 150, No. 1 (July, 1976), 149.
[14] Dale A. Burk, "Let's Give the Bears a Break," *American Forest*, November, 1972, p. 17.
[15] John Craighead, *loc. cit.*, 157.

We feel we have very few of these animals in the state. Some accounts originating in the early days tell of attacks upon humans by grizzlies, but mostly by wounded animals.[16]

According to the Idaho Fish and Game Department:

The grizzly has been protected in Idaho since 1947, although it is lawful for any bear to be taken if it is found to be molesting livestock. For that reason, we do have an occasional grizzly bear killed. The last one that comes to mind is one taken north of the Clark Fork River in northern Idaho about two years ago [i.e. 1961].

We still maintain a listing of about fifty grizzly bears in the state although this is only a rough estimate. We do know that there are a few in eastern Idaho adjacent to Yellowstone National Park, another few in the Bitterroot Range in north central Idaho, and possibly a few more in the Cabinet Range north and west of Lake Pend Oreille.

The one that was killed in the Clark Fork area a couple of years ago, apparently a stock killer, is the only record we have of a grizzly being killed in recent years.[17]

The state of Wyoming, with a vivid history of grizzlies, now considers them game animals. Special hunting seasons are set aside for both grizzly and black bears, and either may be hunted each fall in all areas open for deer and/or elk. Only five to ten grizzlies per season are taken by hunters in this state, with public hunting of bears not permitted in Yellowstone National Park, of course. Most of Wyoming's grizzlies are located in areas bordering the Park and in the Park itself, and the population seems to be remaining stable, according to information from the Wyoming Game and Fish Commission.

A large grizzly-bear closed area was in effect in Montana between 1942 and 1955, and spring hunting has been discontinued throughout the state. More than four hundred silvertips were reported in Montana in 1955–56, exclusive of those in the National Parks. However, this figure is not confirmed by the Montana

[16] Letter to author, October 21, 1963.
[17] Letter to author from E. Kleiss Brown, chief, Information and Education, Idaho Fish and Game Department.

Department of Fish and Game. Present regulations allow an open season on grizzlies, outside the national parks, each fall during the legal elk season. About forty or fifty grizzlies are taken each year, according to Game Department officials, and the kill has been fairly static in recent years, indicating that the grizzly population is holding its own in the wild areas.

"Several stock-killing grizzlies are taken each year by government trappers. There are few records of grizzly attacking humans in our state," a Montana official reports. "Ordinary precaution in grizzly country, such as staying away from females with cubs, is a must."

What chance is there for the grizzly's survival in its present restricted domain? In an article by Co-ordinator Robert F. Cooney, of the Wildlife Restoration Division, National Wildlife Federation, the grizzly bear's future is explored realistically:

> In facing the problem squarely, we must admit that valuable as the grizzly bear is, it cannot be perpetuated in substantial numbers in close proximity with important agricultural activities. Its future, therefore, will depend upon our success in retaining a reasonable amount of wilderness range.
>
> The Wilderness Area Program throughout the West represents an additional important factor. A good example of this is the Bob Marshall Wilderness Area in Montana. This mountainous region covers approximately a million acres, plus a substantial fringe of roadless country beyond its borders. This wilderness area, accessible only by trails, represents the most important single factor in the maintenance of the largest grizzly-bear population in the United States (exclusive of Alaska).
>
> It is obvious that we cannot restore the grizzly to anything like its former numbers or range. We must in fairness to the animals and to the economy of the West, consider the grizzly as a wilderness species. It is upon the preservation of these wilderness areas that the future of the grizzly in the United States will depend.[18]

"Old Ephraim," as the mountain men dubbed him, was ever a source of deep fascination to all who had an opportunity to study

[18] "Wilderness Monarch," *Our Endangered Wildlife* (1955), 17.

him. He was, and is, undoubtedly the most intelligent and most invincible game animal to inhabit this continent, if not the entire world. The Indian and the grizzly lived for many centuries in a state of primeval feud—the white man vanquished the grizzly in one century's time. But each of the men who left a record of their encounters with the big grizzled bears saw something different in his habits and character. Whether this is because of a difference in human observations, a difference in individual bears, or the obvious differences in the subspecies and their habitat is a point of conjecture. The variety of impressions of both early-day and contemporary hunters and naturalists enhances the fascination of this man-maiming, cattle-killing buffoon of the wilds. The collection of grizzly-bear stories presented herewith has been selected to provide a many-faceted account, extending over a period of two centuries. In assembling it from a mass of material, we ended up agreeing with Roger Pocock in *A Man in the Open*:

> The course treatment grizzlies gets from hunters makes them sort of bashful with any strangers. Ye see, b'ars yearns to man, same as the heathen does to their fool gods, whereas bullets, pizen, and deadfalls is sort of discouraging. Their sentiments gets mixed, they acts confused and naturally if they're shot at they'll get hostile, same as you and me. They is misunderstood and that's how nobody has a kind word for grizzlies.[19]

BESSIE DOAK HAYNES AND EDGAR HAYNES

---

[19] (Indianapolis, Bobbs-Merrill, 1912), 84.

CONTENTS

WITH THE MAP MAKERS

THE JOURNEY OF HENRY KELSEY, 1691–92
Henry Kelsey

Henry Kelsey, a young Englishman in the employ of the Hudson's Bay Company, was probably the first white man to set eyes upon the monstrous grizzly bear of the Northwest plains. Kelsey was about twenty years of age when he was "sent up" from Deering's Point[1] to bring the Plains Indians to trade with the company. So incredible was his one-thousand-mile trek from York Fort[2] to the plains of Saskatchewan accompanied only by an Assiniboin chief, that his feat was discredited for over two hundred years. Then, in 1926, Kelsey's journal turned up in North Ireland to verify his amazing exploit.

The following archaic rhyme served as an introduction to *A Journal of a Voyage and Journey Undertaken by Henry Kelsey*[3] and contains the first written record of the "outgrown Bear" of the northern plains. Kelsey had visited Saskatchewan in 1690, although no journal was kept for that expedition. The journal entries for August 18, 19, and 20, 1691, are a fair sample of the terse record kept by a youth who, running out of paper, dispatched a letter

[1] ". . . it is probable that the exact location of Deering's Point will never be positively determined, but the length of Kelsey's voyage up the Saskatchewan corresponds closely with the distance from Cedar Lake to the Carrot River, twenty-six miles up which stream he abandoned his canoes to make his land journey to the country of the Assiniboines, his destination, with its buffalo, grizzly bears and abundance of beaver."—Charles Napier Bell (ed.), *The Journal of Henry Kelsey, 1691–92* (Winnipeg, Dawson Richardson Publications, Limited, 1928), 9, 16.

[2] York Fort was the Hudson's Bay Company post at the mouth of Nelson River, on Hudson Bay.

[3] Arthur G. Doughty and Chester Martin, "A Journal of a Voyage and Journey Undertaken by Henry Kelsey Through God's Assistance to Discover and Bring to Commerce the Naywatomie Poets in Anno 1691," *The Kelsey Papers* (Ottawa, The Public Archives of Canada and the Public Record Office of Northern Ireland, 1929), xx–xxi, 12–13.

written on birch bark with charcoal to his superior at Deering's Point.

So far I have spoken concerning of the spoil
And now will give acco[unt] of that same Country soile
Which hither part is very thick of wood
Affords small nutts w[ith] little cherryes very good
Thus it continues till you leave y[e] woods behind
And then you have beast of severall kind
The one is a black Buffillo great
Another is an outgrown Bear w[hich] is good meat
His skin to gett I have used all y[e] means I can
He is mans food & he makes food of man
His hide they would not me it preserve
But said it was a god & they should Starve
This plain affords nothing but Beast & grass
And over it in three days time we past
getting unto y[e] woods on the other side
It being about forty sixe miles wide
This wood is poplo ridges with small ponds of water
there is beavour in abundance but no Otter
with plains & ridges in the Country throughout
Their Enemies many whom they cannot rout
But now of late they hunt their Enemies
and with our English guns do make y[e] flie
At deerings point after the frost
I set up their a Certain Cross
in token of my being there
Cut out on it y[e] date of year
And Likewise for to veryfie the same
added to it my master sir Edward deerings name
So having not more to trouble you w[ith] all I am
Sir your most obedient & faithful serv. at Command

HENRY KELSEY

August   This day I sent two Indians for to seek for those
y 18th   w[hich] I had sent before to see for y[e] Mountain

4

poets[4] fearing lest they should have come to any damage being so long absent so we pitched y[e] ground Continuing as formerly dist 8 Miles[5]

August y 19th
Now we sett forward again y[e] ground being more Barren then it use to be y[e] Indians having seen great store of Buffillo But kill'd none by Estimation 12 Miles

August y 20th[6]
To day we pitcht to y[e] outtermost Edge of y[e] woods this plain affords Nothing but short Round sticky grass[7] & Buffillo & a great sor[t] of a Bear w[hich] is Bigger then any white Bear & is Neither White nor Black But silver hair'd like our English Rabbit y[e] Buffillo Likewise is not like those to y[e] Northward[8] their Horns growing like an English Ox but Black & short dist: 6 Miles

[4] Kelsey refers to the various Indian tribes as "poets," the "Naywatomie Poets" being Crees and the "Mountain Poets" Assiniboines.

[5] Kelsey entered the estimated distance traveled each day.

[6] On this date by Kelsey's count he had come 404 miles from Deering's Point.

[7] Buffalo grass on the Canadian prairies.

[8] Here Kelsey refers to the musk ox of northern Canada which he had seen in 1689 on an expedition, with an Indian lad, which took him two hundred miles north of Churchill River.

5

LEWIS AND CLARK MEET THE WHITE BEAR
Meriwether Lewis

When President Thomas Jefferson in 1805 commissioned Captains Meriwether Lewis and William Clark to explore the Missouri River and its tributaries to ascertain their practicability as a route to the Pacific Coast, he directed them to make themselves acquainted with all the details of the country through which they passed and the Indian tribes and animals they encountered—especially animals previously unknown in the United States. The journals of both the young leaders of the expedition therefore contain repeated detailed references to the monstrous beast which they designated as the brown, yellow, white, or variegated bear. They claimed this animal to be the fiercest, largest, and most intelligent quadruped on the North American continent and wrote of it with considerable awe. Readers are given a firsthand account of the emotional impact the bears—and the western country itself—made upon Captain Lewis and his men in the following excerpts from Lewis' journal.[1]

Monday April 29th 1805.

SET OUT THIS MORNING at the usual hour; the wind was moderate; I walked on shore with one man. about 8 A.M. we fell in with two brown or yellow (white) bear; both of which we wounded; one of them made his escape; the other after my firing on him purused me seventy or eighty yards; but fortunately had been so badly wounded that he was unable to pursue so closely as to prevent my charging my gun. We again repeated our fire and killed him. It was a male not fully grown; we estimated his weight at 300 lb.

[1] Reuben Gold Thwaites, ed. *Original Journals of the Lewis and Clark Expedition, 1804–1806* (New York, Dodd, Mead and Company, 1904), I, 350–51, and II, 4, 24–25, 33–34, 153–56.

not having the means of ascertaining it precisely. The legs of this bear are somewhat longer than those of the black, as are it's tallons and tusks imcomparably larger and longer. the testicles, which in the black bear are placed pretty well back between the thyes and contained in one pouch like those of the dog and most quadrupeds, are in the yellow or brown bear placed much further forward, and are suspended in separate pouches from two to four inches asunder. It's colour is yellowish brown, the eyes small, black, and piercing; the front of the forelegs near the feet is usually black; the fur is finer, thicker and deeper than that of the black bear. These are all the particulars in which this anamal appeared to me to differ from the black bear; it is a much more furious and formidable anamal, and will frequently pursue the hunter when wounded. It is astonishing to see the wounds they will bear before they can be put to death. The Indians may well fear this anamal equiped as they generally are with their bows and arrows or indifferent fuzees, but in the hands of skillful riflemen they are by no means as formidable or dangerous as they have been represented.

May 6th 1805

.... saw a brown bear swim the river above us, he disappeared before we can get in reach of him; I find that the curiossity of our party is pretty well satisfyed with rispect to this anamal, the formidable appearance of the male bear killed on the 5th added to the difficulty with which they die when even shot through the vital parts, has staggered the resolution [of] several of them, others however seem keen for action with the bear; I expect these gentlemen will give us some amusement sho[r]tly as they [the bears] soon begin to coppolate.

May 11th

.... About 5 P.M. my attention was struck by one of the Party running at a distance towards us and making signs and hollowing as if in distress. I ordered the perogues to put too, and waited untill he arrived; I now found that it was Bratton the man with the soar hand whom I had permitted to walk on shore, he arrived so much out of breath that it was several minutes before

7

he could tell what had happened; at length he informed me that in the woody bottom on the Lar^d side about 1½ [miles] below us he had shot a brown bear which immediately turned on him and pursued him a considerable distance but he had wounded it so badly that it could not overtake him. I immediately turned out with seven of the party in quest of this monster, we at length found his trale and persued him about a mile by the blood through very thick brush of rosebushes and the large leafed willow. We finally found him concealed in some very thick brush and shot him through the skull with two balls; we proceeded [to] dress him as soon as possible, we found him in good order; it was a monstrous beast, not quite so large as that we killed a few days past but in all other rispects much the same. The hair is remarkably long, fine and rich tho' he appears parshally to have discharged his winter coat; we now found that Bratton had shot him through the center of the lungs; notwithstanding which he had pursued him near half a mile and had returned more than double that distance and with his tallons had prepared himself a bed in the earth of about 2 feet deep and five feet long and was perfectly alive when we found him which could not have been less than 2 hours after he received the wound; these bear being so hard to die rather intimidates us all; I must confess that I do not like the gentlemen and had rather fight two Indians than one bear; there is no other chance to conquer them by a single shot but by shooting them through the brains, and this becomes difficult in consequence of two large muscles which cover the sides of the forehead and the sharp projection of the center of the frontal bone, which is also of a pretty good thickness, the flece and skin were as much as two men could possibly carry. by the time we returned the sun had set and I determined to remain here all night, and directed the cooks to render the bear's oil and put it in the kegs which was done. there was about eight gallons of it.

Tuesday, May 14th 1805
. . . one of the party wounded a brown bear very badly, but being alone did not think proper to pursue him. In the evening

8

the men in two of the rear canoes discovered a large brown bear lying in the open grounds about 300 paces from the river, and six of them went out to attack him, all good hunters; they took the advantage of a small eminence which concealed them and got within 40 paces of him unperceived, two of them reserved their fires as had been previously conscerted, the four others fired at the same time and put each his bullet through him, two of the balls passed through the bulk of both lobes of his lungs, in an instant this monster ran at them with open mouth, the two who had reserved their fir[e]s discharged their pieces at him as he came toward them, boath of them struck him, one only slightly and the other fortunately broke his shoulder, this however only retarded his motion for a moment only, the men unable to reload their guns took to flight, the bear pursued and had very nearly overtakén them before they reached the river; two of the party betook themselves among the willows, reloaded their pieces, each discharged his piece at him as they had an opportunity. they struck him several times again but the guns only served to direct the bear to them, in this manner he pursued two of them separately so close that they were obliged to throw aside their guns and pouches and throw themselves into the river altho' the bank was nearly twenty feet perpendicular; so enraged was this anamal that he plunged into the river only a few feet behind the second man he had compelled [to] take refuge in the water, when one of those who still remained on shore shot him through the head and finally killed him; they then took him on shore and buch[er]ed him when they found eight balls had passed through him in different sections; the bear being old the flesh was indifferent, they therefore only took the skin and fleece, the latter made us several gallons of oil. . . .

Friday, June 14th 1805
. . . I set one man about preparing a s[c]affold and collecting wood to dry the meat   Sent the others to bring in the ballance of the buffaloe meat, or at least the part which the wolves had left us, for those fellows are ever at hand and ready to partake with us the moment we kill a buffaloe; and there is no means of

putting the meat out of their reach in these plains; the two men shortly after returned with the meat and informed me that the wolves had devoured the greater part of the meat. about ten O'Clock this morning while the men were engaged with the meat I took my Gun and espontoon and thought I would walk a few miles and see where the rappids termineated above, and return to dinner. accordingly I set out and proceeded up the river[2] about S.W. . . . at the distance of about five miles I arrived at a fall of about 19 feet; the river is here about 400 yds wide . . . I should have returned from hence but hearing a tremendious roaring above me I continued my rout across the point of a hill a few hundred yards further, and was again presented by one of the most beatifull objects in nature, a cascade of about fifty feet perpendicular streching at right angles across the river from side to side to the distance of at least a quarter of a mile. here the river pitches over a shelving rock, with an edge as regular and as straight as if formed by art . . . I had scarcely infixed my eyes from the pleasing object before I discovered another fall above at the distance of half a mile; thus invited I did not think of returning but hurried thither to amuse myself with this newly discovered object. . . . determining as I had proceeded so far to continue my rout to the head of the rappids if it should even detain me all night. . . . I determined to procede as far as the river which I saw discharge itself on the West side of the Missouri convinced that it was [the one] the Indians call *medecine river*. . . . I descended the hill and directed my course to the bend of the Missouri near which there was a herd of at least a thousand buffaloe; here I thought it would be well to kill a buffaloe and leave him untill my return from the river and if I then found that I had not time to get back to camp this evening to remain all night here there being a few sticks of drift wood lying along shore which would answer for my fire, and a few s[c]attering cottonwood trees a few hundred yards below which would afford me at least the semblance of a shelter. . . . I selected a fat buffaloe and shot him very well, through the lungs; while I was gazeing attentively on the poor anamal discharging blood in streams from his mouth and nostrils, expect-

[2] Lewis was at the Great Falls of the Missouri River.

ing him to fall every instant, and having forgotten entirely to reload my rifle, a large white, or reather brown bear, had perceived and crept on me within 20 steps before I discovered him; in the first moment I drew up my gun to shoot, but at the same instant recolected that she was not loaded and that he was too near for me to hope to perform this operation before he reached me, as he was then briskly advancing on me; it was an open level plain, not a bush within miles nor a tree within less than three hundred yards of me; the river bank was sloping and not more than three feet above the level of the water; in short there was no place by means of which I could conceal myself from this monster untill I could charge my rifle; in this situation I thought of retreating in a brisk walk as fast as he was advancing untill I could reach a tree about 300 yards below me, but I had no sooner terned myself about but he pitched at me, open mouthed and full speed. I ran about 80 yards and found he gained on me fast. I then run into the water. the idea struk me to get into the water to such depth that I could stand and he would be obliged to swim, and that I could in that situation defend myself with my espontoon; accordingly I ran haistily into the water about waist deep, and faced about and presented the point of my espontoon, at this instant he arrived at the edge of the water within about 20 feet of me; the moment I put myself in this attitude of defence he sudonly wheeled about as if frightened, declined the combat on such unequal grounds, and retreated with quite as great precipitation as he had just before pursued me. as soon as I saw him run of[f] in that manner I returned to the shore and charged my gun, which I had still retained in my hand throughout this curious adventure. I saw him run through the level open plain about three miles, till he disappeared in the woods on medecine river; during the whole of this distance he ran at full speed, sometimes appearing to look behind him as if he expected pursuit. I now began to reflect on this novil occurrence and indeavored to account for this sudden retreat of the bear. I at first thought that perhaps he had not smelt me before he arrived at the waters edge so near me, but I then reflected that he had pursued me for about 80 or 90 yards before I took [to] the water and on examination saw the grownd toarn with his tallons immediately on the im-p[r]ession of my steps; and the cause of his allarm still remains with me misterious and unaccountable. So it was and I felt myself not a little gratifyed that he had declined the combat.

3

NOTES PERTAINING TO BEARS
David Thompson

David Thompson is, by all odds, one of the great figures of North American exploration. An Englishman, born in London in 1770, he came in 1784 to Fort Churchill as an apprentice of the Hudson's Bay Company. He remained in the fur trade until 1797, ranging from Hudson Bay west to the Athabasca country. He joined the North West Company in the latter year, and in 1797–98 went as far south as the Mandan villages on the upper Missouri, and eastward to the source of the Mississippi.

Thompson's travels carried him also across the Rocky Mountains to the Columbia. Between 1807 and 1810, he had explored most of the Columbia River system and much of present Washington, Oregon, and Idaho. His meticulously detailed maps, now renowned, are still the basis for many present-day maps of western Canada. He knew Astoria, the American outpost of the fur trade, from his visit there in 1811. He died in 1857.

The present selection is taken from Richard Glover's splendidly edited *David Thompson's Narrative*, published by the Champlain Society, Toronto, in 1962, pages 94, 142, and 229–30, by kind permission of the editor and the Champlain Society.

FORMERLY THE BEAVERS WERE VERY NUMEROUS, the many Lakes and Rivers gave them ample space; and the poor Indian[1] had then only a pointed stick shaped and hardened in the fire, a stone Hatchet, Spear and Arrow heads of the same; thus armed he was weak against the sagacious Beaver, who, on the banks of a Lake, made itself a house of a foot thick, or more; composed of earth

---

[1] The Nahathaways, native to the country around Reed Lake House, built by Thompson for the Hudson's Bay Company in 1794 north of the Saskatchewan River.

and small flat stones, crossed and bound together with pieces of wood; upon which no impression could be made but by fire. But when the arrival of the White People had changed all their weapons from stone to iron and steel, and added the fatal Gun, every animal fell before the Indian; the Bear was no longer dreaded, and the Beaver became a desirable animal for food and clothing, and the furr a valuable article of trade; and as the Beaver is a stationary animal, it could be attacked at any convenient time in all seasons, and thus their numbers soon became reduced.

The Old Indians, when speaking of their ancestors, wonder how they could live as the Beaver was wiser, and the Bear stronger, than them, and confess, that if they were deprived of the Gun, they could not live by the Bow and Arrow, and must soon perish. ... The only Bears of this country, are the small black Bear, with a chance Yellow Bear, this latter has a fine furr and trades for three Beavers in barter, when full grown. The Black Bear is common and according to size passes for one or two Beavers, the young are often tamed by the Natives, and are harmless and playful, until near full grown, when they become troublesome, and are killed, or sent into the woods; while they can procure roots and berries, they look for nothing else. But in the Spring, when they leave their winter dens, they can get neither the one nor the other, prowl about, and go to the Rapids where the Carp are spawning; here Bruin lives in plenty; but not content with what it can eat, amuses itself with tossing ashore ten times more than it can devour, each stroke of it's fore paw sending a fish eight or ten yards according to it's size; the fish thus thrown ashore attract the Eagle and the Raven; the sight of these birds flying about, leads the Indian to the place, and Bruin loses his life and his skin. The meat of the Bear feeding on roots and berries becomes very fat and good, and in this condition it enters it's den for the winter; at the end of which time the meat is still good, and has some fat, but [after] the very first meal of fish the taste of the meat is changed for the worse, and soon becomes disagreeable. When a Mahmees Dog, in the winter season has discovered a den, and the Natives go to kill the Bear, on uncovering the top of the den, Bruin is found roused out of it's dormant state, and sitting ready to defend itself; the eld-

14

est man now makes a speech to it; reproaching the bear and all it's race with being the old enemies of Man, killing the children and women, when it was large and strong; but now, since the Manito has made him, small and weak to what he was before, he has all the will, though not the power to be as bad as ever, that he is treacherous and cannot be trusted, that although he has sense he makes bad use of it, and must therefore be killed; parts of the speech have many repetitions to impress it's truth on the Bear, who all the time is grinning and growling, willing to fight, but more willing to escape, until the axe descends on it's head, or [it] is shot; the latter more frequently, as the den is often under the roots of fallen trees, and protected by the branches of the roots.

When a Bear thus killed was hauled out of it's den, I enquired of the Indian who made the speech, whether he really thought the Bear understood him. He replied, "How can you doubt it, did you not see how ashamed I made him, and how he held down his head?" "He might well hold down his head when you were flourishing a heavy axe over it, with which you killed him." On this animal they have several superstitions, and he acts a prominent part in many of their tales. . . . The Black, Brown and Yellow Bears feed on the Berries, the Nuts and any thing else they can catch; one of them was shot that was guarding part of an Antelope, which he had killed and partly eaten; how this clumsy brute could have caught so fleet an animal as the Antelope was a matter of wonder. The bears lay up nothing for their substinence in winter and are then mostly dormant.

. . . from Canada the trade was open to every adventurer, and some of these brought in a great number of Iroquois, Nepissings and Algonquins who with their steel traps had destroyed the Beaver on their own lands in Canada and New Brunswick. . . . Part of these went up the Red Deer River, and about 250 of them came up the Saskatchewan River, in company with the canoes of the Fur Traders to one of the upper Posts called Fort Augustus;[2] where the River passes through fine Plains, upon the banks and in the interior country are numerous herds of Bisons and several

---

[2] Old Fort Augustus was situated on the North Saskatchewan River one mile and a half above the mouth of Sturgeon River.

kinds of Deer, and many Bears of several colours. The Algonquins and Nepissings paid every attention to the advice given to them, and performed the voyage without accident; but the Iroquois treated our warnings with contempt; When advised to be cautious in the hunting of the Bison, especially when wounded; they would laugh and say they killed an ox with the stroke of an axe, and should do the same to the Bisons. The second day in hunting one of them wounded a Bull which ran at him, and although he avoided the full stroke of the head, yet was so much hurt that it was about two months before he was well. The next day as two of them was [sic] crossing a low point of wood near the river, they saw a Bull, fired at and wounded him, the Bull rushed on one of them who to escape ran behind an old rotten stump of a tree of about ten feet high, the furious animal came dash against it, threw it down and the man lay beneath it, the Bull also fell on it, and rolled off. The comrade of the poor fellow ran to the river and hailed the canoes; several of the Men came, the Bison was dying, they took the stump away, but the Iroquois was crushed and dead. These two accidents somewhat lowered their pride as they found that even their guns could not always protect them.

A few days after, as two of them were hunting (they always went by two) they met a coloured Bear, which one of them wounded, the Bear sprung on him, and standing on his hind feet seized the Iroquois hugging him with his forelegs and paws, which broke the bones of both arms above the elbow and with it's teeth tore the skin of the head from the crown to the forehead, for the poor fellow had drawn his knife to defend himself, but could not use it; fortunately his comrade was near, and putting his gun close to the Bear shot him dead. The poor fellow was a sad figure, none of us were surgeons, but we did the best we could, but for want of proper bandageing his arms were three months in getting well. These accidents happening only to the Iroquois made them superstitious and they concluded that some of the Algonquins had thrown bad medicine on them, and a quarrel would probably have taken place had we not been with them. These accidents were the fault of their mode of hunting, being accustomed to hunt only timid animals, and keeping about one hundred yards from each other, to cover more ground did very well for Deer; but to hunt the animals of the upper countries as the Bison and Bear and which are fierce and dangerous, requires the two hunters to be close to each other, the one reserving his fire in case of the wounded animal being able to attack them; they were faulty in their hunting until experience taught them better. . . .

4

THE PHILADELPHIA BEAR CUBS
John Davidson Godman, M.D.

The following excerpt from John Davidson Godman's *American Natural History* is doubly intriguing because it is one of the first zoology-textbook descriptions of the grizzly bear, and because it includes a letter written to President Thomas Jefferson by Zebulon Montgomery Pike[1] answering the President's query about a pair of grizzly cubs then on display at Peale's Museum in Philadelphia. Written only two years after the return of Lewis and Clark from the expedition to the west authorized by Jefferson, the letter is indicative of the President's continuing interest in the newly explored country and all it contained. One can imagine Jefferson, after having seen the ferocious bears first described by Captain Lewis, sitting down to write Pike for information about their acquisition.

John Davidson Godman studied medicine in Baltimore but soon found that he had no liking for village practice. He took his family to Ohio for several years, then returned to study anatomy in Philadelphia, and, in 1826, was called to fill the chair of anatomy at the newly established Rutger's Medical College in New York. An ardent student of the zoology of North America, he published a number of articles on zoological subjects that were later incorporated into a natural history which went through a number of printings between 1826 and 1860. The material used here is from Godman's *American Natural History, Volume I, To which is added His Last Work, The Ramblings of a Naturalist*, pages 94–97 and 99–101, published at Philadelphia in 1842 by R. W. Pomeroy. All editions of Godman's natural history are extremely rare, but copies may sometimes be found in university zoology libraries.

[1] Explorer and army officer who led the western expedition on which Pikes Peak was discovered and named.

Two CUBS OF THE GRIZZLY BEAR were sometime since kept at Peale's (now the Philadelphia) Museum. When first received they were quite small, but speedily gave indication of that ferocity for which this species is so remarkable. As they increased in size they became exceedingly dangerous, seizing and tearing to pieces every animal they could lay hold of, and expressing extreme eagerness to get at those accidently brought within sight of their cage, by grasping the iron bars with their paws and shaking them violently, to the great terror of spectators, who felt insecure while witnessing such displays of their strength. In one instance an unfortunate Monkey was walking over the top of their cage, when the end of the chain which hung from his waist dropped through within reach of the Bears. They immediately seized upon it, dragged the screaming Monkey through the narrow aperture, tore him limb from limb, and devoured his mangled carcass almost instantaneously. At another time, a small Monkey thrust his arm through the Bear cage, one of them immediately seized him and, with a sudden jerk tore the whole arm and shoulder-blade from the body and devoured it before anyone could interfere. They were still cubs, and very little more than half-grown when their ferocity became so alarming as to excite continual apprehension lest they should escape, and they were killed to prevent such an event.

The following letter is relative to the two Grizzly Bears above mentioned:

Washington, Feb. 3d., 1808.

Sir: — I had the honor of receiving your note last evening, and in reply to the inquiries of Mr. Peale can only give the following notes:

The Bears were taken by an Indian in the mountain which divides the western branch of the Río del Norte and some small rivers, which discharge their waters into the east side of the Gulf of California, near the dividing line between the provinces of Biscay and Sonora. We happened at the time to be marching along the foot of those mountains, and fell in with the Indian who had them, when I conceived the idea of bringing them to the United States. Although then more than 1600 miles from our frontier

19

post, Natchitoches, I purchased them of the savage, and for three or four days made my men carry them in their laps on horseback. As they would eat nothing but milk, they were in danger of starving. I then had a cage prepared for both, which was carried on a mule, lashed between two packs, but always ordered them to be let out the moment we halted, and not shut up again until we were prepared to march. By this treatment they became exceedingly docile when at liberty, following my men, whom they learned to distingiush from the Spanish dragoons, by their feeding them, and encamping with them, like dogs through our camps, the small villages and forts where we halted. When well supplied with sustenance they would play like young puppies with each other and the soldiers, but the instant they were shut up and placed on the mule, they became cross, as the jostling of the animal knocked them against each other. They were sometimes left exposed to the scorching heat of a vertical sun for a day without any food or a drop of water, in which case they would worry and tear each other, until nature was exhausted, and they could neither fight nor howl any longer. They will be one year old on the first of next month, March, 1808—and, as I am informed, they frequently arrive at the weight of eight hundred pounds.

Whilst in the mountains we sometimes discovered them [grizzly bears] at a distance, but in no instance were we ever able to come up with one, which we eagerly sought, and *that* being the most inclement season of the year, induces me to believe they seldom or never attack a man unprovoked, but defend themselves courageously; an instance of this kind occurred in New Mexico, whilst I sojourned in that province: three of the natives attacked a bear with their lances, two of whom he killed, and wounded the third, before he fell the victim.

With sentiments of the
highest respect and esteem
Your obedient servant,
Z. M. PIKE

His Excellency, Thomas Jefferson
President of the United States

The Grizzly Bear is remarkably tenacious of life, and on many occasions numerous rifle balls have been fired into the body of an individual, without much apparent injury. Governor Clinton[2]

[2] DeWitt Clinton, governor of New York (1817–21, 1825–28).

says that "Dixon, an Indian, told a friend of his, that this animal had been seen fourteen feet long; that, notwithstanding its ferocity, it had been occasionally domesticated; and that an Indian belonging to a tribe on the head waters of the Mississippi had one in a reclaimed state which he sportively directed to go into a canoe belonging to another tribe of Indians, then returning from a visit. The bear obeyed, and was struck by an Indian. Being considered as one of the family, this was deemed an insult, resented accordingly, and produced a war between these nations."

Mr. John Dougherty, a very experienced and respectable hunter, who accompanied Major Long's party[3] during their expedition to the Rocky Mountains . . . relates the following instance of the great strength of the Grizzly Bear: Having killed a Bison, and left the carcass for the purpose of procuring assistance to skin and cut it up, he was very much surprised, on his return, to find that it had been dragged off whole to a considerable distance, by a Grizzly Bear, and was then placed in a pit, which the animal had dug for its reception. This Bear strikes a very violent blow with its forepaws, and the claws inflict dreadful wounds. One of the cubs belonging to the Philadelphia Museum struck the other a blow over part of its back and shoulder, which produced a large wound like a sabre cut. It is stated in Long's Expedition that a hunter received a blow from the forepaw of a Grizzly Bear, which destroyed his eye, and crushed his cheek bone.

The Grizzly Bear is unable to climb trees, like other Bears: he is much more intimidated by the voice than the aspect of man; and on some occasions, when advancing to attack an individual, he has turned and retired, merely in consequence of the screams extorted by fear. The degree of ferocity exhibited by the Grizzly Bear, appears to be considerably influenced by the plenty or scarcity of food in the region which it inhabits. Prior to the time of Lewis and Clarke's expedition, nothing very satisfactory was known in relation to this Bear; and it was not until the publication of Long's Expedition to the Rocky Mountains, that a correct

[3] Stephen Harriman Long, who explored the upper Mississippi region in 1817 and in 1819-20 explored the Rocky Mountains.

scientific description was given by that distinguished naturalist, Say.[4]

It may with certainty be distinguished from all the known species of this genus by its elongated claws, and the rectilinear or slightly arched figure of its facial profile. . . . On the front of the Grizzly Bear the hair is short, and between and anterior to the eyes it is very much so. On the rest of the body, it is long and very thickly set, being blacker and coarser on the legs, feet, shoulders, throat, behind the thighs, and beneath the belly. On the snout it is paler. The ears are short and rounded, the forehead somewhat convex, or arcuated; and the line of the profile continues on the snout, without any indentations between the eyes. . . . The eyes are quite small, and have no remarkable supplemental lid. The iris is of a light reddish-brown, or burnt sienna color. The muffle of the nostrils is black, and the sinus very distinct and profound. The lips are capable of being extended anteriorly, especially the upper one.

The claws of the fore-feet are slender and elongated and the fingers have five sub-oval naked tubercles, separated from the palm, each other, and the base of the claws, by dense hair. The anterior half of the palm is naked, and is of an oval figure transversely; the base of the palm has a rounded naked tubercle encircled by hair.

The soles of the (hind) feet are naked, and the nails are more curved and not so long as those of the fore-paws. The nails are not in the least diminished at the tip, but they grow sharper at that part only by lessening from beneath.

The color of the Grizzly Bear varies very considerably, according to age and its particular state of pelage. Hence they have been described as brown, white, variegated, by Lewis and Clarke although evidently of the same species judging by all other characteristics; in advance life the colour is that peculiar mixture of white, brown, and black, which has procured for the bear the appropriate name of "grizzly."

[4] Thomas Say, noted naturalist who was one of the members of the expedition to the Rocky Mountains in 1819 and 1820, commanded by Maj. Stephen H. Long.

FUR TRAPPERS AND MOUNTAIN MEN

5

ADVENTURES OF WILLIAM CANNON AND
JOHN DAY WITH GRIZZLY BEARS

Washington Irving

The rich historical worth of Washington Irving's *Astoria; or Anecdotes of an Enterprise Beyond the Rocky Mountains*, owing to the researches of Edgeley W. Todd, makes it more than ever a book to heed, particularly for the light it throws upon the American fur trade in the Far West at the dramatic period of its beginnings under John Jacob Astor, the founder of Astoria, Oregon, in 1810. Irving, already a greatly respected figure on both sides of the Atlantic, published his book in 1836. The following selection is taken from Todd's masterly edition of *Astoria*, published in 1964 by the University of Oklahoma Press, pages 231 and 234–38.

MR. HUNT[1] AND HIS PARTY were now on the skirts of the Black Hills, or Black Mountains, as they are sometimes called; an extensive chain, lying about a hundred miles east of the Rocky Mountains, and stretching in a northeast direction from the south fork of the Nebraska, or Platte River, to the great north bend of the Missouri. . . .

Baffled in his attempts to traverse this mountain chain, Mr. Hunt skirted along it to the southwest, keeping it on the right; and still in hopes of finding an opening. At an early hour one day, he encamped in a narrow valley on the banks of a beautifully clear but rushy pool; surrounded by thickets bearing abundance of wild cherries, currents, and yellow and purple gooseberries.

[1] Mr. Wilson Price Hunt, of New Jersey, the fourth partner in the American Fur Company, and selected by John Jacob Astor to lead the overland expedition to the mouth of the Columbia River and to represent him in the contemplated establishment of the Astoria post.

While the afternoon's meal was in preparation, Mr. Hunt and Mr. M'Kenzie ascended to the summit of the nearest hill, from whence, aided by the purity and transparency of the evening atmosphere, they commanded a vast prospect on all sides. Below them extended a plain, dotted with innumerable herds of buffalo. Some were lying down among the herbage, others roaming in their unbounded pastures, while many were engaged in fierce contests . . . their low bellowings reaching the ear like the hoarse murmurs of the surf on a distant shore. . . .

On returning to the camp, Mr. Hunt found some uneasiness prevailing among the Canadian voyageurs. In straying among the thickets they beheld tracks of grizzly bears in every direction, doubtless attracted thither by the fruit. To their dismay, they now found that they had encamped in one of the favorite resorts of this dreaded animal. The idea marred all the comfort of the encampment. As night closed, the surrounding thickets were peopled with terrors; insomuch that, according to Mr. Hunt, they could not help starting at every little breeze that stirred the bushes.

The grizzly bear is the only really formidable quadruped of our continent. He is the favorite theme of the hunters of the far West, who describe him as equal in size to a common cow and of prodigious strength. He makes battle if assailed, and often, if pressed by hunger, is the assailant. If wounded, he becomes furious and will pursue the hunter. His speed exceeds that of a man but is inferior to that of a horse. In attacking he rears himself on his hind legs, and springs the length of his body. Woe to horse or rider that comes within the sweep of his terrific claws, which are sometimes nine inches in length, and tear everything before them.

At the time we are treating of, the grizzly bear was still frequent on the Missouri and in the lower country, but, like some of the broken tribes of the prairie, he has gradually fallen back before his enemies, and is now chiefly to be found in the upland regions, in rugged fastnesses like those of the Black Hills and the Rocky Mountains. Here he lurks in caverns, or holes which he has digged in the sides of hills, or under the roots and trunks of fallen trees. Like the common bear, he is fond of fruits, and mast, and roots, the latter of which he will dig up with his foreclaws. He is carnivorous also, and will even attack and conquer the lordly buffalo, dragging his huge carcass to the neighborhood of his den, that he may prey upon it at his leisure.

The hunters, both white and red men, consider this the most heroic game. They prefer to hunt him on horseback, and will venture so near as sometimes to singe his hair with the flash of the rifle. The hunter of the grizzly bear, however, must be an experienced hand, and know where to aim at a vital part; for of all quadrupeds, he is the most difficult to be killed. He will receive repeated wounds without flinching, and rarely is a shot mortal unless through the head or heart.

That the dangers apprehended from the grizzly bear, at this night encampment, were not imaginary, was proved on the following morning. Among the hired men of the party was one William Cannon, who had been a soldier at one of the frontier posts, and entered into the employ of Mr. Hunt at Mackinaw. He was an inexperienced hunter and a poor shot, for which he was much bantered by his more adroit comrades. Piqued at their raillery, he had been practicing ever since he had joined the expedition, but without success. In the course of the present afternoon, he went forth by himself to take a lesson in venerie, and, to his great delight, had the good fortune to kill a buffalo. As he was a considerable distance from the camp, he cut out the tongue and some of the choice bits, made them into a parcel, and slinging them on his shoulders by a strap passed round his forehead, as the voyageurs carry packages of goods, set out all glorious for the camp, anticipating a triumph over his brother hunters. In passing through a narrow ravine, he heard a noise behind him, and looking round beheld, to his dismay, a grizzly bear in full pursuit, apparently attracted by the scent of the meat. Cannon had heard so much of the invulnerability of this tremendous animal, that he never attempted to fire, but, slipping the strap from his forehead, let go the buffalo meat and ran for his life. The bear did not stop to regale himself with the game, but kept on after the hunter. He had nearly overtaken him when Cannon reached a tree, and, throwing down his rifle, scrambled up it. The next instant Bruin was at the foot of the tree; but, as this species of bear does not

27

climb, he contented himself with turning the chase into a blockade. Night came on. In the darkness Cannon could not perceive whether or not the enemy maintained his station; but his fears pictured him rigorously mounting guard. He passed the night, therefore, in the tree, a prey to dismal fancies. In the morning the bear was gone. Cannon warily descended the tree, gathered up his gun, and made the best of his way back to the camp, without venturing to look after his buffalo meat.

While on this theme we will add another anecdote of an adventure with a grizzly bear, told of John Day, the Kentucky hunter, but which happened at a different period of the expedition. Day was hunting in company with one of the clerks of the Company, a lively youngster, who was a great favorite with the veteran, but whose vivacity he had continually to keep in check. They were in search of deer, when suddenly a huge grizzly bear emerged from a thicket about thirty yards distant, rearing himself upon his hind legs with a terrific growl, and displaying a hideous array of teeth and claws. The rifle of the young man was leveled in an instant, but John Day's iron hand was as quickly upon his arm. "Be quiet, boy! Be quiet!" exclaimed the hunter between his clenched teeth, and without turning his eyes from the bear. They remained motionless. The monster regarded them for a time, then, lowering himself on his forepaws, slowly withdrew. He had not gone many paces before he again returned, reared himself on his hind legs, and repeated his menace. Day's hand was still on the arm of his young companion; he again pressed it hard, and kept repeating between his teeth, "Quiet boy!—keep quiet!—keep quiet!"—though the latter had not made a move since his first prohibition. The bear again lowered himself on all fours, retreated some twenty yards further, and again turned, reared, showed his teeth, and growled. This third menace was too much for the game spirit of John Day. "By Jove!" exlaimed he, "I can stand this no longer," and in an instant a ball from his rifle whizzed into the foe. The wound was not mortal; but, luckly, it dismayed instead of enraging the animal, and he retreated into the thicket.

Day's young companion reproached him for not practicing

the caution which he enjoined upon others. "Why, boy," replied the veteran, "caution is caution, but one must not put up with too much, even from a bear. Would you have me suffer myself to be bullied all day by a varmint?"

6

A WOUNDED BEAR
Alexander Ross

In his writings Alexander Ross has left us a rich heritage of information on the climactic years of the Northwest fur trade. The young Scotchman joined John Jacob Astor's Pacific Fur Company in 1810, going around the Horn in the *Tonquin* to help establish Fort Astoria at the mouth of the Columbia River. When the American concern was taken over by the North West Company during the War of 1812, Ross elected to remain with the Northwesters, and when these staid English traders were subsequently absorbed by the more aggressive Hudson's Bay Company, he stayed to participate in one of the most exciting and hazardous eras in North American history. After his retirement Ross settled near the Red River in Manitoba, where he wrote several extraordinary accounts of the turbulent and competitive Columbia River fur trade.

In *The Fur Hunters of the Far West: A Narrative of Adventures in the Oregon and Rocky Mountains*, published in London in 1855, Ross has given us an authoritative and dramatic narrative which has long been considered the classic source material on the Columbia River fur trade. We have extracted the following incredible account of an Indian bear hunt from Kenneth A. Spaulding's ably edited version of Volume I of this rare work, published under the title of *The Fur Hunters of the Far West*, at Norman, by the University of Oklahoma Press in 1956, pages 99, 101, and 111–12.

AT THE OUTSET we proceeded up the North or Sun-tea-coot-acoot River[1] for three days, then turning to the right we took to the woods, steering our course in the eye of the rising sun nearly

[1] The North Thompson River, in southern British Columbia.

midway between Thompson's River on the south and Fraser's River on the north. . . .

We had now resolved to follow our guide, having every confidence in his knowledge of the country; but instead of taking us by an easterly direction, he bent his course almost due north for about sixty miles when we reached a small river called Ke-low-na-skar-am-ish, or Grizzly Bear River,[2] which we ascended in nearly an easterly direction for six days until it became so narrow that we could have jumped over it. While following this little stream, we passed several beaver lodges and other ravages of that animal. In many places the trees were cut down, and the course of the water stopped and formed into small lakes and ponds by the sagacious and provident habits of the beaver. In one place forty-two trees were cut down, at the height of about eighteen inches from the root within the compass of half an acre. We now began to think we had found the goose that lays the golden eggs; this was but of short duration. . . .

Along Grizzly Bear River we shot four elk, twenty-two deer, two otters, two beavers and three black bears without stepping out of our way; but the bears were poor, and the only cause we could assign for it was the scarcity of berries and fish. These animals generally frequent fruit and fish countries. . . .

In one of the thickets as we passed along, our guide took us a little out of our way to show us what he called a bear's haunt or wintering den, where that animal according to Indian theory remains in a dark and secluded retreat without food or nourishment for months together, sucking its paws! But there was nothing remarkable about the place. The entrance to the lair or den was through a long and winding thicket of dense brush wood; but its hiding place was not in a hole under ground but on the surface, deeply imbedded among the fallen leaves. The snow is often many feet deep, and their hiding place is discovered only by an air hole over the den resembling a small funnel, sometimes not two inches in diameter, through which the breath issues; but so concealed from view that none but the keen eye of the savage can find it out.

[2] The Adams River.

31

In this den the bear is said to lie in a torpid state from December till March. They do not lie together in families but singly, and when they make their exit in the spring, they are very sleek and fat. To their appearance at this season I can bear ample testimony, having frequently seen them. But no sooner do they leave their winter quarters and begin to roam about than they get poor and haggard. The bear is said never to winter twice in the same place. In their retreats they are often found out and killed by the Indians without making the least resistance. . . .

After passing some time looking around us, we descended and encamped at the edge of the small and insignificant stream called Canoe River, celebrated among North Westers for the quality of the birch bark. So completely were its banks overhung and concealed with heavy timber, that it was scarcely visible at the short distance of fifty yards. It is a mere rill among rivers, in some places not more than fifteen paces broad. Its course is almost due south, and flows over a stony bottom, with low banks, clear cold water, and strong current. Here our guide told us that in two days' moderate travel we could reach its mouth, where it enters the Columbia near Portage Point. . . .

Soon after my arrival from Canoe River,[3] I was invited by the chiefs of my post to accompany a party of the natives on a bear hunting expedition for a few days. On these occasions they felt flattered by their trader accompanying them. The party were all mounted on horseback to the number of seventy-three, and exhibited a fine display of horsemanship. After some two miles' travel we commenced operations. Having reached the hunting ground the party separated into several divisions. We then perambulated the woods, crossed rivers, surrounding thickets, and scampered over hill and dale with yell and song for the greater part of two days, during which time we killed seven bears, nine wolves and eleven small deer; one of the former I had the good luck to shoot myself. In the evening of the third day however, our sport was checked by an accident. One of the great men, the

[3] Ross is speaking of the return to his post as trader at Shuswap Lake, forty miles north of Nelson, British Columbia.

chief Pasha of the hunting party named Ta-tack-it, It-tso-augh-an, or Short Legs, got severely wounded by a female bear.

The only danger to be apprehended on these savage excursions is by following the wounded animal into a thicket, or hiding place; but with the Indians the more danger the more honour, and some of them are foolhardy enough to run every hazard in order to strike the last fatal blow, in which the honour lies, sometimes with a lance, tomahawk or knife, at the risk of their lives. No sooner does a bear get wounded than it immediately flies for refuge to some hiding place unless too closely pursued, in which case it turns round with savage fury on its pursuers, and woe awaits whatever is in the way.

The bear in question had been wounded, and taking shelter in a small coppice the bush was instantly surrounded by the horsemen, when the more bold and daring entered it on foot armed with gun, knife and tomahawk. Among the bush rangers on the present occasion was the chief Short Legs, who, while scrambling over some fallen timber, happened to stumble near to where the the wounded and enraged bear was concealed; but too close to be able to defend himself before the vicious animal got hold of him. At that moment I was not more than five or six paces from the chief; but could not get a chance of shooting so I immediately called out for help, when several mustered around the spot. Availing ourselves of the doubtful alternative of killing her, even at the risk of killing the chief, we fired and as good luck would have it shot the bear and saved the man, then carrying the bear and wounded chief out of the bush we laid both on open ground. The sight of the chief was appalling. The scalp was torn from the crown of the head down over the eyebrows! The chief was insensible, and for some time we all thought him dead; but after a short interval his pulse began to beat and he gradually showed signs of returning animation.

But it was a curious and somewhat interesting scene to see the party approach the spot when the accident happened. Not being able to get a chance of shooting they threw their guns from them and could scarcely be restrained from rushing on the fierce ani-

33

mal with their knives only. The bear all the time kept looking first at one then at another, and casting her fierce and flaming eyes around the whole of us, as if ready to make a spring at each; yet she never let go her hold of the chief but stood over him. Seeing herself surrounded by so many enemies, she moved her head from one position to another and these movements gave us ultimately an opportunity of dispatching her.

The misfortune produced a long and clamorous scene of mourning among the chief relations and we hastened home carrying our dead bears along with us, and arrived at the camp early in the morning of the fourth day. The chief remained for three days speechless. In cutting off the scalp and dressing the wound we found the skull, according to our imperfect knowledge of anatomy, fractured in two or three places, and at the end of eight days I extracted a bone measuring two inches long, of an oblong form, and another of about an inch square, with several small pieces, all from the crown of the head! The wound, however, gradually closed up and healed excepting a small spot about the size of an English shilling. In fifteen days, by the aid of Indian medicine he was able to walk about, and at the end of six weeks from the time he got wounded, he was on horseback again at the chase.

The tide of sympathy for the great man's misfortune did not run high for at best he was but an unprincipled fellow, an enemy to the whites and hated by his own people. Many were of opinion that the friendly bear had at last rid us of an unfriendly chief; but to the disappointment of all he set the bear and wounds both at defiance, and was soon, to our great annoyance, at his old trade of plotting mischief!

7

JOE MEEK'S ADVENTURES WITH THE GRIZZLIES
Frances Fuller Victor[1]

Joseph Meek was probably the least modest of all the famous fur trappers and apparently was a man to whom exciting adventures and narrow escapes just naturally happened. He joined William Sublette's Rocky Mountain Fur Company in 1828 at the age of nineteen, living the life of a mountain man until settling in Oregon's Willamette Valley. Accredited with having awakened Congress to the need for territorial government for Oregon when he traveled to Washington with the news of the Whitman massacre, his picturesque appearance and backwoods mannerisms attracted so much attention in the national capital that he was appointed the first United States marshal for Oregon Territory when it was created.

"Uncle Joe's" adventures with the Yellowstone grizzlies, told in his own outlandish vernacular to Mrs. Victor late in his life, illustrate perfectly the flair for storytelling for which Meek was famous. It is taken from Franois Fuller Victor's *River of the West*,[2] published in 1870. This rare volume, which contains an

[1] Frances Fuller Victor began her literary career with a San Francisco newspaper. She became a member of Hubert H. Bancroft's staff, moving to Oregon in 1865 and "ghost writing" the histories of the Northwest Coast, Oregon and Montana, Washington, Nevada, Colorado and Wyoming, and volumes VI and VII of *The History of California* which bore Bancroft's name and became the cornerstones for most latter-day histories of the western states. Although accurate in most details, these works contain occasional errata which have been perpetuated even in present-day writings. The footnotes are particularly interesting, containing much intimate biographical information on early settlers in the West.

[2] Victor, Frances Fuller, *The River of the West. Life and Adventure In the Rocky Mountains and Oregon; Embracing Events in the Life-time of a Mountain Man and Pioneer; with the Early History of the North-Western Slope, including an Account of the Fur Traders, the Indian Tribes, the Overland Immigration, the Oregon Missions, and the Tragic Fate of Rev. Dr. Whitman and Family. Also, a Description of the Country, Its Condition, Prospects, and Re-*

immense treasury of information on early days in the Oregon country, has been reprinted in a facsimile edition by Long's Colege Book Company, of Columbus, Ohio.

1830. THE WHOLE COUNTRY lying upon the Yellowstone and its tributaries, and about the head-waters of the Missouri, at the time of which we are writing, abounded not only in beaver, but in buffalo, bear, elk, antelope, and many smaller kinds of game. Indeed the buffalo used then to cross the mountains into the valleys about the head-waters of the Snake and Colorado Rivers, in such numbers that at certain seasons of the year, the plains and river bottoms swarmed with them. Since that day they have quite disappeared from the western slope of the Rocky Mountains, and are no longer seen in the same numbers on the eastern side.

Bear, although they did not go in herds, were rather uncomfortably numerous, and sometimes put the trapper to considerable trouble, and fright also; for very few were brave enough to willingly encounter the formidable grizzly, one blow of whose terrible paw, aimed generally at the hunter's head, if not arrested, lays him senseless and torn, an easy victim to the wrathful monster. A gunshot wound, if not directed with certainty to some vulnerable point, has only the effect to infuriate the beast, and make him trebly dangerous. From the fact that the bear always bites his wound, and commences to run with his head thus brought in the direction from which the ball comes, he is pretty likely to make a straight wake towards his enemy, whether voluntarily or not; and woe be to the hunter who is not prepared for him, with a shot for his eye, or the spot just behind the ear, where certain death enters.

In the frequent encounters of the mountain-men with these huge beasts, many acts of wonderful bravery were performed, while some tragedies, and not a few comedies were enacted.

From something humorous in Joe Meek's organization, or

---

sources, Its Soil, Its Climate, and Scenery; Its Mountains, Rivers, Valleys, Deserts, and Plains; Its Inland Waters, and Natural Resources (Hartford, Connecticut, and Toledo, Ohio, R. W. Bliss & Company; Newark, Bliss & Company; San Francisco, R. J. Trumbull & Company, 1870), 90–94, 138–40, 194–95, and 218–23.

some wonderful "luck" to which he was born, or both, the greater part of his adventures with bears, as with men, were of a humorous complexion; enabling him not only to have a story to tell, but one at which his companions were bound to laugh. One of these which happened during the fall hunt of 1830, we will let him tell for himself:

"The first fall on the Yellowstone, Hawkins and myself were coming up the river in search of camp, when we discovered a very large bar³ on the opposite bank. We shot across, and thought we had killed him, fur he laid quite still. As we wanted to take some trophy of our victory to camp, we tied our mules and left our guns, clothes, and everything except our knives and belts, and swum over to whar the bar war. But instead of being dead, as we expected he sprung up as we come near him, and took after us. Then you ought to have seen two naked men run! It war a race for life, and a close one, too. But we made the river first. The bank war about fifteen feet high above the water, and the river ten or twelve feet deep; but we didn't halt. Overboard we went, the bar after us, and in the stream about as quick as we war. The current war very strong, and the bar war about half way between Hawkins and me. Hawkins was trying to swim down stream faster than the current war carrying the bar, and I war a trying to hold back. You can reckon that I swam! Every moment I felt myself being washed into the yawning jaws of the mighty beast, whose head war up the stream, and his eyes on me. But the current war too strong for him, and swept him along as fast as it did me. All this time, not a long one, we war looking for some place to land where the bar could not overtake us. Hawkins war the first to make the shore, unknown to the bar, whose head war still up stream; and he set up such a whooping and yelling that the bar landed too, but on the opposite side. I made haste to follow Hawkins, who had landed on the side of the river we started from, either by design or good luck; and then we traveled back a mile or more to whar our mules war left—a bar on one side of the river and *two bares* on the other! . . ."

³ "Mr. Meek's pronunciation is southern. He says 'thar,' and 'war,' and 'bar' . . ."—*The River of the West, vi.*

37

Whenever a trapper could get hold of any sort of story reflecting on the courage of a leader, he was sure at some time to make him aware of it, and these anecdotes were sometimes sharp answers in the mouths of careless camp-keepers. Bridger was once waylaid by Blackfeet, who shot at him, hitting his horse in several places. The wounds caused the animal to rear and pitch, by reason of which violent movements Bridger dropped his gun, and the Indians snatched it up; after which there was nothing to do except to run, which Bridger accordingly did. Not long after this, as was customary, the leader was making a circuit of the camp examining the camp-keeper's guns, to see if they were in order, and found that of one Maloney, an Irishman, in a very dirty condition.

"What would you do," asked Bridger, "with a gun like that, if the Indians were to charge on the camp?"

"Be Jasus, I would throw it to them, and run the way ye did," answered Maloney, quickly. It was sometime after this incident before Bridger again examined Maloney's gun.

A laughable story in this way went the rounds of the camp in this fall of 1830. Milton Sublette was out on a hunt with Meek after buffalo, and they were just approaching the band on foot, at a distance apart of about fifty yards, when a large grizzly bear came out on a thicket and made after Sublette, who, when he perceived the creature, ran for the nearest cotton-wood tree. Meek in the meantime, seeing that Sublette was not likely to escape, had taken sure aim, and fired at the bear, fortunately killing him. On running up to the spot where it laid, Sublette was discovered sitting at the foot of a cotton-wood, with his legs and arms clasped tightly around it.

"Do you always climb a tree in that way?" asked Meek. . . .

"I'll be d——d, Meek, if I didn't think I was twenty feet up that tree when you shot"; answered the frightened Booshway;[4] and from that time the men never tired of alluding to Milton's manner of climbing a tree. . . .

[4] Leaders or chiefs, corrupted from the French *bourgeois*, and borrowed from the Canadians.—*ibid.*, 149.

1833.[5] The cold was not the only enemy in camp that winter, but famine threatened them. The buffalo had been early driven east of the mountains, and the other game was scarce. Sometimes a party of hunters were absent for days, even weeks, without finding more game than would subsist themselves. As the trappers were all hunters in the winter, it frequently happened that Meek and one or more of his associates went on a hunt in company, for the benefit of the camp, which was very hungry at times.

On one of these hunting expeditions that winter, the party consisting of Meek, Hawkins, Doughty, and Antoine Claymore, they had been out nearly a fortnight without killing anything of consequence, and had clambered up the side of the mountain on the frozen snow, in hopes of finding some mountain sheep. As they traveled along under a projecting ledge of rocks, they came to a place where there were the impressions in the snow of enormous grizzly bear feet. Close by was an opening in the rocks, revealing a cavern, and to this the tracks in the snow conducted. Evidently the creature had come out of its winter den, and made just one circuit back again. At these signs of game the hunters hesitated—certain it was there, but doubtful how to obtain it.

At length Doughty proposed to get up on the rocks above the mouth of the cavern and shoot the bear as he came out, if somebody would go in and dislodge him.

"I'm your man," answered Meek.

"And I too," said Claymore.

"I'll be d——d if we are not as brave as you are," said Hawkins, as he prepared to follow.

On entering the cave, which was sixteen or twenty feet square, and high enough to stand erect in, instead of one, three bears were discovered. They were standing, the largest one in the middle, with their eyes staring at the entrance, but quite quiet, greeting the hunters only with a low growl. Finding that there was a bear apiece to be disposed of, the hunters kept close to the wall,

[5] The trappers were camped at the junction of the Portneuf and Missouri rivers.

and out of the stream of light from the entrance, while they advanced a little way, cautiously, towards their game, which, however, seemed to take no notice of them. After maneuvering a few minutes to get nearer, Meek finally struck the large bear on the head with his wiping-stick, when it immediately moved off and ran out of the cave. As it came out, Doughty shot, but only wounded it, and it came rushing back, snorting, and running around in a circle, till the well directed shots from all three killed it on the spot. Two more bears now remained to be disposed of.

The successful shot put Hawkins in high spirits. He began to hallo and laugh, dancing around, and with the others striking the next largest bear to make him run out, which he soon did, and was shot by Doughty. By this time their guns were reloaded, the men growing more and more elated, and Hawkins declaring they were "all Daniels in the lions' den, and no mistake." This, and similar expressions, he constantly vociferated, while they drove out the third and smallest bear. As it reached the cave's mouth, three simultaneous shots put an end to the last one, when Hawkins' excitement knew no bounds. "Daniel was a humbug," said he. "Daniel in the lions' den! Of course it was winter, and the lions were sucking their paws! Tell me no more of Daniel's exploits. We are as good Daniels as he ever dared to be. Hurrah for these Daniels!" With these expressions, and playing many antics by way of rejoicing, the delighted Hawkins finally danced himself out of his "lion's den," and set to work with the others to prepare for a return to camp.

Sleds were soon constructed out of the branches of the mountain willow, and on these light vehicles the fortunate find of bear meat was soon conveyed to the hungry camp in the plain below. And ever after this singular exploit of the party, Hawkins continued to aver, in language more strong than elegant, that the Scripture Daniel was a humbug compared to himself, and Meek, and Claymore. . . .

1835. In December, Bridger's command went into winter quarters in the bend of the Yellowstone. Buffalo, elk and bear were in great abundance, all that fall and winter. Before they went to camp, Meek, Kit Carson, Hawkins, and Doughty were trapping together on the Yellowstone, about sixty miles below. They had made their temporary camp in the ruins of an old fort, the walls of which were about six feet high. One evening, after coming in from setting their traps, they discovered three large grizzly bears in the river bottom, not more than half a mile off, and Hawkins went out to shoot one. He was successful in killing one at the first shot, when the other two, taking fright, ran towards the fort. As they came near enough to show that they were likely to invade camp, Meek and Carson, not caring to have a bear fight, clambered up a cotton-wood tree close by, at the same time advising Doughty to do the same. But Doughty was tired, and lazy besides, and concluded to take his chances where he was; so he rolled himself in his blanket and laid quite still. The bears, on making the fort, reared up on their hind legs and looked in as if meditating taking it for a defence.

The sight of Doughty lying rolled in his blanket, and the monster grizzlys inspecting the fort, caused the two trappers who were safely perched in the cotton-wood to make merry at Doughty's expense; saying all the mirth-provoking things they could, and then advising him not to laugh, for fear the bears should seize him. Poor Doughty, agonizing between suppressed laughter and growing fear, contrived to lie still however, while the bears gazed upward at the speakers in wonder, and alternately at the suspicious looking bundle inside the fort. Not being able to make out the meaning of either, they gave at last a grunt of dissatisfaction, and ran off into a thicket to consult over these strange appearances; leaving the trappers to enjoy the incident as a very good joke. For a long time after, Doughty was reminded how close to the ground he laid, when the grizzlys paid their compliments to him.

Such were the every-day incidents from which the mountain-men contrived to derive their rude jests, and laughter-provoking reminiscences. . . .

1836. It happened . . . during this autumn, that while the main camp was in the valley of the Yellowstone, a party of eight trappers, including Meek and a comrade named Stanberry, were trapping together on the Mussel Shell, when the question as to which was the bravest man got started between them, and at length, in the heat of controversy, assumed such importance that it was agreed to settle the matter on the following day according to the Virginia code of honor, *i.e.*, by fighting a duel, and shooting at each other with guns, which hitherto had only done execution on bears and Indians.

But some listening spirit of the woods determined to avert the danger from these two equally brave trappers, and save their ammunition for its legitimate use, by giving them occasion to prove their courage on the instant. While sitting around the camp-fire discussing the coming event of the duel at thirty paces, a huge bear, already wounded by a shot from the gun of their hunter who was out looking for game, came running furiously into camp, giving each man there a challenge to fight or fly.

"Now," spoke up one of the men quickly, "let Meek and Stanberry prove which is the bravest, by fighting the bear!" "Agreed," cried the two as quickly, and both sprang with guns and wiping-sticks in hand, charging upon the infuriated beast as it reached the spot where they were awaiting it. Stanberry was a small man, and Meek a large one. Perhaps it was owing to this difference of stature that Meek was first to reach the bear as it advanced. Running up with reckless bravado Meek struck the creature two or three times over the head with his wiping-stick before aiming to fire, which however he did so quickly and so surely that the beast fell dead at his feet. This act settled the vexed question. Nobody was disposed to dispute the point of courage with a man who would stop to strike a grizzly before shooting him: therefore Meek was proclaimed by the common voice to be "cock of the walk" in that camp. The pipe of peace was solemnly smoked by himself and Stanberry, and the tomahawk buried never more to be resurrected between them, while a fat supper of bear meat celebrated the compact of everlasting amity.

It was not an unfrequent occurrence for a grizzly bear to be run into camp by the hunters, in the Yellowstone Country where this creature abounded. An amusing incident occurred not long after that just related, when the whole camp was at the Cross Creeks of the Yellowstone, on the south side of that river. The hunters were out, and had come upon two or three bears in a thicket. As these animals sometimes will do, they started off in a great fright, running towards camp, the hunters after them, yelling, frightening them still more. A runaway bear, like a runaway horse, appears not to see where it is going, but keeps right on its course no matter what dangers lie in advance. So one of these animals having got headed for the middle of the encampment, saw nothing of what lay in its way, but ran on and on, apparently taking note of nothing but the yells in pursuit. So sudden and unexpected was the charge which he made upon camp, that the Indian women, who were sitting on the ground engaged in some ornamental work, had no time to escape out of the way. One of them was thrown down and run over, and another was struck with such violence that she was thrown twenty feet from the spot where she was hastily attempting to rise. Other objects in camp were upset and thrown out of the way, but without causing so much merriment as the mishaps of the two women who were so rudely treated by the monster.

It was also while the camp was at the Cross Creeks of the Yellowstone that Meek had one of his best fought battles with a grizzly bear. He was out with two companions, one Gardiner, and Mark Head, a Shawnee Indian. Seeing a very large bear digging roots in the creek bottom, Meek proposed to attack it, if the others would hold his horse ready to mount if he failed to kill the creature. This being agreed to he advanced to within about forty paces of his game, when he raised his gun and attempted to fire, but the cap bursting he only roused the beast, which turned on him with a terrific noise between a snarl and a growl, showing some fearful looking teeth. Meek turned to run for his horse, at the same time trying to put a cap on his gun; but when he had almost reached his comrades, their horses and his own took fright at the bear now close on his heels, and ran, leaving him alone with the now fully infuriated beast. Just at the moment he succeeded in getting a cap on his gun, the teeth of the bear closed on his blanket capote which was belted around the waist, and the suddenness and force of the seizure turning him around, as the skirt of his capote yielded to the strain and tore off at the belt. Being now nearly face to face with his foe, the intrepid trapper thrust his gun into the creature's mouth and attempted again to fire, but the gun being double triggered and not set, it failed to go off. Perceiving the difficulty he managed to set the triggers with the gun still in the bear's mouth, yet no sooner was this done than the bear succeeded in knocking it out, and firing as it slipped out, it hit her too low down to inflict a fatal wound and only served to irritate her still farther.

In this desperate situation when Meek's brain was rapidly working on the problem of live Meek or live bear, two fresh actors appeared on the scene in the persons of two cubs, who seeing their mother in difficulty seemed desirous of doing something to to assist her. Their appearance seemed to excite the bear to new exertions, for she made one desperate blow at Meek's empty gun with which he was defending himself, and knocked it out of his hands, and far down the bank or sloping hillside where the struggle was now going on. Then being partially blinded by rage, she seized one of her cubs and began to box it about in a most unmotherly fashion. This diversion gave Meek a chance to draw his knife from the scabbard, with which he endeavored to stab the bear behind the ear; but she was too quick for him, and with a blow struck it out of his hand, as she had the gun, nearly severing his forefinger.

At this critical juncture the second cub interfered, and got a boxing from the old bear, as the first one had done. This too, gave Meek time to make a movement, and loosening his tomahawk from his belt, he made one tremendous effort, taking deadly aim, and struck her just behind the ear, the tomahawk sinking into the brain, and his powerful antagonist lay dead before him. When the blow was struck he stood with his back against a little bluff of rock, beyond which it was impossible to retreat. It was his last chance, and his usual good fortune stood by him. When the struggle was over the weary victor mounted the rock behind him and looked down upon his enemy slain, and "came to the conclusion that he was satisfied with bar-fighting."

8

KIT CARSON'S STIRRING ADVENTURES WITH TWO GRIZZLY BEARS
Edward S. Ellis[1]

The following account of Kit Carson's adventure with two grizzlies is from Edward S. Ellis' *Kit Carson*,[2] published in 1889 as a pulp adventure for boys. For a more authentic account of the mountain man who explored the western half of the United States from St. Louis to California we must go to M. Morgan Estergreen's *Kit Carson: A Portrait in Courage*, published by the University of Oklahoma Press in 1962, or Edwin L. Sabin's *Kit Carson Days*, published in Chicago by A. C. McClurg Publishing Company in 1914. However, the excerpt reprinted here gives a vivid picture of Kit Carson in an exceedingly uncomfortable situation which adult readers will appreciate.

As CARSON'S ENGAGEMENT WITH CAPTAIN LEE was ended, he decided to do as he had done before—arrange an expedition of his own. He had but to make known his intentions, when he had more applications than he could accept. He selected three, who it is needless to say had no superiors in the whole party. The little company then turned the heads of their horses toward Laramie River.

At that day, the section abounded with beaver, and although

---

[1] Edward Sylvester Ellis' first book, *Seth Jones; or, the Captive of the Frontier*, published in 1860, sold 600,000 copies, becoming the forerunner of the dime-novel "thrillers" which glutted America in the second half of the nineteenth century. While superintendent of the Trenton, New Jersey, schools, and later, Ellis wrote prolifically on adventure and hero themes for young boy readers. He also wrote inspirational American biographical and historical books for children and adults and published a great deal of material dealing with topics of the day.

[2] Edward S. Ellis, *Kit Carson* (Chicago and New York, M. A. Donahue Company, 1889).

the summer is not the time when their fur is in the best condition, the party trapped on the stream and its tributaries until cold weather set in. They met with far greater success, than could have come to them had they stayed with the principal company of trappers. But they had no wish to spend the winter alone in the mountains and gathering their stock together, they set out to rejoin their old companions.

One day, after they had gone into camp, Carson, leaving his horse in charge of his friends, set out on foot to hunt some game for their evening meal. They had seen no signs of Indians, though they never forgot to be on their guard against them. Game was not very abundant and Carson was obliged to go a long ways before he caught sight of some elk grazing on the side of a hill. Well aware of the difficulty of getting within gunshot of the timid animals, the hunter advanced by a circuitous course toward a clump of trees, which would give him the needed shelter; but while creeping toward the point he had fixed upon as one from which to fire, the creatures scented danger and began moving off. This compelled him to fire at long range, but he was successful and brought down the finest of the group.

The smoke was curling upward from the rifle of Carson, when he was startled by a tremendous crashing beside him, and, turning his head, he saw two enormous grizzly bears making for him at full speed. They were infuriated at this invasion of their home, and were evidently resolved on teaching the hunter better manners by making their supper upon him.

Carson had no time to reload his gun: had it been given him he would have made short work of one of the brutes at least, but as it was, he was deprived of even that privilege. Fortunate indeed would he be if he could escape their fury.

The grizzly bear is the most dreaded animal found on this continent. He does not seem to feel the slightest fear of the hunter, no matter whether armed or not, and, while other beasts are disposed to give man a wide berth, old "Ephraim," as the frontiersmen call him, always seems eager to attack him. His tenacity of life is extraordinary. Unless pierced in the head or heart, he will continue his struggles after a dozen or score of rifle balls have been buried in his body. So terrible is the grizzly bear, that an Indian can be given no higher honor than the privilege of wearing a necklace made from his claws,—the distinction being permitted only to those who have slain one of the animals in single-handed combat.

No one understood the nature of these beasts better than Kit Carson and he knew that if either of the animals once got his claws upon him, there would not be the faintest chance of escape. The only thing therefore that could be done was to run.

There were not wanting men who were fleeter of foot than Carson, but few could have overtaken him when he made for the trees on which all his hopes depended. Like the blockade runner, closely pursued by the man of war, he threw overboard all the cargo that could impede his speed. His long, heavy rifle was flung aside, and the short legs of the trapper doubled under him with amazing quickness as he strove as never before to reach the grove.

Fortunately the latter was not far off, and, though the fierce beasts gained rapidly upon him, Carson arrived among the timber a few steps in advance. He had no time even to select a tree, else he would have chosen a different one, but making a flying leap, he grasped the lowermost limb and swung upward, at the moment the foremost grizzly was beneath him. So close in truth was his pursuer that the hunter distinctly felt the sweeping blow of his paw aimed at the leg which whisked beyond his reach just in the nick of time.

But the danger was not over by any means. The enthusiastic style in which the bears entered into the proceedings proved they did not mean that any trifles should stop them. They were able to climb the tree which supported Carson,[3] and he did not lose sight of the fact. Whipping out his hunting knife; he hurriedly cut off a short thick branch and trimmed it into a shape that would have made a most excellent shillaleh [*sic*] for a native of the Green Isle.

He had hardly done so, when the heads of the bruins were thrust upward almost against his feet. Carson grasped the club

[3] Authorities generally agree that mature grizzly bears cannot climb trees because of their great weight and the anatomy of their paws.

47

with both hands and raising it above his shoulders brought it down with all his might upon the nose of the foremost. The brute sniffed with pain, threw up his head and drew back a few inches— just enough to place the other nose in front. At that instant, a resounding whack landed on the rubber snout and the second bear must have felt a twinge all through his body.

Though each blow caused the recipient to recoil, yet he instantly returned, so that Carson was kept busy pounding the noses as if he was an old fashioned farmer threshing wheat with a flail.

It was a question with Carson which would last the longer— the club or the snouts, but in the hope of getting beyond their reach, he climbed to the topmost bough, where he crouched into the smallest possible space. It was idle, however, to hope they would overlook him, for they pushed on up the tree which swayed with their weight.

The nose of the grizzly bear is one of the most sensitive portions of his body, and the vigorous thumps which the hunter brought down upon them, brought tears of pain to their eyes. But while they suffered, they were roused to fury by the repeated rebuffs, and seemed all the more set on craunching [*sic*] the flesh and bones of the insignificant creature who defied them.

It must have been exasperating beyond imagination to the gigantic beasts, who feared neither man nor animal to find themselves repeatedly baffled by a miserable being whom they could rend to pieces with one blow of their paws, provided they could approach nigh enough to reach him.

They came up again and again; they would draw back so as to avoid those stinging strokes, sniff, growl, and push upward, more eager than ever to clutch the poor fellow, who was compressing himself between the limb and the trunk, and raining his blows with the persistency of a pugilist.

They were finally forced to desist for a few minutes in order to give their snouts time to regain their tone. The bulky creatures looked at each other and seemed to say, "That's a mighty queer customer up there; he doesn't fight fairly, but we'll fetch him yet."

Once more and for the last time, they returned to the charge, but the plucky scout was awaiting them, and his club whizzed through the air like the piston rod of a steam engine. The grizzlies found it more than they could stand, and tumbling back to solid earth they gave up the contract in disgust. Carson tarried where he was until they were beyond sight, when he descended and hastily caught up and re-loaded his rifle, having escaped, as he always declared, by the narrowest chance of all his life.

9

THE SAGA OF HUGH GLASS

George Frederick Augustus Ruxton

Students of the fur trade in the West have long regarded the
writings of George Frederick Ruxton as classics of their kind,
unexcelled for authenticity, color, and pithiness. Ruxton was ex-
pelled from the Royal Military Academy at Sandhurst, England,
at the age of fifteen. From that time until his death in St. Louis
in 1848, he led a life of fabulous adventure. After a daring period
on the Continent, he served in Canada for a time as an officer of
the British army. It was during this service that he became in-
fatuated with the North American wilderness. Following an ad-
venture-filled episode in Morocco at the age of twenty-three and
exploration in South Africa at twenty-four, he embarked upon an
arduous journey from Mexico City, northward through the interior of Mexico to Santa Fe, thence into Colorado and overland to St. Louis, traveling alone or with a succession of skittish
servants. It was on this journey that he gathered the colorful
material which was published first as a series of articles in English periodicals.

Ruxton was the first writer to depict the Old West realistically.
He wrote picturesquely of the life led by mountain men and fur
trappers, often using the rough jargon of this rough tribe of men,
so that his writings literally breathe life. Unfortunately this marvelous record of early days in the West has not been available to
modern readers until recent times. Clyde and Mae Reed Porter
methodically gathered together letters Ruxton wrote to his family from America and other previously unpublished material and
combined them with Ruxton's stories of his adventures in America
under the title, *Ruxton of the Rockies*, edited by LeRoy R. Hafen
and published by the University of Oklahoma Press, at Norman,
Oklahoma, in 1950. The following legend of Hugh Glass ap-

pears on pages 252–55 of this book. For another version read J. Cecil Alter, "A Famous Bear Story," *Jim Bridger*, Norman, University of Oklahoma Press, 1962, pages 38–42.

THE GRIZZLY BEAR is the fiercest of the *ferae naturae* of the mountains. His great strength and wonderful tenacity of life render an encounter with him anything but desirable, and therefore it is a rule with the Indians and white hunters never to attack him unless backed by a strong party. Although, like every other wild animal, he usually flees from man, yet at certain seasons, when maddened by love or hunger, he not unfrequently charges at first sight of a foe, when, unless killed dead, a hug at close quarters is anything but a pleasant embrace, his strong hooked claws stripping the flesh from bones as easily as a cook peels an onion. Many are the tales of bloody encounters with these animals which the trappers delight to recount to the greenhorn, to enforce their caution as to the foolhardiness of ever attacking the grizzly bear.

Some years ago a trapping party was on their way to the mountains, led, I believe, by old Sublette, a well-known captain of the West. Amongst the band was one John [Hugh] Glass, a trapper who had been all his life in the mountains, and had seen, probably, more exciting adventures, and had had more wonderful and hairbreadth escapes, than any of the rough and hardy fellows who make the West their home, and whose lives are spent in a succession of perils and privations. On one of the streams running from the Black Hills, a range of mountains northward of the Platte, Glass and a companion were one day setting their traps, when, on passing through a cherry thicket which skirted the stream, the former, who was in advance, descried a large grizzly bear quietly turning up the turf with his nose, searching for yampa roots or pig nuts, which there abounded. Glass immediately called his companion, and both, proceeding cautiously, crept to the skirt of the thicket, and, taking steady aim at the animal, whose broadside was fairly exposed at the distance of twenty yards, discharged their rifles at the same instant, both balls taking effect, but not inflicting a mortal wound. The bear, giving a groan of pain, jumped with all four legs from the ground, and, seeing the wreaths of smoke hanging at the edge of the brush, charged at once in that direction, snorting with pain and fury.

"Harraw, Bill!" roared out Glass, as he saw the animal rushing towards them, "we'll be made meat of as sure as shootin'!" and, leaving the tree behind which he had concealed himself, he bolted through the thicket, followed closely by his companion. The brush was so thick that they could scarcely make their way through, whereas the weight and strength of the bear carried him through all obstructions, and he was soon close upon them.

About a hundred yards from the thicket was a steep bluff, and between these points was a level piece of prairie; Glass saw that his only chance was to reach this bluff, and, shouting to his companion to make for it, they both broke from the cover and flew like lightning across the open space. When more than half way across, the bear being about fifty yards behind them, Glass, who was leading, tripped over a stone and fell to the ground, and just as he rose to his feet, the beast, rising on his hind feet, confronted him. As he closed, Glass, never losing his presence of mind, cried to his companion to load up quickly, and discharged his pistol full into the body of the animal, at the same moment that the bear, with blood streaming from its nose and mouth, knocked the pistol from his hand with one blow of its paw, and, fixing its claws deep into his flesh, rolled with him to the ground.

The hunter, notwithstanding his hopeless situation, struggled manfully, drawing his knife and plunging it several times into the body of the beast, which, furious with pain, tore with tooth and claw the body of the wretched victim, actually baring the ribs of flesh and exposing the very bones. Weak with loss of blood, and with eyes blinded with the blood which streamed from his lacerated scalp, the knife at length fell from his hand, and Glass sank down insensible, and to all appearance dead.

His companion, who, up to this moment, had watched the conflict, which, however, lasted but a few seconds, thinking that his turn would come next, and not having had presence of mind even to load his rifle, fled with might and main back to camp, where he narrated the miserable fate of poor Glass. The captain of the band of trappers, however, dispatched the man with a com-

panion back to the spot where he lay, with instructions to remain
by him if still alive, or to bury him if, as all supposed he was,
defunct, promising them at the same time a sum of money for
so doing.

On reaching the spot, which was red with blood, they found
Glass still breathing, and the bear, dead and stiff, actually lying

upon his body. Poor Glass presented a horrifying spectacle: the flesh was torn in strips from his chest and limbs, and large flaps strewed the ground; his scalp hung bleeding over his face, which was also lacerated in a shocking manner.

The bear, besides the three bullets which had pierced its body, bore the marks of the fierce nature of Glass's final struggle, no less than twenty gaping wounds in the breast and belly testifying to the gallant defence of the mountaineer.

Imagining that, if not already dead, the poor fellow could not possibly survive more than a few moments, the men collected his arms, stripped him even of his hunting shirt and moccasins, and, merely pulling the dead bear off the body, mounted their horses, and slowly followed the remainder of the party, saying, when they reached it, that Glass was dead, as probably they thought, and that they had buried him.

In a few days the gloom which pervaded the trappers' camp, occasioned by the loss of a favourite companion, disappeared, and Glass's misfortune, although frequently mentioned over the campfire, at length was almost entirely forgotten in the excitement of the hunt and Indian perils which surrounded them.

Months elapsed, the hunt was over, and the party of trappers were on their way to the trading fort with their packs of beaver. It was nearly sundown, and the round adobe bastions of the mud-built fort were just in sight, when a horseman was seen slowly approaching them along the banks of the river. When near enough to discern his figure, they saw a lank cadaverous form with a face so scarred and disfigured that scarcely a feature was discernible. Approaching the leading horsemen, one of whom happened to be the companion of the defunct Glass in his memorable bear scrape, the stranger, in a hollow voice, reining in his horse before them, exclaimed, "Hurraw, Bill, my boy! you thought I was gone under that time, did you? But hand me over my horse and gun, my lad; I ain't dead yet by a dam sight!"

What was the astonishment of the whole party, and the genuine horror of Bill and his worthy companion in the burial story, to hear the well-known, though now much altered, voice of John Glass, who had been killed by a grizzly bear months before, and comfortably interred, as the two men had reported, and all had believed!

There he was, however, and no mistake about it; and all crowded round to hear from his lips, how, after the lapse of he knew not how long, he had gradually recovered, and being without arms, or even a butcher knife, he had fed upon the almost putrid carcase of the bear for several days, until he had regained sufficient strength to crawl, when, tearing off as much of the bear's meat as he could carry in his enfeebled state, he crept down the river, and suffering excessive torture from his wounds, and hunger, and cold, he made the best of his way to the fort, which was some eighty or ninety miles from the place of his encounter with the bear, and, living the greater part of the way upon roots and berries, he after many, many days, arrived in a pitiable state, from which he had now recovered, and was, to use his own expression, "as slick as a peeled onion."

CALIFORNIA GRIZZLIES

10

EARLY CALIFORNIA REMINISCENCES
General John Bidwell

Many present-day Californians may read with skepticism General Bidwell's tale of galloping grizzlies in the Upper Sacramento River Valley, but the fact remains that California grizzly bears were the largest carnivorous animals in the Old West, weighing several hundred pounds, and were much too numerous in many parts of the state for comfort. Andrew Sublette was mauled to death by one of these brutes within the present boundaries of Santa Monica; meat hunters for the gold camps and sports hunters from the East and Europe helped eliminate the big bears, and they gradually diminished in number as their habitat was put under cultivation.

General Bidwell was one of the leaders of the first party of settlers to come to California in 1841. He took an active part in Frémont's Bear Flag revolt in 1846 and in 1849 purchased Rancho Chico and surrounding area, where he founded the rich agricultural economy of the Chico Valley. The story reprinted here first appeared in an uncopyrighted pamphlet entitled *Echoes of the Past*, printed by the *Chico Advertiser* in 1914, pages 74–79. Other material contained in the rare little booklet had previously appeared in serial form in *Century Magazine* in 1890. This charming and informative pamphlet is quite rare. Fortunately, it has been republished (General John Bidwell, *Echoes of the Past* [New York, The Citadel Press, 1962]) and is available to Americana enthusiasts.

MY FIRST OCCUPATION in California was for Sutter at Bodega and Fort Ross, in removing the property purchased from the Russians to Sacramento. When all the cattle (wild cattle I mean, for all the cattle were considered wild, except a few which had been

broken in to milk or to work as oxen) had been removed to Sacramento, there still remained from 150 to 200 head so wild that
they seldom could be seen in the day time. Late in the evening,
when it was almost dark, they would emerge from their impenetrable hiding places to eat grass. They were wilder than any deer,
buffalo, elk or antelope, possessing the keenest vision and hearing.
It was almost impossible to kill them, the country being so hilly
and brushy. They were so wild that for a year I never killed one
because the deer, antelope, etc. would get between me and the
game, and if I scared a deer, they knew that meant danger,
and ran. I thought I had seen wild animals, but I confess they
were the wildest I had ever seen.

All these cattle had been brought here from Mexico. Of horses
there were thousands in the San Joaquin Valley. I have seen herds
twenty miles long on the west side. The men at Sutter's Fort were
very orderly, showing that, when men are beyond the law and
the customs of civilization, there springs up a common law among
themselves. There was no law by which to regularly govern the
men, yet there was no trouble except with a degraded set of
mountaineers hovering around the Indian rancheria, trading beads
and whiskey, and sleeping in the rancheria. There was no such
thing as murder till as late as 1845. Sutter had a distillery in 1845.

On my way home some of my horses strayed away and I
borrowed a mule and a horse from a man Manuel Vaca at what
is now Vacaville. Subsequently my horses returned, but Vaca's
mule and horse had been stolen from me and he wanted $50 for
the mule and $25 for the horse. These figures seemed amazing, for,
in fact, the best horses sold from $5 to $10 and the best mules
from $10 to $15. It would take me three months to earn the
$75 at the salary I was getting, and I decided to scour the country
for these wonderful animals. Peter Lassen, whose name now at-
taches to Lassen Peak and Lassen county, Joe Bruheim, a German
living at what is now Nicolus, accompanied me. We heard that
a party had started for Oregon and decided to overtake them, as
in those days it was deemed a wise precaution to look out for
your horses when a party left for Oregon.

Approaching Butte Creek, where we camped for the first time

after leaving Hock Farm, we had an episode among the grizzly bears. In the spring of the year they lived principally on the plains, and especially in the little depressions on the plains. The first we saw made for the timber two or three miles distant, soon another, and another and more, all bounding away toward the creek. At one time there were sixteen in the drove. Of course we chased them, but had no desire to overtake them; there were too many. As they advanced, one of the largest diverged to the left, and I pursued him alone. He was the largest I had ever seen, and his hair was long and shaggy, and I had the keenest desire to shoot him. I rode almost onto him, but every time I raised the gun the horse commenced bucking. My desire to shoot the bear became so great that it overcame my prudence, and I charged as near as I dared and dismounted, intending to get a shot, and mount again before he could get me. But the moment I was on the ground it was all I could do to hold the horse, which jumped and plunged and sawed my hands with the rope. When I could look toward the bear, I found he had stopped, reared, and was looking toward me and the horse. My hair, I think, stood straight up, and I was delighted when the bear turned and ran from me. I soon mounted the horse, and saw him plunge into the timber and make off.

Horses and mules are always frightened at the sight and smell of grizzly bears. It was difficult to keep our horses, as they snorted and tried to get away all night.

The next morning we were early in the saddle, and on our way, and in a few miles ride took further lessons in the pastime of chasing grizzly bears. I pursued a large one and a very swift one. When following you must run by the side and not immediately behind him, for he can more easily catch you if you do.

I was chasing too directly behind him and before I could turn, so close was I, that when he turned and struck, his claws touched the tail of my horse, and for a hundred yards at every jump he struck my horse's tail. Coming to better ground we soon left the bear in the distance, and as soon as he turned I turned after him. I heard him plunge into a stream and swim across it. Stationing myself where I could see him when he came out, as he stood on his hind feet, I shot. The blood spurted out of his nostrils two or three feet high, and he bounded about one hundred yards and died. These scenes were common—of daily and almost hourly occurrences. . . .

We were now on the trail of the Oregon company, which lay on the east bank of the Sacramento River. The streams flowing into it, with the exception of Butte Creek, had at that time, not been named. Seeing some of the Sabine pine on a stream where we camped, we named it Pine Creek. . . .

Crossing Antelope Creek, and following the trail of the Oregon party, we came to the Sacramento River opposite the site of Red Bluff. Here the company had crossed the river and were encamped on the opposite bank. They had no wagons, simply pack animals. The stream at that time was considerably swollen, deep, swift and cold. With simply a small hatchet, scarcely larger than a tomahawk, I set about making a raft to cross, which was no easy task to construct of dry willow brush and such dead sticks as we could secure with our means. At last it was completed, being sufficient merely to hold me above water; however, to secure a dry passage if possible, a second story was built on it, consisting of fine, dry brush, tied securely. In size it resembled somewhat a small load of hay. Fearing that I could not manage it alone, I persuaded a wild Indian to go with me. He consented to go with great reluctance, but a few beads and a cotton handkerchief were so tempting that he could not resist. The only things we could get to propel the raft were willow poles, and none of them were long enough to touch the bottom when we started into the stream; so we had to use them as paddles. We were high and dry when we started, but the displacement of the water by the brush was so little, and the material became so quickly water-logged, that the raft was soon under water. The swift current carried us so rapidly down that it was with difficulty we got over at all, but we finally got across one or two miles below. The most of the time we were up to our arms in cold water, and only knew by the brush under our feet that we were on the raft at all. If men ever labored for their lives we did. Safely on land, however, I soon made my way to the camp of the Oregon company. . . . I at once made known my object which was to find the mule and the horse, which I had lost at Sacramento. These men at once declared that if the animals were there, and if I could identify them, I could have them, but nearly all protested that there were no such animals there, and they all agreed to drive up all the horses and mules they had for my inspection. As a result I soon found my animals and demanded their surrender. There was some opposition, but Ben Kelsey, a very resolute man, and on this occasion a very useful one to me, declared that I should have them. Then all opposition being withdrawn, the animals were driven to the river and made to swim across. My object being accomplished, I at once set out upon my return.

11

OF BEARS IN THE NIPOMO HILLS
Rocky Dana and Marie Harrington

Juan Francisco Dana was the fourth son born to Captain William Goodwin Dana and Maria Josefa Petra del Carmen, daughter of Don Carlos Antonio Carrillo, resident of Santa Barbara and later provisional governer of Mexican California. Captain Dana arrived on the coast of California in 1825, when the Mexicans first opened their ports to foreign ships. He married Señorita Carrillo the following year after waiting months for the permission necessitated by the fact that he was neither Mexican nor Roman Catholic.

Juan Francisco was born in Santa Barbara village and grew up in the Spanish-American atmosphere of San Luis Obispo County, near the present-day town of Nipomo, on the land grant acquired by his father after his Mexican naturalization. *The Blond Ranchero: Memories of Juan Francisco Dana*, compiled by Rocky Dana, grandson of Juan Francisco, assisted by Marie Dana Harrington (no relation), is a rich treasury of memorabilia of golden days in California, before guided-missile launching pads, oil wells, and tourist accommodations came to the verdant Nipomo Hills. The picture presented has the warmth that gave life on the early California ranchos a distinctly different flavor than was ever found elsewhere in America. The charming little book was published in Los Angeles in 1960 by Dawson's Book Shop. Our selection appears on pages 83–92 and is reprinted here by the kind permission of Mr. Glen Dawson and Marie Harrington.

OLD BRUIN WAS A SMART FELLOW and I had many run-ins with his tribe from the time I could ride a horse. My father had a warehouse at Cave Landing when I was a youngster and I would often be told to go with one of our Indians and take a carreta-load[1]

---

[1] A *carreta* is a heavy, wooden cart.

of hides and tallow if a ship were expected. Our "leather dollars" —pesos de cuero—would be exchanged for commodities that we could not produce on Nipomo such as coffee, sugar, chocolate, and clothing or furniture from the United States for our women folk.

After we loaded the carreta, we would usually visit awhile with the captain and often hear about our far-off kinsfolk in Boston. Then we would head south for home following the beachline, crossing and recrossing the sandunes on the way. Believe me, the oxen had to pull hard to keep the carrettas from bogging in the deep sand. They had a hard time of it for the carreta wheels were cut from single sections of sycamore trees and the carretas were very heavy even when unloaded.

On one of these trips everything went along well until we reached the Oso Flaco region.[2] Sure enough, the carreta got stuck in the sand and the poor oxen could not budge it. The Indian poked and poked with his garrocha[3] but finally had to give up. While we were tugging away, two bears came out of the nearby monte.[4] We had a side of bacon in the carreta that day and the smell had probably attracted them. They stood less than 50 feet from us—just stood and looked at us!

We surely were in a predicament for we couldn't get that carreta going and we couldn't unload with the bears around. If we unyoked the oxen and left, we were pretty sure there wouldn't be any supplies left on our return either! Maybe it sounds childish but I got the idea to make a dummy! I gathered sticks of wood from the nearby brush and took some of the new clothes we had got at Cave Landing. The family might yell but they would yell more if Old Bruin took their supplies. My Indian companion was good and frightened by this time but I told him I was sure the bears would have hurt us when they first spotted us if they were going to hurt us at all. So we unyoked the oxen, the Indian got behind me on my horse and off we started for Casa de Dana, driving the animals ahead of us. We arrived home quite late that

[2] Region of the "thin bears."
[3] An iron pointed staff.
[4] The Spanish word for mountain.

. night and had plenty of explaining to do about the missing carreta.

Early the next morning we started back for Oso Flaco with the strongest oxen team that we had on the rancho. We were very surprised to find a lot of bear tracks in the sand circling the untouched carreta. It looked as if more bears had been attracted by the smell of bacon during the night. Apparently they didn't come any nearer than 15 feet despite the milling and circling that went on. Maybe they thought the scent came from the "man" on the cart. Strange as it may seem, no damage at all was done the carreta or its contents. We hitched the oxen to the carreta and finally got it out of the sand and on its way. We didn't see any more bears on the return trip although we kept a sharp outlook.

During later years as a vaquero on our rancho I had many meetings with Old Bruin. One time in the hills back of Nipomo I lassoed a bear, wrapping the riata around the saddle horn, preparing to drag the bear down the hill. But my lasso tightened when I had gone only a little way and the bear choked to death . . . which ended a possible bull and bear fight!

Tio Juan Price had the same experience one day although the bear remained very much alive. Tio Juan wanted his riata but he didn't dare go near the bear to get it back. He suddenly got an idea as he looked at a nearby oak tree. When Mr. Bruin was opposite the tree, Tio Juan rode his horse rapidly around the tree several times, securely binding the bear. He then tied the riata and went home. Later, he returned with a rifle and finished off that bear.

There's an old saying that if you give a monkey a bottle of soda pop he will open it and try to drink the contents. I've seen a seagull pick up a clam, fly to a certain height and drop the clam so the shell will break and the gull has a tasty supper. Bears also have their own method of getting tidbits.

One day I was riding along La Canada de los Alisos[5] when suddenly my horse perked up his ears and started trembling. Ahead of me, on the edge of a nearby monte, I saw a young bear busily killing bees. He was so busy he hadn't heard or seen us approach.

[5] Alder Canyon.

I pulled my horse to the side of the trail and watched Mr. Bruin. As each bee came out of a hole in the tree, the bear made just one swipe with his paw. Once in a while a bee would escape and Mr. Bruin would scamper off, soon returning. He continued this for some time until one bee which had been struck but not killed, had enough life left in him to get revenge. So he struck and Mr. Bruin turned tail, running down the trail as fast as he could with the bee after him!

I rode over to the tree where a pile of dead bees were on the ground. This long process was Mr. Bruin's patient way of getting at the honey in the tree trunk. If he had stayed a little longer, he probably would have got all the bees in that trunk and the honey comb as well. At any rate, I didn't wait to find out how many more bees were left—I took off too!

Of all the bears I have seen in my long life, the one the rancheros[6] in our section of the state called El Casador, or the Hunter, was the giant of the lot and probably cost more damage to stock than any other single bear around us. He finally killed so many cattle and sheep that several rancheros, including Don Francisco

[6] Ranchers.

Branch, Don Diego Olivera and our family, got together and offered a reward to the person killing this beast.

Don Diego owned a rifle which used larger bullets than any used by the rancheros in the central coast country. At last, one day Don Diego shot El Casador in one paw—part of the paw was shot off but the huge beast escaped and for a long time after the tracks of his mutilated paw were his dreaded "calling card" after a killing. His tracks were easily identified especially if the sand or soil was soft and it got so that every time a calf was missing or any other stock for that matter, El Casador got the blame.

One day my brother, Ramon, and I went deer hunting. Before long, we saw four deer. Ramon followed them into a monte while I stayed on the edge of the thicket. In just a few minutes my brother returned saying he couldn't find the deer. I thought that was strange so I went into the monte. Within a few yards I saw deer tracks—and also found the reason for Ramon's quick return! El Casador was in the neighborhood! I let the deer go too as I had visions of that great beast tearing me apart. My rifle wasn't anywhere big enough for bear hunting. Needless to say, there were strained relations between Ramon and me going back to Nipomo.

Thoughts of El Casador haunted me all that night. The next day I found myself saddling my horse and heading back for that monte. I rode over the same ground but couldn't find any fresh tracks. I was just about to give up when I came across some fresh tracks with the well-known mutilated paw mark. I followed them as they led into the monte. Pretty soon I wished I hadn't gone into the thicket for I heard a great noise and saw coming toward me, the biggest and fiercest-looking bear I had ever seen. I didn't need intuition to tell me that El Casador and I were finally meeting. My horse was trembling and so were my knees. I opened fire but the charges didn't even seem to bother the brute. On he came and on I fired and the last shot took effect for the mighty hunter crashed to the ground.

I don't think I ever did see a bigger or fatter bear in my whole life. His claws were very sharp and my horse and I would have been torn to shreds if El Casador had ever got near enough to us.

I didn't waste any time in galloping home to tell the family that I had shot El Casador. Some of the family were sitting around a stove talking, when I arrived and they thought I was telling a tall tale when I told them that if they had stuck the bear's head into the stove opening his nose would have hit the bottom of the grate and his eyes would have still been outside that stove. After laughing awhile, some of the hardy ones agreed to return to the monte with me and bring back the trophy.

I had the laugh on everyone when they first laid eyes on the late El Casador. Their eyes fairly bugged from their sockets as mine had a few hours earlier. We skinned the bear on the spot. We cut his thick layer of fat into strips to take home to be rendered. We got a big barrel of tallow as a result and used it for a long time to grease our carreta wheels and for other greasing jobs around the rancho.

We examined his paws to see if it really was El Casador—sure enough, we found the large bullet which proved Don Francisco had wounded the monarch of the Nipomo Hills.

I don't remember what became of that huge skin—I'm sure we never used it for a rug as it retained a strong scent and even the horses didn't like it.

Speaking about the Oso Flaco region—when I was young, there was a great monte there of tangled vines, blackberry, poison oak and all sorts of other growth. There were many bears around there and a favorite story of a very thin bear—an oso flaco—that lived in the monte. Rancheros, passing by on horseback, often saw this lean bear and when telling where they had been would say usually:

"Pasemos cerca donde esta el oso flaco." (We passed near where the lean bear is.)

Today this region, which has taken its name from this lean bear, is a rich agricultural section and the lean bear would be a fat bear indeed if he were living.

Up at the town of San Lus [sic] Obispo, when it was young, we had bull and bear fights in the old plaza. These were held up into the 1860's. The bull ring stood where the Anderson Hotel is now and Jeff Anderson used to tell how disappointed he was as a boy because his parents wouldn't let him see one of these fights.

When there was to be a contest, Old Bruin would be brought down from the hills to the bull-ring where one of his legs would be secured to the end of a chain. The other end of the chain was wrapped around a strong post in the middle of the ring. Then the bull would be let loose. The bull always seemed to remember that he was the protector of the herd, facing his natural enemy and as a result, the fight was always fierce and furious.

But not all the fights took place at the pueblo. Many a time a vaquero would see a spectacular fight right out on the open range. Many a time the bull was killed as a result of these accidental meetings.

All the rancheros had their experiences with bears. Don Francisco Branch had many run-ins. He and his wife, Dona Manuela Carlona de Branch, had settled on their rancho before our father had brought his family to Nipomo. The Branch's rancho was in a very wild country, thick with montes and full of willows and cottonwoods in which lions and wildcats as well as bears, made their haunts.

One time a bear—and it may have been El Casador—killed one of Don Francisco's cows and left the partially-eaten carcass where it had fallen. Thinking the bear would return, Don Francisco and a friend dug a pit nearby, putting a brush cover over it. They got into the pit with their rifles. But their plans backfired for that night a she-bear and her cub came along instead of the expected El Casador or a lesser giant.

The men decided to kill the cub before attacking the mother and she certainly was enraged and I can't blame her. The maddened bear ran around in circles, leaped against trees and tore great hunks of bark from them all night long. The two hunters kept mighty quiet, they told us later, and were glad to creep away with their lives the next morning after the bear had left the spot.

Another time Don Francisco saw a grizzly busily eating berries which grew wild in one of the many thickets along the Arroyo Grande.[7] He looked for a good spot to get a bead on the bear

[7] Big Creek.

and it's a good thing that he looked good and hard—because he saw not one, but nine bears all shoveling berries by the pawfuls into their big mouths as fast as they could! He didn't lose much time in getting away from that place!

Don Francisco had a trusted retainer named Mike who worked for him for many years and in fact, outlived him. "Old Mike," as he was called, lived at the Arroyo Grande adobe until he died in 1877 when he was an old man and blind. But in his young days he was an Indian fighter and vaquero. He, too, outwitted Mr. Bruin many times. I remember one time a bear had come down near the Branch adobe and killed a calf. So Mike took the skin with the head still attached, put it over himself and crawled out to the chaparral not far from the house. Sure enough, pretty soon a bear appeared. Mike took a good aim and neatly put a bullet right into Old Bruin's head. Don Francisco had been watching from the adobe and was a relieved man when it was over.

Bruin didn't come too near our casa very often—not nearly as often as coyotes did. For a long time, coyotes made off with a lot of our chickens which puzzled my mother as she knew the birds roosted high in an oak tree at nights near the house. One day she asked one of our old Indian servants about it and he gave such a queer explanation that we all laughed at him. But he said he would prove he was right that very night.

It was full moonlight that night and we hid under a willow tree that faced the oak tree. Pretty soon a coyote came along and started to circle the oak tree. He circled and circled and sure enough, it wasn't long before a silly chicken fell to the ground! Right after her, another chicken fell! At this point we rushed out from our hiding place and scared off the coyote.

The old Indian said to me the next morning: "Juan, tonight you be the coyote!"

So that night he tied a short rope around the tree trunk and told me to take the other end and circle around the tree. I did and sure enough, pretty soon down dropped a mesmerized chicken!

"Eat him, Coyote!" the Indian shouted at me in great mirth. I guess eventually I did help to eat that chicken—only it was in a stew!

12

TAMING A GRIZZLY
Major Horace Bell

Probably no other man was better qualified to write of early days in Southern California than Major Horace Bell. He was a gold miner at Hangtown while still in his teens, a ranger in pursuit of the notorious Joaquín Murieta when barely past his majority, an aide to General William Walker in the celebrated Nicaraguan filibuster a few years later; and he was continuously involved in political and social activities among the Argonauts for half a century. As the publisher of a prickly little newspaper, *The Porcupine*, in which he lambasted the grasping *gringos* who victimized Spanish Californios and dominated Southern California politics, and as an attorney who defended the rights of the Californios in court, Bell became the target of much scurrilous and scathing acrimony. His joining the Union forces made him even less popular in a community which was predominantly in sympathy with the Confederate cause. Later years brought him honor, however,

The following vivid description of the manner in which the California vaqueros lassoed grizzly bears is reprinted from Major Bell's *Reminiscences of a Ranger; or, Early Days in Southern California*, published in Los Angeles in 1881 by Yarnell, Caystile and Mathes, Printers, where it appears on pages 255–56. This extremely rare book was reprinted in 1927 by Wallace Hebbard, Publisher, at Santa Barbara, and this edition, too, is quite rare.

AT THE TIME of which I write early in the '50s the grizzly bears were more plentiful in Southern California than pigs; they were, in fact, so numerous in certain localities [such] as Topango, Malibu, La Laguna de Chico, Lopez and other places, as to make the rearing of cattle utterly impossible. These ferocious brutes were the terror of the aboriginal tribes, and dreaded by the California

Spaniard, whose only weapon of offensive warfare against them was the *riata* and lance, more commonly called in *gringo* parlance, the *lazo*.

When burly bruin, in quest of *carne*, would boldly emerge from his lair in the fastnesses of the Sierra and make his appearance on the plain, he ran nine chances out of ten of losing his scalp. When beset by three or four *lazadores*, he was most generally overpowered and spitted, and this is the way in which that most wonderful feat, lassoing of a grizzly, was performed by those most formidable men on horseback, whose like will never more be known—the California ranchero. When he was seen on the open plain a party of the most intrepid, cool-headed, well-mounted and expert *lazadores* surrounded him. Bruin, finding himself corraled, seats himself upright on his haunches, and takes the defensive position of the pugilist. A *lazador* now approaches him and swings his *riata*. There must be no mistake about it; the bear must be caught by one of his forefeet. That is the first thing to be done . . . the monster may be 2,000 pounds weight, and if caught around the body or neck, he takes told of that *riata* and draws in the horse and rider hand over fist, as easily as a fisherman would draw in a catfish. The coil of the *lazo* describes a rapid circle, Whizz! Whirr! Bruin's eyes wall from side to side in the vain endeavor to know where the blow is about to fall, and his two immense arms gyrate wildly, as though he intends to make the left, right, front and rear parry at one and the same time and motion. *Whizz, Whirr, Whirr, Whip* goes the *riata*, and lord grizzly is caught by the forepaw. In the twinkling of an eye, *whizz, whirr, whip*, goes another *riata*, and the astonished monster is caught by the other forefoot. He now angrily, and with gnashing teeth and terrific growls, stands erect, and waltzes around like a grenadier; but the next thing he knows, *whizz, whirr, whirr whip*, and a *riata* tightens on his hind foot and before he can enter his growling protest, he is caught by the other hind foot, and is tripped up and falls heavily upon his back, where he struggles desperately for life; but four well-trained horses, and four cool-headed, fearless riders, with their terrible *riatas* are too much for him; and in a few minutes the monster, with groans and growls, with a heaving chest

73

and dilating eyes, surrenders at discretion and lies on his back as helpless as a child. Whereupon he is approached by one or two lookers-on and is dispatched with their lances.

13

BULL-AND-BEAR FIGHTS, I
Major Horace Bell

The reader is taken back in time to Spanish California in the following chapter from Major Horace Bell's *On the Old West Coast*,[1] edited by Lanier Bartlett and published in New York by William Morrow and Company in 1930. The story of the picturesque fiesta, where a vicious bull-and-bear fight was the afternoon's main entertainment, may have been published originally in Bell's fiery newspaper, *The Porcupine*. Bell is said to have had the tenderfoot in mind as he wrote about the old frontier days. If so, any added "color" only intensifies the excitement and lends reality to his narration which, for lack of minutiae, might have been lost to present-day readers and posterity.

"Bulls-and-Bear Fights" appears on pages 108–13 of *On the Old West Coast* and is reprinted here with the kind permission of the publishers.

IN THE GREAT FIESTAS OF TIMES PAST at the Missions and Presidios there was always a bull and bear fight for the entertainment of the crowd. The last one on record that I know of took place at Pala, a branch of *asistencia* at the once great Mission San Luis Rey, in the mountains of San Diego County; nearly fifty years ago. One of the American newspapers in California published an account of it written by a correspondent who was present. I have the clipping of that and as it is a better-written description than I could produce myself, I give it herewith:

The bear was an ugly grizzly that for years had roamed the pine-clad region of Palomar Mountain, rising six thousand feet

[1] Major Horace Bell, *On the Old West Coast. Being Further Reminiscences of a Ranger*, edited by Lanier Bartlett. (New York, William Morrow and Company, Inc., Publishers, 1930).

75

above the little Mission. Tied to a huge post in the center of the old adobe-walled quadrangle he stood almost as high as a horse, a picture of fury such as painter never conceived. His hind feet were tethered with several turns of a strong rawhide reata, but were left about a yard apart to give full play. To the center of this rawhide, between the two feet, was fastened another heavy reata, doubled and secured to a big loop made of doubled reatas thrown over the center post. The services of a man on horseback with a long pole were constantly needed to keep the raging monster from chewing through the rawhide ropes.

By the time the bear had stormed around long enough to get well limbered up after being tied all night the signal was given, the horseman effected his disappearance and in dashed a bull through an open gate. He was of the old long-horn breed but of great weight and power. He had been roaming the hills all summer, living like a deer in the chaparral of the rough mountains and was as quick and wild as any deer. He, too, like old bruin, had been captured with the noosed lazo in a sudden dash of horsemen on a little flat he crossed to go to a spring at daylight and felt no more in love with mankind than did the bear. As he dashed across the arena it looked as if the fight was going to be an unequal one, but the bear gave a glance that intimated that no one need waste sympathy on him.

No creature is so ready for immediate business as is the bull turned loose in an amphitheater of human faces. He seems to know they are there to see him fight and he wants them to get their money's worth. So, as soon as the gate admits him, he goes for everything in sight with the dash of a cyclone. Things that outside he would fly from or not notice he darts at as eagerly as a terrier for a rat the instant he sees them in the ring.

This bull came from the same mountains as the bear and they were old acquaintances, though the acquaintance had been cultivated on the run as the bull tore with thundering hoofs through the tough manzanita or went plunging down the steep hillside as the evening breeze wafted the strong scent of the bear to his keen nose. But now, in the arena, he spent no time looking for a way of escape but at a pace that seemed impossible for even the

great weight of the bear to resist he rushed across the ring directly at the enemy as if he had been looking for him all his life.

With wonderful quickness for so large an animal the bear rose on his hind legs and coolly waited until the long sharp horns were within a yard of his breast. Then up went the great paws, one on each side of the bull's head, and the sharp points of the horns whirled up from horizontal to perpendicular, then almost to horizontal again as bull and bear went rolling over together. In a twinkling the bear was on his feet again, but the bull lay limp as a rag, his neck broken.

In rode four horsemen and threw reatas around the feet of the dead bull, while the grizzly did his ferocious best to get at them. As they dragged the body of the vanquished victim out one gate, the runway to the bullpen was opened once more and a second bull, a big black one with tail up as if to switch the moon, charged into the arena. On his head glistened horns so long and sharp that it seemed impossible for the bear ever to reach the head with his death-dealing paws before being impaled.

But this problem did not seem to worry the grizzly. He had not been living on cattle for so many years without knowing a lot about their movements. When this new antagonist came at him he dodged as easily as a trained human bullfighter, and as the bull shot past him down came one big paw on the bovine's neck with a whack that sounded all over the adobe corral. A chorus of shouts went up from the rows of swarthy faces, with here and there a white face, as the victim, turning partly over, went down with a plunge that made one of his horns plow up dirt, then break sharp off under the terrific pressure of his weight and momentum.

The bull was not done for; he tried to rise and bruin made a dash for him, but his tethers held him short of his goal. In a second the bull got to his feet and wheeled around with one of those short twists that makes him so dangerous an antagonist. But once he is wheeled around his course is generally straight ahead and a quick dodger can avoid him; however, he is lightning-like in his charge and something or somebody is likely to be over-hauled in short order. So it was this time and before the bear could recover from the confusion into which he had been thrown by being brought up short by his tether, the bull caught him on the shoulder with his remaining horn.

Few things in nature are tougher than the shoulder of a grizzly bear and a mere side swing without the full weight of a running bull behind it was insufficient to make even this sharp horn penetrate. The bear staggered, but the horn glanced from the ponderous bone, leaving a long gash in the shaggy hide. This only angered bruin the more. He made a grab for the head of the bull but again was frustrated by the reatas which allowed him only a limited scope of action.

The bull returned to the charge as soon as he could turn himself around and aimed the long horn full at his enemy's breast. But just as the horn seemed reaching its mark the grizzly grabbed the bull's head with both paws and twisted it half round, with the nose inward. The nose he seized in his great white teeth and over both went in a swirl of dust while the crowd roared and cheered.

Now one could see exactly why cattle found killed by bears

always have their necks broken. Bears do not go through the slow process of strangling or bleeding their victims, but do business on scientific principles.

This time the grizzly rose more slowly than before, nevertheless he rose, while the bull lay still in death.

The owners of the bear now wanted to stop the show but from all sides rose a roar of *"Otro! Otro! Otro! Otro toro!"* "Another! Another! Another! Another bull!"

The owners protested that the bear was disabled and was too valuable to sacrifice needlessly; that a dead bull was worth as much as a live one, and more, but that the same arithmetic did not hold good for a bear. The clamor of the crowd grew minute by minute, for the sight of blood gushing from the bear's shoulder was too much for the equilibrium of an audience like this one.

Soon another bull shot toward the center of the arena. Larger than the rest but thinner, more rangy, he opened negotiations with even more vigor, more speed. With thundering thump of great hoofs, his head wagging from side to side, eyes flashing green fire, he drove full at the bear with all his force. The grizzly was a trifle clumsy this time and as he rose to his hind feet the bull gave a twist of his head that upset the calculations of the bear. Right into the base of the latter's neck went a long sharp horn, at the same time that the two powerful paws closed on the bull's neck from above. A distinct crack was heard. The bull sank forward carrying the bear over backward with a heavy thump against the big post to which he was tied.

Again the horsemen rode in to drag out a dead bull. But the grizzly now looked weary and pained. Another pow-wow with his owners ensued while the crowd yelled more loudly than ever for another bull. The owners protested that it was unfair, but the racket rose louder and louder for the audience knew that there was one bull left, the biggest and wildest of the lot.

The crowd won, but bruin was given a little more room in which to fight. Vaqueros rode in and while two lassoed his forepaws and spread him out in front, the other two loosened his ropes behind so as to give him more play. He now had about half the length of a reata. Allowing him a breathing spell, which

79

he spent trying to bite off the reatas, the gate of the bullpen was again thrown open.

Out dashed an old Red Rover of the hills and the way he went for the bear seemed to prove him another old acquaintance. He seemed anxious to make up for the many times he had flown from the distant scent that had warned him that the bear was in the same mountains. With lowered head turned to one side so as to to aim one horn at the enemy's breast he cleared the distance in half a dozen leaps.

The bear was still slower than before in getting to his hind feet and his right paw slipped as he grabbed the bull's head. He failed to twist it over. The horn struck him near the base of the neck and bull and bear went rolling over together.

Loud cheers for the bull rose as the bear, scrambling to his feet, showed blood coming from a hole in his neck almost beside the first wound. Still louder roared the applause as the bull regained his feet. Lashing his sides with his tail and bounding high in fury he wheeled and returned to the fray. The bear rolled himself over like a ball and would have been on his feet again safely had not one foot caught in the reata which tied him to the post. Unable to meet the bull's charge with both hind feet solid on the ground he fell forward against his antagonist and received one horn full in the breast, up to the hilt.

But a great grizzly keeps on fighting even after a thrust to the heart. Again he struggled to his feet, the blood gushing from the new wound. With stunning quickness in so large an animal the bull had withdrawn his horn, gathered himself together and returned to the charge. The bear could not turn in time to meet him and with a heavy smash the horn struck him squarely in the shoulder forward of the protecting bone. Those who have seen the longest horns driven full to the hilt through the shoulder of a horse—a common sight in the bull-fights of Mexico—can understand why the bear rolled over backward to rise no more.

14

BULL-AND-BEAR FIGHTS, II
J. D. Borthwick

J. D. Borthwick's account of three years in the California gold
fields is an outstanding chronicle of one of the high spots in California history. Little is known about this writer and talented artist,
but his book is well written and is a unique detailed record of the
mining camps along the western slope of the Sierras. Borthwick's
lithographs of life in the Mother Lode country are considered the
finest pictorial record produced of the period of the gold rush
for action, fidelity, and quiet humor.

The following vivid description of a gala event at Moquelumne
Hill, near the present town of Placerville, California, is taken from
Three Years in California, 1851–54, published in Edinburgh,
Scotland, by Blackford and Sons in 1857, pages 237 and 243–300.
It is generously illustrated with Borthwick's remarkable drawings.
Needless to say, this book is very rare. One thousand copies were
reprinted for the California Centennial in 1948 by Biobooks of
Oakland, and this edition is also rare and expensive.

AT THE TIME OF MY ARRIVAL in Moquelumne Hill, the town was
posted all over with placards, which I had also observed stuck
upon trees and rocks by the roadside as I travelled over the mountains. They were to this effect:

"War! War! ! War! ! !
The celebrated Bull-killing Bear,
GENERAL SCOTT
will fight a Bull on Sunday the 15th inst.
at 2 P.M.
at Moquelumne Hill.
"The bear will be chained with a twenty-foot chain

in the middle of the arena. The Bull will be perfectly wild, young, of the Spanish breed and the best that can be found in the country. The Bull's horns will be of their natural length, and *not sawed off to prevent accidents!* The Bull will be quite free in the arena, and not hampered in any way whatever."

The proprietors then went on to say that they had nothing to do with the humbugging which characterised the last fight, and begged confidently to assure the public that this would be the most splendid exhibition ever seen in the country.

I had often heard of these bull-and-bear fights as popular amusements in some parts of the State, but had never yet had an opportunity of witnessing them; on Sunday the 15th, I found myself walking up toward the arena, among the crowd of miners and others of all nations, to witness the performance of the redoubted General Scott.

The amphitheatre was a roughly but strongly built wooden structure, uncovered of course; and the outer enclosure, which was of boards about ten feet high, was a hundred feet in diameter, and enclosed a very strong five-barred fence. From the top of this rose tiers of seats, occupying the space between the arena and the outside enclosure.

As the appointed hour drew near, the company continued to arrive till the whole place was crowded; while, to beguile the time till the business of the day should commence, two fiddlers—a white man and a gentleman of colour—performed a variety of appropriate airs.

The scene was gay and brilliant, and was one which would have made a crowded opera-house appear gloomy and dull by comparison. The shelving bank of human beings which encircled the place was like a mass of bright flowers. The most conspicuous objects were the shirts of the miners, red, white, and blue being the fashionable colours, among which appeared bronzed and bearded faces under hats of every hue; revolvers and silver-handled bowie knives glanced in the bright sunshine; and among the crowd were numbers of gay Mexican blankets, and red and blue French bonnets; while here and there the fair sex was represented by a few Mexican women in snowy-white dresses, puffing their cigaritos in delightful anticipation of the exciting scene which was to be enacted. Over the heads of the highest circle of spectators was seen mountain beyond mountain fading away in the distance; and on the green turf of the arena lay the great center of attraction, the hero of the day, General Scott.

He was, however, not yet exposed to the public gaze, but was confined in his cage, a heavy wooden box lined with iron, with open iron bars on one side, which for the present was boarded over. From the centre of the arena a chain led into the cage, and at the end of it no doubt the bear was to be found. Beneath the scaffolding on which sat the spectators were two pens, each containing a very handsome bull, showing evident signs of indignation at his confinement. Here also was the bar, without which no place of public amusement would be complete.

There was much excitement among the crowd at the result of the battle, as the bear had already killed several bulls; but an idea prevailed that in former fights the bulls had not had fair play, being tied by a rope to the bear, and having the tips of their horns sawed off. But on this occasion the bull was to have the advantage. . . .

The bear made his appearance before the public in a very bearish manner. . . . He floundered half-way round the ring at the length of his chain, and commenced to tear up the earth with his fore-paws. He was a grizzly bear of pretty large size, weighing about twelve-hundred pounds.

The next thing to be done was to introduce the bull. The bars between his pen and the arena were removed . . . he did not seem to like the prospect, and was not disposed to move till pretty sharply poked from behind, when, making a furious dash at the red flag which was being waved in front of the gate, he found himself in the ring face to face with General Scott. . . .

The bull was a very beautiful animal, of dark purple colour marked with white. His horns were regular and sharp, and his coat was as smooth and glossy as a racer's. He stood for a moment taking a survey of the bear, the ring, and the crowds of people; but not liking the appearance of things in general, he wheeled

83

round, and made a splendid dash at the bars, which had already been put up between him and his pen, smashing through them with as much ease as the man in the circus leaps through a hoop of brown paper. . . . Again persuaded to enter the arena . . . he put down his head and charged furiously across the arena. The bear received him crouching down, and though one could hear the bump of the bull's head and horns upon his ribs, he was quick enough to seize the bull by the nose before he could retreat. This spirited commencement of the battle was hailed with uproarious applause. . . .

The bear, lying on his back, held the bull's nose firmly between his teeth and embraced him round the neck with his forepaws, while the bull made the most of his opportunities in stamping on the bear with his hind-feet. At last the General became exasperated at such treatment, and shook the bull savagely by the nose, when a promiscuous scuffle ensued, which resulted in the bear throwing his antagonist to the ground with his forepaws. For this feat the bear was cheered immensely, and it was thought he would make short work of him; but apparently wild beasts do not tear each other to pieces so easily as is generally supposed. . . . the bull soon regained his feet, and, disengaging himself, retired to the other side of the ring, while the bear again crouched down in his hole.

After standing a few minutes, steadily eyeing the General, the bull made another rush at him. Again poor bruin's ribs resounded, but again he took the bull's nose into chancery. The bull, however, quickly disengaged himself, and was making off, when the General, not wishing to part with him so soon, seized his hind-foot between his teeth, and, holding on by his paws as well, was thus dragged round the ring before he quitted his hold.

This round terminated with shouts of delight from the excited spectators, and it was thought the bull might have a chance after all. He had been severely punished, however; his nose and lips were a mass of bloody shreds, and he lay down to recover himself. But he was not allowed to rest very long, being poked up with sticks by men outside, which made him very savage. He made several feints to charge them through the bars. . . . He was eventually worked up to such a state of fury as to make another charge at the bear. The result was much the same as before, only that when the bull managed to get up after being thrown, the bear still had hold of the skin of his neck.

In the next round both parties fought more savagely than ever, and the advantage was rather in favor of the bear: the bull seemed to be quite used up, and to have lost all chance of victory.

The conductor of the performances then mounted the barrier, and, addressing the crowd, asked them if the bull had not had fair play, which was unanimously allowed. He then stated that for two hundred dollars he would let in the other bull, and the three should fight it out till one or all were killed.

This proposal was received with loud cheers, and two or three men going round with hats soon collected the required amount. The people were intensely excited and delighted with the sport. A man sitting next to me, who was a connoisseur in bear-fights, and passionately fond of the amusement, informed me that this was "the finest fight ever fit in the country."

The second bull was equally handsome as the first, and in as good condition. On entering the arena, he seemed to understand the state of affairs at once. Glancing from the bear to the other bull standing at the opposite side of the arena, with drooping head and bloody nose, he seemed to divine at once that the bear was their common enemy, and rushed at him full tilt. The bear, as usual, pinned him by the nose; but this bull did not take such treatment so quietly as the other: struggling violently, he soon freed himself, and, wheeling round he caught the bear on the hind-quarters and knocked him over; while the other bull, who had been quietly watching the proceedings, thought this a good opportunity to pitch in also; and rushing up, he gave the bear a dig in the ribs on the other side before he had time to recover. . . .

After another round or two with the fresh bull, it was evident he was no match for the bear, and it was agreed to conclude the performance. The bulls were then shot to put them out of pain, and the company dispersed, all apparently satisfied that it had been a very splendid fight.

The reader can form his own opinion as to the character of an exhibition such as I have endeavored to describe. For my own part, I did not at first find the actual spectacle so disgusting as I had expected I should; for as long as the animals fought with spirit, they might have been supposed to be following their natural instincts; but when the bull had to be urged and goaded on to return to the charge, the cruelty of the whole proceeding was too apparent; and when the two bulls at once were let in upon the bear, all idea of sport or fair play was at an end, and it became a scene which one would rather have prevented than witnessed.

In these bull-and-bear fights the bull sometimes kills the bear at the first charge, by plunging his horns beween the ribs, and striking a vital part. Such was the fate of General Scott in the next battle he fought, a few weeks afterwards; but it is seldom that the bear kills the bull outright, his misery being in most cases ended by a rifle-ball when he can no longer maintain the combat.

I took a sketch of the General the day after the battle. He was in the middle of the now deserted arena, and was in a particularly savage humour. He seemed to consider my intrusion on his solitude as a personal insult for he growled most savagely, and stormed about in his cage, even pulling at the iron bars in his efforts to get out. I could not help thinking what a mess he would have made of me if he had succeeded in doing so; but I regarded with peculiar satisfaction the massive architecture of his abode; and, taking a seat a few feet from him, I lighted my pipe, and waited until he should quiet down into an attitude, which he soon did, though very sulkily, when he saw that he could not help himself.

He did not seem to be much the worse for the battle, having but one wound, and that appeared to be only skin deep.

Such a bear as this, alive, was worth about fifteen hundred dollars. The method of capturing them is a service of considerable danger, and requires a great deal of labour and constant watching.

A spot is chosen in some remote part of the mountains, where it has been ascertained that bears are pretty numerous. Here a species of cage is built, about twelve feet square and six feet high, constructed of pine logs, and fastened after the manner of a log cabin. This is suspended between two trees, six or seven feet off the ground, and inside is hung a huge piece of beef, communicating by a string with a trigger, and down comes the trap, which has more the appearance of a log cabin suspended in the air than anything else. A regular locomotive cage, lined with iron, has also to be taken to the spot, to be kept in readiness for bruin's accommodation, for the pine-log trap would not hold him long, he would soon eat and tear his way out of it. The enterprising bear-catchers have therefore to remain in the neighborhood and keep a sharp look-out.

Removing the bear from the trap to the cage is the most dangerous part of the business. One side of the trap is so contrived as to admit of being opened or removed, and the cage is drawn up along side, with the door also open, when the bear has to be persuaded to step into his new abode, in which he travels down to the more populous parts of the country, to fight bulls for the amusement of the public.

SOME PET GRIZZLY CUBS

15

LADY WASHINGTON
Theodore H. Hittell

Imagine the panic which would ensue if a bearded, uncouth fellow (not a beatnik type) led four or five full-grown grizzly bears along Sutter Street in San Francisco someday next week! In the late 1850's James Capen Adams and his special pets, Lady Washington and Ben Franklin, together with several other half-ton bears, were a common sight in the town above Golden Gate. The following condensed selections from *The Adventures of James C. Adams*[1] take the reader with "Grizzly" Adams to Washington Territory, where Lady Washington and Ben Franklin were captured. Adams brought quite a menagerie back to Portland after this hunting expedition and experienced some difficulty in booking passage to California for his charges, some of which were destined for Eastern zoos.

Theodore H. Hittell, who wrote about Adams' amazing exploits, was a San Francisco newspaperman who became fascinated with the hunter's yarns. Hittell says, in a letter to William H. Wright, author of *The Grizzly Bear*,[2] that Adams "knew little about geography and could not locate himself except in very general terms . . . that Adams did not, on any occasion, appear to exaggerate, and told nothing improbable, though [he] had to wonder how [Adams] could remember so distinctly the particulars of his various hunts." What a pity that the chronicle of "Grizzly" Adams is a rare book.

I HAD LONG WISHED to see Oregon and Washington territories, whose fame was known to the world, even before that of Cali-

[1] Theodore H. Hittell, *The Adventures of James C. Adams, Mountaineer and Grizzly Bear Hunter of California* (San Francisco, Towne and Bacon, 1860), 21, 23–25, 27–31, 33, 37, 40, 67–71.
[2] See Chapters 22 and 23 below.

fornia; and having now a business object, I resolved that they should be the first regions I would visit. I accordingly left my mountain fastness . . . laid in a stock of ammunition, exchanged my oxen for mules and pack saddles, and gathered such information regarding the northern countries and roads to them as could be obtained. . . .

Without stopping to examine the country, or hunt more than necessary, we[3] hastened on for two weeks to the Klamath region; whence we struck down through that wilderness which lies between the Cascades and Blue Mountains. We saw much to interest us, on this travel, in the mountains, plains, forests, streams, and Indians of Southern Oregon, but pushed ahead as rapidly as possible, leaving the lofty heads of Mount Jefferson and Mount Hood to our left, and at length, well worn with fatigue, turned the great bend of the Columbia, crossed Lewis's River, and struck out into the country lying to the northeastward. We came at last to a desirable valley among the hills, where grass and water were abundant, about ten miles distant from an Indian village or rancheria; and, turning out our mules, we made camp; and this constituted our headquarters during the entire summer. . . .

The region of eastern Washington, where we were now encamped, contains many fine animals; but chief among them is the powerful one often denominated the curly-haired brown bear, which is in reality, however, but a variety of the grizzly species and cousin-germain of the monster of California. There are several varieties of the grizzly bear; or, to speak more properly, perhaps, the species has a wide range, extending from the British Possessions on the north to New Mexico on the south, and from the eastern spurs of the Rocky Mountains to the Pacific Ocean. He was once frequently found on the lower part of the Missouri, and on the Mississippi River; but by degrees has been driven back, until now, his range east of the Rocky chain is much circumscribed. His size, general appearance, and character, vary with the part of this great region in which he is found; for although

[3] Two young Tuolumne Indians, whom Adams called Tuolumne and Stanislaus, and a young man named William Sykesey accompanied the hunter to Washington Territory.

courageous and ferocious in the Rocky Mountains, he is there neither so large or so terrible as in the Sierra Nevada, where he attains his greatest size and strength.

The grizzly of the Rocky Mountains seldom, if ever, reaches the weight of a thousand pounds; the color of his hair is almost white; he is more disposed to attack man than the same species in in other regions, and has often been known to follow upon the human track for several hours at a time. It was this bear which first became known to the enlightened world; and from him the species was appropriately named grizzly. Among hunters, he is known as the Rocky Mountain white bear, to distinguish him from other varieties.

The California grizzly sometimes weighs as much as two thousand pounds. He is of a brown color, sprinkled with grayish hairs. When aroused, he is, as has been said before, the most terrible of all animals in the world to encounter; but ordinarily will not attack man, except under peculiar circumstances. It is of this animal that the most extraordinary feats of strength are recorded. It is said, with truth, that he can carry off a full-grown horse or buffalo, and that, with one blow of his paw, he can stop a mad bull in full career. When roused, and particularly when wounded, there is no end to his courage; he fights till the last spark of life expires, fearing no odds, and never deigning to turn his heel upon the combat. It is to him that the appellations of science *ursus ferox* and *ursus horribilis,* are peculiarly applicable.

The grizzly of Washington and Oregon territories resembles the bear of California, with the exception that he rarely attains so large a size, and has a browner coat. His hair is more disposed to curl and is thicker, owing to the greater coldness of the climate. He is not so savage, and can be hunted with greater safety than either the California or Rocky Mountain bear. In New Mexico, the grizzly loses much of his strength and power, and upon the whole is a rather timid and spiritless animal.

Not far from my camp, there was an extensive tract of chaparral, covering the side of a broad mountain and skirting a beautiful valley of tender herbage. My attention was attracted to it by indications of large bears; and, after a short reconnaissance, I dis-

93

covered on the mountainside the den of an old grizzly with two yearling cubs. The animals were in the habit of descending into the valley every night, and had worn a trail, along which they almost invariably passed in their excursions. I immediately determined, if possible, to slay this dam, and make myself master of her offspring, which were two of the finest looking beasts I had ever seen.

To resolve to do a thing, and to do that thing, are different matters; and so I found them on this occasion. There seemed, however, to be but one plan of action,—to waylay the dam; and, in accordance with it, I concealed myself one morning near the trail, when the animals were coming up from the valley. I had both my rifles well charged lying at my side; and, as the old beast approached, I drew Kentucky, and planted a half-ounce ball in her breast. She fell, but almost instantly recovered herself and rushed towards me; when, seizing my second rifle, I fired a second shot through her open mouth into her brain. It is often the case that the grizzly will live for several hours after being pierced even through the head or heart, and perform prodigies of strength; but in this instance, fortunately for me, perhaps, life lasted but a few minutes.

As soon as the dam expired, I seized a lasso, which lay at my side, and rushed towards the cubs. I had imagined it would be a matter of ease, with the dam once out of the way, to secure them; but soon learned my mistake. As I rushed at them, they retreated; as I pursued, they broke away, and doubling, shot past with a rapidity of motion which defied all my skill. I chased a long time without success; and, finally, when they and I were nearly worn out, they suddenly turned and made so violent an attack upon me that I was compelled, for my personal safety, to betake myself to a tree, and was glad to find one to climb. Although but little more than a year old, I saw that they had teeth and claws which were truly formidable.

It was a ludicrous situation which I occupied in that tree; and it makes me laugh now to think how a hunter of great bears was thus besieged by little ones. However, there I sat, and there was no help for it. The cubs tried to climb after me, and it was necessary to pound their paws to keep them down; and I shall never forget how they snapped their jaws; and how wickedly they looked, when they were satisfied I was beyond their reach. Had they been fully grown grizzlies and thus driven me, like the sage Nestor of antiquity, to seek refuge in the branches, it might have been a long time before it would have been their good pleasure to withdraw; but the cubs did not understand the art of starving an enemy; and, in the course of half an hour, went off to their dead mother. They had shown enough, however, to make me give up the idea of taking them by the plan proposed; and, as I left the place, I began contriving other kinds of expedients for their capture.

The plan hit upon at last was to procure horses from the Indians; for it seemed to me that, if we could chase the cubs into the plain, and pursue them on horseback, we could certainly take them with our lassos. Accordingly, the same day, I mounted a mule, and, taking a quantity of dried venison as a present, rode down to the village, which I found to be under the sway of a hard-headed but good-natured old Indian potentate, named Kennasket. This chief, for divers good reasons, doubtless, placed little reliance in the white man; but he seemed pleased with my present and conversation, and finally consented to loan me three good horses, with which, however, he sent a brave, whom we called Pompey, to see to their safe return.

Having thus procured horses, three of us, well mounted, took the field the next morning before daylight, and repaired to the neighborhood of the dead bear, where the cubs still remained. It was my intention to drive them down the trail to the open valley, so that our lassos could be used with effect; and I therefore directed my comrades to conceal themselves and be ready to rush forward. Having dismounted, I then made a circuit, and getting upon the trail above the position of the animals, moved slowly down towards them. In many places the bushes were so thick that I had to creep under them upon my hands and knees; and, as my rifle was never out of my hands, it may be conceived that the path was not without its annoyances.

Upon drawing near the spot, a most interesting sight presented

95

itself to my eyes. The cubs lay, with their paws upon the body of their dead mother, as if endeavoring to draw the accustomed warmth from it. Their appearance was so pleasing, so child-like, that, for a few moments, I could only stop and gaze. At first they did not observe me; but, on a slight movement, they suddenly sprang to their feet, and, as they did so, I dashed forward, whirling my cap. They bounded down the trail; I followed, thinking we surely had them now; but, unfortunately, my comrades, too anxious to act, prematurely left their places; and the cubs, frightened by the display, bounded aside from the trail, and, getting into the chaparral, escaped.

The next morning, we endeavored to try the same plan over, but, on going to the place, I found that the body of the dam had been devoured during the previous afternoon by vultures or buzzards; and of the cubs nothing was to be seen. I was now put to my wits to know what to do; for some time it appeared that nothing could be accomplished; but, finally, the idea occurred to me that, as there was but one spring in the valley, the animals would have to visit it for water, and that there was the place to take them. I therefore determined to watch the spring; and, as soon as it began to grow dark that evening, selected a place of concealment, where, the result of the experiment being uncertain, and the remainder of the party choosing to return to camp, I was left alone. . . .

I tried to beguile the time by a severe exercise of thought upon other subjects; but, in a short time, I fell into a doze, then into a sleep, and was not awakened until midnight, when the cubs unexpectedly passed by me. The moon shone, and they were plainly to be seen; but they had evidently been at the spring, and were now on their return to the mountain. They had outwitted me! I instantly sprang from my concealment and rushed after them; but in vain,—before I could overtake them, they reached the chaparral; and thus, for the third time, my endeavors failed. . . .

Being now certain that the grizzly cubs visited the spring, I ordered out all my forces the next evening, and concealed them about the place, with strict instructions not to move out but upon a signal. We commenced at sundown and watched till midnight. Once in a while a band of antelopes, a couple of deer, or a pack of wolves would approach; but they were allowed to come and go undisturbed. The stars, which rose in the evening, passed over our heads, and had sunk far down into the west; and faint streaks of light already played upon the eastern horizon, when, all at once, a yelping on the mountain, in the direction of the den, gave the welcome notification of the approach of the cubs. We now all stood watching every shadow and catching every sound. Presently the little bears ran past us, plunged their noses in the water, wallowed a few minutes, and then, crawling out, began tumbling and wrestling on the grass. At this moment, I gave the whistle; and sinking the spurs into our horses' sides, and swinging our lassos about our heads, we dashed forwards. The cubs, frightened by our sudden and unexpected attack, separated and ran in different directions. I pursued one, and my comrades the other.

My cub, which proved to be a female, bounded into the plain, and required a long chase. She ran quite a mile before it was possible for me to throw the lasso, which was no sooner over her head than she poked it off, and started on again. I followed several miles, and threw the lasso over her again and again, as many as seven times; before it kept its place; but it finally did retain its hold, and she was mine. I immediately sprang from my horse, and, whipping out a muzzle and cords from my pockets, soon had her bound head and foot. She was so beautiful that I had to stop and admire her for some time, before going to see what my comrades had done.

They, too, had succeeded. Indeed, they flattered themselves that they had excelled the old hunter,—a hallucination in which I indulged them awhile for amusement. When the cubs separated, they had pursued theirs, which proved to be a male, a long distance, until he ran into a chaparral so thick and interlaced that he became completely entangled. They then dismounted, and seized him with their hands in such a manner that, though all were more or less scratched and bitten, they succeeded in securing and binding him,—and well was he bound; never in my life before or since have I seen an animal so completely tied up and wound

97

about. They had then procured a long pole, and slinging the bear upon it, had borne him upon their shoulders to the spring. All this they told me with great glee, enjoying their supposed triumph over me. I asked to be shown the place where they had captured him; and when they pointed it out, I remarked that they had an easier place to catch their bear than I mine; but they had got bitten and scratched, which I had not. This speech puzzled them. "Look at your hands," said I; "mine are not scratched in that way; there is no blood here"; and then I told them my story. "And," said I, "she is the prettiest little animal in all the country." Sykesey and Tuolumne thought I was joking and wanted a proof; but, looking them straight in the eyes, I asked if they had ever known the old hunter to lie. No, they replied, they had never known that he ever did.

Such was the manner in which my bear, Lady Washington, one of the companions of my future hunting life, was captured. From that time to this, she has always been with me; and often she has shared my dangers and privations, borne my burdens and partaken of my meals. The reader may be surprised to hear of a grizzly companion and friend; but Lady Washington has been both to me. He may hardly credit the accounts of my nestling up between her and the fire to keep both sides warm under the winter colds of the mountains; but they are all true; let him only read on.

As the cubs were now caught, the next matter was to get them to camp; and upon this question various opinions were held. Sykesey proposed taking them bound upon horseback; Tuolumne preferred making a drag of grass, fastening them upon it, and pulling them along; but there were objections to both these plans. We finally determined to make an experiment with the male cub, by putting a strap of buckskin about his neck, attaching lariats on both sides, and leading him. This arrangement, however, did not work as well as anticipated; and the animal worried himself so much, by prancing and leaping to one or the other side, that, by the time, we got to camp, he was completely worn out. However, we doused him into water, and, as soon as he was cooled and refreshed, chained him up to a tree.

99

On account of the above difficulties, I proposed making for Lady Washington a kind of box of dry hide, and packing her in on horseback; but my Indian friend Pompey, said, No, that he would procure a cart, which would answer much better. This cart, he said, was of a kind sometimes used by the Indians for hauling their goods from place to place, and consisted of a tongue, axletree, two solid wooden wheels, and a body of green hide. I had never seen a vehicle of the kind, but from the description it seemed to be the very thing required, and I sent him off at once to procure it; and he promised to meet me where the bear lay three hours before dark.

Agreeably to our understanding, I rode out about the middle of the afternoon to the spot, and found the cub lying where she had been left, but fretting considerably with her situation. I passed the time admiring her, and looking for Pompey; but it grew nearly sundown, and he did not make his appearance. I fired my rifle several times as a signal; and at last, as the sun went down, a faint shout replied, appearing to come from a great distance; but this was caused by an intervening hill; and in a few minutes Pompey, with a cart drawn by two horses, came up, followed by three Indians on foot.

I had to stand amazed at the novelty of the vehicle they had brought. It answered the description given of it, but was entirely different from my idea, being one of the most rude and aboriginal carriages possible. The harness consisted of strips of dry elk-hide, rubbed in the hands until pliable, and fastened together with strings of the same. The traces were made of like strips, twisted. There were no collars, but only broad bands of hide in place of them. The tongue of the cart was short, and held up between the horses by strings attached to the shoulder-bands; but there was no breeching, and this astonished me most of all. I asked the Indians how they could keep the cart from running upon the horses' legs when going down hill. Pompey replied, that an Indian's cart was made to go only forwards, and it was a bad horse that could not keep out of the way of it. This answer amused me, and I should have asked many more questions; but the night approached, and we therefore, without more ado, hastily lashed the cub on the cart, and Pompey, jumping upon one of the horses, started off at so round a rate that I found it difficult to keep up. The Indians on foot put themselves to a fast trot, and being good runners, lagged not behind in the race.

On the road to camp, upon getting within a mile of it, we suddenly came upon a pack of wolves, at a spot where they appeared, by remarkable good fortune, to have found a choice bit of carrion. The Indians cried out *Lobos,* as both they and the Spaniards call wolves, and asked me to kill them. At that time, wolves had no value in my eyes, but, to please the Indians, I dismounted, and, crawling towards the pack, which had gorged themselves, and were now howling and fighting over what was left, as is the habit of these gluttonous creatures, fired at them. My shot was random, there not being light enough to see; but I succeeded, by firing into their midst, in boring one through the middle, and soon heard him draw his breath through blood. At this the Indians were exceedingly delighted, and, with almost one voice, asked for the skin. I had always supposed that wolf skins were valueless; but now learned that they are highly prized by these northern Indians, who make leggings of them. So much, indeed, did they prize it, that they would not suffer the precious carcass to be tied on the cart with the bear, for fear of its being torn, and insisted upon carrying it themselves. So anxious were they for lobos leggings, that I at once engaged them for a grand antelope hunt, by a promise of wolf skins.

After this, we proceeded, without further incident, to camp, where a quantity of roasted bear-steaks, tea made of a fragrant herb of the mountains, and a rousing, comfortable, big fire awaited us. . . .

The high state of training to which several of my bears were brought, will form an interesting part of my story; and, as they subsequently became my constant companions in all my wanderings and upon many of my hunts, the manner in which they were educated deserves careful and particular mention. It is with bears as it is with children,—although much allowance is to be made for the stock from which they spring, yet, if the right course be taken, their natural characters may be modified and improved to such a degree as to be a subject of wonder. . . .

My pets now amounted to four; the black cubs, which had been taken on our way through Oregon, and the grizzlies, lately taken. The former, which were quite young, and which were by nature of much milder disposition than the grizzly cubs, were already tame enough to follow us about camp, almost like dogs. They were frequently allowed to run perfectly free, and would play around us without the slightest desire to leave. On the contrary, they became so much attached to our persons that it was difficult to prevent them following wherever we went. If we moved but a short distance, they would jump and pursue; and such was their watchfulness, that it was almost impossible to escape their vigilance. . . .

One night I resolved to try a new experiment with the black cubs; this was to have them sleep by me. Upon spreading my blanket to retire, I drove a stake near my feet, and tied them to it. Making them lie down side by side, I then spread a corner of the blanket over them, and felt as responsible and proud as any *pater familias* in the abodes of civilization. During the night, my fondlings were a little troublesome, and required me to rise several times; but, with a little judicious boxing of their ears, they lay still at last, and we all passed a reasonably comfortable night.

With the grizzlies there was much more difficulty; not only on account of their natural ferocity; but because they were more than a year old. From the day on which they were captured, we were compelled to keep them chained; and, although, they became by degrees more familiar, they did not show any disposition whatever to acknowledge a master. Lady Washington, whom I had treated with the greatest kindness, was particularly violent, and invariably would jump and snap at me, whenever within her reach. On one occasion, when she had nearly injured me seriously, I came to the determination to give her a castigation that would make her recollect me; and I called my comrades to witness, and, if necessary assist me in, this first lesson of subjection.

I stepped back into a ravine, cut a good stout cudgel, and

approaching with it in my hand, began vigorously warming her jacket. This made her furious; it would, indeed, be difficult to describe her violence, the snarls she uttered, and the frothing anger she exhibited,—not that she was hurt, but she was so dreadfully aroused. My comrades, in view of the danger, cautioned me to desist; but, notwithstanding their fears and remonstrances, I continued trouncing her back, until finally she acknowledged herself well corrected, and lay down exhausted. It is, beyond question a cruel spectacle to see a man thus taking an animal and whipping it into subjection; but when a bear has once grown up, untutored, as large as the Lady was, this is the only way to lay the foundation of an education,—and the result proved the judiciousness of my course. In a short time afterward I patted her shaggy coat; and she gradually assumed a milder aspect, which satisfied me that the lesson had been beneficial, and that she would not soon forget it. As she became calmer, I gave her a greater length of chain; and, upon feeding her, she ate kindly and heartily, and gave good promise of what she afterwards became,—a most faithful and affectionate servant.

A week or two after this, I resumed the training of Lady Washington, being determined that her education should not suffer for want of tuition. Every day she had been taught a little; but this was rather to keep her in mind of the first lesson, than to give her a new one. On this latter occasion, having removed the chain and attached a lariat to her collar, I led her about the camp, and found her much more tractable than was to have been expected. A little stubbornness she indeed showed at first; but a few raps on her back reminded her of the duties she owed, and entirely removed the necessity of any more trouncing for the time being. Her education was as yet by no means complete; but, even in learning this much, she had made remarkable proficiency.

The male grizzly cub, which had been named Jackson, was even more difficult to be managed than Lady Washington. Upon an attempt being made to lead him, he would sit doggedly still, refusing to move, and growling defiantly. When his chain was pulled, he would place his paw upon it and bristle up, as much as to say, "At your peril!" Indeed, all my endeavors to do anything with him, peaceably, were ineffectual; and, as he seemed to be becoming fixed in his obstinacy, I determined to treat him also with the necessary severity. Accordingly, mounting a mule, having attached a lariat, one end to his collar and the other to the pommel of the saddle, I dragged him along by main force. After being pulled thus a short distance, he leaped at the mule's legs; but she kicked, and laid him sprawling on the grass. Being but little injured, however, he soon got up again; but was a sadder and wiser bear than ever before; for, although he braced himself for a few minutes against my invitations to come along, he soon found it was of no use to resist the odds against him, and sulkily followed, wherever I was pleased to lead.

After leading him about, thus, for some time, I jumped down from my mule, took the lariat in my hand, and led him in that manner; feeling certain that his evil spirit was overcome, and that there was no danger in doing so. At one time, in a fit of returning obstinacy, he sat down and refused to move; but a few whacks over the haunches recalled him to his proper senses, and he again followed me. In fine, upon tying him to his tree, I felt safe in approaching, patting him upon the head, and scratching his neck, —actions which are grateful to the bear as well as to most other animals; and he received these favors with a pleasant countenance. It was easy to see that he might be considered as reclaimed. . . .

Such was the commencement of my bear taming; the subsequent steps, and account of the various degrees of docility to which my pets arrived, are woven almost inseparably into my narrative. From all my experience, and from what has reached me in the way of unquestionable information, the conviction is pressed upon my mind that the grizzly bear possesses a nature which, if taken in time and carefully improved, may be the perfection of animal goodness. . . .

I resolved to remain at camp and train my pets, and particularly Lady Washington, who had now become tame enough to follow me without leading. The thought struck me of teaching her to carry a pack; and getting an old flour-bag, and filling it with sand, I lashed it upon her shaggy back. It was barely bound on, however, before she threw her head around, seized it with her teeth and tore a great hole, and the sand ran out. I talked to her, tried to make her understand what was wanted, and reproved her with a stick, but it was of no use; she grew angry, and I found that it was not prudent to carry the affair any further that day, so I busied myself with Jackson, the wolves, and the little black bears, all of which improved rapidly.

A few days after this, an adventure occurred in which the Lady played an important part. Having determined to build another trap, we all set forth to the spot selected, which was about four miles distant. Being anxious all the time to accustom the Lady to my companionship, I allowed her to follow me. It was a little hazardous, perhaps, to take her so great a distance, but so firm was my confidence in her training as to overrule all objection. She followed like a dog, and during the whole day remained at my side, partaking of my lunch at noon.

Towards evening, as we got ready to start home, I gave my rifle to Stanislaus, and directed him, with Sykesey and Tuolumne, to make a circuit and kill what game they could, while I would go direct to camp with the Lady. They went off in one direction, and I started in another, with nothing to defend myself except my pistol and bowie-knife. I had not gone far before several deer, grazing on a hill-side, attracted my attention; and though it was foolish to attempt to shoot them with a pistol, my ambition was such that I could not think of allowing the opportunity to pass without an attempt. Accordingly, I tried to creep around to a spot from which to fire with advantage; and, coming to a thicket, commenced crawling through the brush, the Lady following in my wake. But before advancing more than a hundred yards, I felt my position was dangerous; there certainly were bears about, and if one should attack me, being without a rifle, I would have but a poor chance. The deer, it is true, still remained grazing, and this was the first time the Old Hunter ever refused an opportunity of killing a deer when he was in need of provision; but the risks seemed too great, and the chance of success too small, and finally, I turned around and began backing out. Suddenly, Lady Washington gave a snort and chattered her teeth. I wheeled around at this, and directly behind the Lady, full in sight, standing upon his hind legs and wickedly surveying us, stood a savage old grizzly. That he had hostile intentions, all his actions clearly showed; and there I was, almost without arms, and with the Lady as well as myself to take care of.

In this emergency, I seized the chain with which the Lady was usually tied, and which was now wrapped about her neck, and unwound it as noiselessly as possible. I was then about to move to a tree which stood near, when the enemy dropped upon his all fours, came a little nearer, and rose again. Here was a dilemma. I knew from the nature of the beast that if I moved now, I was to expect him either to instantly attack or precipitately fly, —but the former much more probably than the latter. I did not wish to hasten an unforeseen determination on his part, however, and therefore stood stock-still, with my pistol in my hand; and thus we both, motionless as stone, eyed each other. It is difficult to tell how long the bear would have gazed without acting,—not long, probably; seeing his indecision, I resolved to turn it to my advantage; and suddenly discharging the pistol, rattling the iron chain, and at the same time yelling with all my might, I had the gratification of seeing the enemy turn tail and run, as if frightened out of his wits. Not satisfied with this, I followed after him yelling and shouting, with the Lady growling and the chain clanking. It seemed as if a thousand devils had sprung up all at once in the wilderness, and the old bear tore through the bushes as if each particular one was after him.

Such was the first instance in which Lady Washington, my faithful friend and constant companion for years afterwards, stood side by side with me in the hour of danger and dire alarm; and from that time I felt for her an affection which I have seldom given to any human being.

16

BABY SYLVESTER

Bret Harte

The reader is guaranteed to find this richly humorous story of
a baby grizzly's sojourn in a San Francisco boarding house both
charming and entertaining. Bret Harte created the "local color"
story, now one of modern literature's classic forms, when directed
to do a series of local California sketches for the *Overland
Monthly*. His mastery of the picturesque details and deft handling
of sentiment and wit are evident in "Baby's" misadventures; he had
a remarkable journalistic discernment for odd mannerisms and
unusual settings and a dramatic ability to appeal to the reader's
five senses. His stories first appeared in the San Francisco *Golden
Era* in 1857 and, collected into book form, became wonderfully
successful. The story of Baby Sylvester was included in *The Tales
of the Argonauts and Other Sketches*, published in Boston in 1875
by The Regent Press, pages 173–98.

IT WAS AT A LITTLE MINING-CAMP in the California Sierras that
he first dawned upon me in all his grotesque sweetness.

I had arrived early in the morning, but not in time to intercept
the friend who was the object of my visit. He had gone "prospecting,"—so they told me on the river,—and would not probably
return until late in the afternoon. They could not say what direction he had taken; they could not suggest that I would be likely
to find him if I followed. But it was the general opinion that I
had better wait. . . .

Where could I wait?

Oh! anywhere,—down with them on the river-bar, where
they were working, if I liked. Or I could make myself at home
in any of those cabins that I found lying around loose. Or perhaps

it would be cooler and pleasanter for me in my friend's cabin on the hill. Did I see those three large sugar-pines, and, a little to the right, a canvas roof and chimney, over the bushes? Well, that was my friend's,—that was Dick Sylvester's cabin . . . I would find some books in the shanty. I could amuse myself with them; or I could play with the baby.

Do what?

But they had already gone. I leaned over the bank, and called after their vanishing figures,—

"What did you say I could do?"

The answer floated slowly up on the hot, sluggish air,—

"Plá-a-y with the ba-by."

. . . I must have been mistaken. My friend was not a man of family; there was not a woman within forty miles of the river camp; he never was so passionately devoted to children as to import a luxury so expensive. I must have been mistaken.

I turned my horse's head toward the hill. . . . A golden lizard, the very genius of desolate stillness, had stopped breathless upon the threshold of one cabin; a squirrel peeped impudently into the window of another; a woodpecker, with the general flavor of undertaking which distinguishes that bird, withheld his sepulchral hammer from the coffin-lid of the roof on which he was professionally engaged, as we passed. For a moment I half regretted that I had not accepted the invitation to the river-bed; but, the next moment, a breeze swept up the long, dark cañon, and the waiting files of the pines beyond bent toward me in salutation. . . .

Unsaddling my horse in a little hollow, I unslung the long *riata* from the saddle-bow, and, tethering him to a young sapling, turned toward the cabin. But I had gone only a few steps, when I heard a quick trot behind me; and poor Pomposo, with every fiber tingling with fear, was at my heels. I looked hurriedly around. . . . I examined the ground carefully for rattlesnakes, but in vain. Yet here was Pomposo shivering from his arched neck to his sensitive haunches, his very flanks pulsating with terror. I soothed him as well as I could, then walked to the edge of the wood, and peered into its dark recesses. The bright flash of a bird's wing, or the quick dart of a squirrel, was all I saw. I confess it was with something of superstitious expectation that I again turned towards the cabin. . . .

I threw myself on the couch, and tried to read. But I soon exhausted my interest in my friend's library, and lay there staring through the open door on the green hillside beyond. . . . The slumbrous droning of bumblebees outside the canvas roof, the faint cawing of rooks on the opposite mountain, and the fatigue of my morning ride, began to droop my eyelids. I pulled the *serape* over me, as a precaution against the freshening mountain breeze, and in a few moments was asleep.

I do not remember how long I slept. I must have been conscious, however, during my slumber, of my inability to keep myself covered by the *serape;* for I awoke once or twice, clutching it with a despairing hand as it was disappearing over the foot of the couch. Then I became suddenly aroused to the fact that my efforts to retain it were resisted by some equally persistent force; and letting it go, I was horrified at seeing it swiftly drawn under the couch. At this point I sat up, completely awake; for immediately after, what seemed to be an exaggerated muff began to emerge from under the couch. Presently it appeared fully, dragging the *serape* after it. There was no mistaking it now: it was a baby-bear,—a mere suckling, it was true, a helpless roll of fat and fur, but unmistakably a grizzly cub!

I cannot recall any thing more irresistibly ludicrous than its aspect as it slowly raised its small, wondering eyes to mine. It was so much taller on its haunches than its shoulders, its forelegs were so disproportionately small, that, in walking, its hind-feet invariably took precedence. It was perpetually pitching forward over its pointed, inoffensive nose, and recovering itself always, after these involuntary somersaults with the gravest astonishment. To add to its preposterous appearance, one of its hind-feet was adorned by a shoe of Sylvester's, into which it had accidentally and inextricably stepped. As this somewhat impeded its first impulse to fly, it turned to me; and then, possibly recognizing in the stranger the same species as its master, it paused. Presently it slowly raised itself on its hind-legs, and vaguely and deprecat-

ingly waved a baby-paw, fringed with little hooks of steel. I took
the paw, and shook it gravely. From that moment we were friends.
The little affair of the *serape* was forgotten.

Nevertheless, I was wise enough to cement our friendship by
an act of delicate courtesy. Following the direction of his eyes, I
had no difficulty in finding on a shelf near the ridgepole the sugar-
box and the square lumps of white sugar that even the poorest
miner is never without. While he was eating them, I had time
to examine him more closely. His body was a silky, dark, but
exquisitely-modulated gray, deepening to black in his paws and
muzzle. His fur was excessively long, thick, and soft as eider-
down; the cushions of flesh beneath perfectly infantine in their
texture and contour. He was so very young, that the palms of
his half-human feet were still tender as a baby's. Except for the
bright blue, steely hooks, half sheathed in his little toes, there
was not a single harsh outline or detail in his plump figure. . . .
Your caressing hand sank away in his fur with dreamy langour.
To look at him long was an intoxication of the senses; to pat him
was a wild delirium; to embrace him, an utter demoralization of
the intellectual faculties.

When he had finished the sugar, he rolled out of the door with
a half-diffident, half-inviting look in his eyes as if he expected me
to follow. I did so; but the sniffing and snorting of the keen-
scented Pomposo in the hollow not only revealed the cause of
his former terror, but decided me to take another direction. After
a moment's hesitation, he concluded to go with me, although
I am satisfied, from a certain impish look in his eye, that he fully
understood and rather enjoyed the fright of Pomposo. As he
rolled along at my side, with a gait not unlike a drunken sailor,
I discovered that his long hair concealed a leather collar around
his neck, which bore for its legend the single word "Baby!" I
recalled the mysterious suggestion of the two miners. This, then
was the "baby" with whom I was to "play."

How we "played"; how Baby allowed me to roll him down
hill, crawling and puffing up again each time with perfect good
humor; how he climbed a young sapling after my Panama hat,
which I had "shied" into one of the top-most branches; how, after

getting it, he refused to descend until it suited his pleasure; how, when he did come down, he persisted in walking about on three legs, carrying my hat, a crushed and shapeless mass, clasped to his breast with the remaining one; how I missed him at last, and finally discovered him seated on a table in one of the tenantless cabins, with a bottle of syrup between his paws, vainly endeavoring to extract its contents,—these and other details of that eventful day I shall not weary the reader with now. Enough of that, when Dick Sylvester returned, I was pretty well fagged out, and the Baby was rolled up, an immense bolster, at the foot of the couch, asleep. Sylvester's first words after our greeting were,—

"Isn't he delicious?"

"Perfectly. Where did you get him?"

"Lying under his dead mother, five miles from here," said Dick, lighting his pipe. "Knocked her over at fifty yards: perfectly clean shot; never moved afterwards. Baby crawled out, scared, but unhurt. She must have been carrying him in her mouth, and dropped him when she faced me; for he wasn't more than three days old, and not steady on his pins. He takes the only milk that comes to the settlement, brought up by Adams Express at seven o'clock every morning. They say he looks like me. Do you think so?" asked Dick with perfect gravity, stroking his hay-colored mustachios, and evidently assuming his best expression.

I took leave of baby early the next morning in Sylvester's cabin, and, out of respect to Pomposo's feelings, rode by without any postscript of expression. But the night before I had made Sylvester solemnly swear that, in the event of any separation between himself and Baby, it should revert to me. "At the same time," he had added, "it's only fair to say that I don't think of dying just yet, old fellow; and I don't know of anything else that would part the cub and me."

Two months after this conversation, as I was turning over the morning's mail at my office in San Francisco, I noticed a letter bearing Sylvester's familiar hand. But it was post-marked "Stockton," and I opened it with some anxiety at once. Its contents were as follows:—

"O FRANK!—Don't you remember what we agreed upon

anent the baby? Well, consider me as dead for the next six months, or gone where cubs can't follow me,—East. I know you love the baby; but do you think, dear boy,—now, really, do you think you *could* be a father to it? Consider this well . . . and let me know speedily; for I've got him as far as this place, and he's kicking up an awful row in the hotel-yard, and rattling his chain like a maniac. Let me know by telegraph at once.

SYLVESTER.

"P.S.—Of course he's grown a little, and doesn't take things always as quietly as he did. He dropped rather heavily on two of Watson's 'purps' last week, and scratched old Watson himself bald headed, for interfering. You remember Watson? For an intelligent man, he knows very little of California fauna. How are you fixed for bears on Montgomery Street, I mean in regard to corrals and things?

S."

"P.P.S.—He's got some new tricks. The boys have been teaching him to put up his hands with them. He slings an ugly left.

S."

I am afraid that my desire to possess myself of Baby overcame all other considerations; and I telegraphed an affirmative at once to Sylvester. When I reached my lodgings late that afternoon, my landlady was awaiting me with a telegram. It was two lines from Sylvester,—
"All right. Baby goes down on night-boat. Be a father to him.

S."

It was due, then, at one o'clock that night. For a moment I was staggered at my own precipitation. I had as yet made no preparations, had said nothing to my landlady about her new guest. I expected to arrange every thing in time; and now, through Sylvester's indecent haste, that time had been shortened twelve hours.

Something, however, must be done at once. I turned to Mrs. Brown. I had great reliance in her maternal instincts: I had that still greater reliance common to our sex in the general tender-heartedness of pretty women. But I confess I was alarmed. . . . So I tried a business *brusquerie,* and placing, the telegram in her hand, said hurriedly, "We must do something about this at once. It's perfectly absurd; but he will be here at one to-night. Beg thousand pardons; but business prevented my speaking before"—and paused out of breath and courage.

Mrs. Brown read the telegram gravely, lifted her pretty eyebrows, turned the paper over, and looked on the other side, and then, in a remote and chilling voice, asked me if she understood me to say that the mother was coming also.

"Oh, dear no!" I exclaimed with considerable relief. "The mother is dead, you know. Sylvester, that is my friend who sent this, shot her when the baby was only three days old." But the expression of Mrs. Brown's face at this moment was so alarming, that I saw that nothing but the fullest explanation would save me. Hastily, and I fear not very coherently, I told her all.

She relaxed sweetly. She said I had frightened her with my talk. . . . Indeed, I think my picture of poor Baby, albeit a trifle highly colored, touched her motherly heart. . . . Still I was not without some apprehension. It was two months since I had seen him; and Sylvester's vague allusion to his "slinging an ugly left" pained me. I looked at sympathetic little Mrs. Brown; and the thought of Watson's pups covered me with guilty confusion.

Mrs. Brown had agreed to sit up with me until he arrived. One o'clock came, but no Baby. Two o'clock, three o'clock, passed. It was almost four when there was a wild clatter of horses' hoofs outside, and with a jerk a wagon stopped at the door. In an instant I had opened it, and confronted a stranger. Almost at the same moment, the horses attempted to run away with the wagon.

The stranger's appearance was, to say the least, disconcerting. His clothes were badly torn and frayed; his linen sack hung from his shoulders like a herald's apron; one of his hands was bandaged; his face scratched; and there was no hat on his dishevelled head. To add to the general effect, he had evidently sought relief from his woes in drink; and he swayed from side to side as he clung to the door-handle, and, in a very thick voice, stated that he had "suthin" for me outside. When he had finished, the horses made another plunge.

Mrs. Brown thought they must be frightened at something.

"Frightened!" laughed the stranger with bitter irony. "Oh, no! Hossish ain't frightened! On'y ran away four timesh comin' here. Oh, no! Nobody's frightened. Every thin's all ri.' Ain't it, Bill?" he said, addressing the driver. "On'y been overboard twish; knocked down a hatchway once. Thash nothin'! On'y two men unner doctor's han's at Stockton. Thash nothin'! Six hunner dollarsh cover all dammish."

I was too much disheartened to reply, but moved toward the wagon. The stranger eyed me with an astonishment that almost sobered him.

"Do you reckon to tackle that animile yourself?" he asked, as he surveyed me from head to foot.

I did not speak, but, with an appearance of boldness I was far from feeling, walked to the wagon, and called "Baby!"

"All ri'. Cash loose them straps, Bill, and stan' clear."

The straps were cut loose; and Baby, the remorseless, the terrible, quietly tumbled to the ground, and rolling to my side, rubbed his foolish head against me.

I think the astonishment of the two men was beyond any vocal expression. Without a word, the drunken stranger got into the wagon, and drove away.

And Baby? He had grown, it is true, a trifle larger; but he was thin, and bore the marks of evident ill usage. His beautiful coat was matted and unkempt; and his claws, those bright steel hooks, had been ruthlessly pared to the quick. His eyes were furtive and restless; and the old expression of stupid good humor had changed to one of intelligent distrust. . . .

I had great difficulty in keeping Mrs. Brown from smothering him in blankets, and ruining his digestion with the delicacies of her larder; but I at last got him completely rolled up in the corner of my room, and asleep. I lay awake some time later with plans for his future. I finally determined to take him to Oakland—where I had built a little cottage, and always spent my Sundays—the very next day. And in the midst of a rosy picture of domestic felicity, I fell asleep.

When I awoke, it was broad day. My eyes at once sought the corner where Baby had been lying; but he was gone. I sprang from my bed, looked under it, searched the closet, but in vain. The door was still locked; but there were the marks of his blunted claws upon the sill of the window that I had forgotten to close. He had evidently escaped that way. But where? The window opened upon a balcony, to which the only other entrance was through the hall. He must still be in the house.

My hand was already upon the bell-rope; but I stayed it in time. If he had not made him self known, why should I disturb the house? I dressed myself hurriedly, and slipped into the hall. The first object that met my eyes was a boot lying upon the stairs. It bore the marks of Baby's teeth; and, as I looked along the hall, I saw too plainly that the usual array of freshly blackened boots and shoes before the lodgers' doors was not there. As I ascended the stairs, I found another, but with the blackening carefully licked off. On the third floor were two or three more boots, slightly mouthed; but at this point Baby's taste for blacking had evidently palled. A little farther on was a ladder, leading to an open scuttle. I mounted the ladder, and reached the flat roof, that formed a continuous level over the row of houses to the corner of the street. Behind the chimney on the very last roof something was lurking. It was the fugitive Baby. He was covered with dust and dirt and fragments of glass. But he was sitting on his hind-legs, and was eating an enormous slab of peanut candy, with a look of mingled guilt and infinite satisfaction. He even, I fancied, slightly stroked his stomach with his disengaged fore-paw as I approached. He knew that I was looking for him; and the expression of his eye said plainly, "The past, at least, is secure."

I hurried him, with the evidences of his guilt, back to the scuttle, and descended on tiptoe to the floor beneath. Providence favored us; I met no one on the stairs; and his own cushioned tread was inaudible. I think he was conscious of the dangers of detection; for he even forebore to breathe, or much less chew the last mouthful he had taken; and he skulked at my side with the sirup dropping from his motionless jaws. I think he would have silently choked to death just then, for my sake; and it was not until I had reached my room again, and threw myself panting on the sofa, that I saw how near strangulation he had been. He gulped once or twice apologetically, and then walked to the corner of his own accord, and rolled himself up like an immense sugarplum, sweating remorse and treacle at every pore.

I locked him in when I went to breakfast, when I found Mrs. Brown's lodgers in a state of intense excitement over certain mysterious events of the night before, and the dreadful revelations of the morning. It appeared that burglars had entered the block from the scuttles; that, being suddenly alarmed, they had quitted our house without committing any depredation, dropping even the boots they had collected in the halls; but that a desperate attempt had been made to force the till in the confectioner's shop on the corner, and that the glass show-case had been ruthlessly smashed. A courageous servant in No. 4 had seen a masked burglar, on his hands and knees, attempting to enter their scuttle; but, on her shouting, "Away wid yees!" he instantly fled.

I sat through this recital with cheeks that burned uncomfortably; nor was I the less embarrassed, on raising my eyes, to meet Mrs. Brown's fixed curiously and mischievously on mine. As soon as I could make my escape from the table, I did so, and, running rapidly up stairs, sought refuge from any possible inquiry in my own room. Baby was still asleep in the corner. It would not be safe to remove him until the lodgers had gone down town; and I was revolving in my mind the expediency of keeping him until night veiled his obtrusive eccentricity from the public eye, when there came a cautious tap at my door. I opened it. Mrs. Brown slipped in quietly, closed the door softly, stood with her back against it, and her hand on the knob, and beckoned me mysteriously towards her. Then she asked in a low voice,—

"Is hair-dye poisonous?"

I was too confounded to speak.

"Oh, do! you know what I mean," she said impatiently. "This stuff." She produced suddenly from behind her a bottle with a

Greek label so long as to run two or three times spirally around it from top to bottom. "He says it isn't a dye: it's a vegetable preparation for invigorating"—

"Who says?" I asked despairingly.

"Why, Mr. Parker, of course!" said Mrs. Brown, severely, with the air of having repeated the name a great many times,— "the old gentleman in the room above. The simple question I want to ask," she continued with the calm manner of one who has just convicted another of gross ambiguity of language, "is only this: If some of this stuff were put in a saucer, and left carelessly on the table, and a child, or a baby, or a cat, or any young animal, should come in the window, and drink it up,—a whole saucer full,—because it had a sweet taste, would it be likely to hurt them?"

I cast an anxious glance at Baby, sleeping peacefully in the corner and a very grateful one at Mrs. Brown, and said I didn't think it would.

"Because," said Mrs. Brown loftily as she opened the door, "I thought, if it was poisonous, remedies might be used in time. Because," she added suddenly, abandoning her lofty manner, and wildly rushing to the corner with a frantic embrace of the unconscious Baby, "because, if any nasty stuff should turn its bo+ful hair a horrid green, or a naughty pink, it would break its own muzzer's heart, it would!"

But, before I could assure Mrs. Brown of the inefficiency of hair-dye as an internal application, she had darted from the room.

That night, with the secrecy of defaulters, Baby and I decamped from Mrs. Brown's. Distrusting the too emotional nature of that noble animal, the horse, I had recourse to a hand-cart, drawn by a stout Irishman, to convey my charge to the ferry. Even then, Baby refused to go, unless I walked by the cart, and at times rode in it.

"I wish," said Mrs. Brown, as she stood by the door, wrapped in an immense shawl, and saw us depart, "I wish it looked less solemn,—less like a pauper's funeral."

I must admit, that, as I walked by the cart that night, I felt very much as if I were accompanying the remains of some humble friend to his last resting-place; and that, when I was obliged to ride in it, I never could entirely convince myself that I was not helplessly overcome by liquor, or the victim of an accident, *en route* to the hospital. But at last we reached the ferry. On the boat, I think no one discovered Baby, except a drunken man, who approached me to ask for a light for his cigar, but who suddenly dropped it, and fled in dismay to the gentlemen's cabin, where his incoherent ravings were luckily taken for the earlier indications of *delirium tremens*.

It was nearly midnight when I reached my little cottage on the outskirts of Oakland; and it was with a feeling of relief and security that I entered, locked the door, and turned him loose in the hall, satisfied that henceforward his depredations would be limited to my own property. He was very quiet that night; and after he had tried to mount the hat-rack, under the mistaken impression that it was intended for his own gymnastic exercise, and knocked all the hats off, he went peacefully to sleep on the rug. . . .

GRIZZLY HUNTERS OF THE OLD WEST

17

HUNTING IN THE WEST
Theodore Roosevelt

If proof were needed that Old Ephraim was indeed the king of beasts, it is provided by Theodore Roosevelt's suspense-filled account of his first grizzly kill. This selection from the works of America's former President and most famous big-game hunter permits the reader to participate in camp life and the excitement of the hunt, so acute are the author's descriptions of his surroundings and so adept his comments on hunting activities. When Roosevelt comes upon the half-human tracks of the silvertipped bear for the first time, one senses his great excitement; when he "counts coup" on the enormous grizzly, one shares his elation.

This chronicle of the taking of Roosevelt's most prized trophy is one of many enthralling hunting tales contained in his book, *Hunting Trips of a Ranchman: Sketches of Sports on the Northern Cattle Plains*, published in New York and London in 1885 by G. P. Putnam's Sons and The Knickerbocker Press. The excerpt reprinted here appears on pages 306–14 of this book.

IT WAS STILL EARLY in September, and the weather was cool and pleasant, the nights being frosty and pleasant; every two or three days there was a flurry of light snow which rendered the labor of tracking much more easy. Our fare was excellent, consisting of elk venison, mountain grouse, and small trout; the last caught in one of the beautiful little lakes that lay almost up by the timber line. To us, who had for weeks been accustomed to make small fires from dried brush, or from sage-brush roots, which we dug out of the ground, it was a treat to sit at night before the roaring fire and crackling pine logs; as the old teamster quaintly put it, we had at last come to a land "where the wood grew on trees."

Sometimes we hunted in company; sometimes each of us went out alone; the teamster, of course, remaining to guard the camp and cook. One day we had separated; I reached camp early in the afternoon and waited a couple of hours before Merrifield put in an appearance.

At last I heard a shout—the familiar long-drawn *Eikoh-h-h* of the cattleman, and he came in sight, galloping at full speed down an open glade waving his hat, evidently having had good luck. When he reined in we saw that he had packed behind his saddle the fine glossy pelt of a black bear. Better still, he announced that he had been off about ten miles to a perfect tangle of ravines and valleys where bear sign was very thick; and not of black bear either, but of grizzly.

The black bear (the only one we got on the mountains) he had run across by accident, while riding up a valley in which there was a patch of dead timber grown up with berry bushes. He noticed a black object which he first took to be a charred stump. . . . On coming near, however, the object suddenly took to its heels. He followed over frightful ground until the pony stumbled and fell down. By this time he was close on the bear which had just reached the edge of the woods. Picking himself up, he rushed after it, hearing growling ahead of him; after running fifty yards the sound stopped and he stood listening. He saw and heard nothing until he happened to cast his eyes upward and there was the bear, almost overhead and about 25 feet up a tree. In as many seconds afterwards it came down to the ground with a bounce, dead.

Merrifield's tale made me decide to shift camp. . . . Next morning we were off and by noon we pitched camp by a clear brook, in a valley with steep, wooded sides, but with good feed for the horses in the open bottom. We rigged the canvas wagon sheet into a small tent, sheltered by the trees from the wind, and piled great pine logs nearby where we wished to place the fire. . . .

That afternoon we went out and I shot a fine bull elk. I came home alone toward nightfall, walking through a reach of burnt forest, where there was nothing but charred tree-trunks and black mould. When nearly through it I came across the huge, half-human footprints of a great grizzly, which must have passed by within a few minutes. It gave me rather an eerie feeling in the silent, lonely woods, to see for the first time the unmistakable proofs that I was in the home of the mighty lord of the wilderness. I followed the tracks in the fading twilight until it became too dark to see them any longer, and then shouldered my rifle and walked back to camp.

Next day we went off on a long tramp through the woods and along the sides of the canyons. There were plenty of berry bushes growing in clusters; and all around these there were fresh tracks of bear. On visiting the place where Merrifield had killed the black bear, we found that the grizzlies had been there before us, and had utterly devoured the carcass with cannibal relish. Hardly a scrap was left, and we turned our steps toward where lay the bull elk I had killed. It was quite late in the afternoon when we reached the place. The grizzly had evidently been at the carcass during the preceding night, for his great footprints were in the ground all around it, and the carcass itself was gnawed and torn, and partially covered with earth and leaves—for the grizzly has a curious habit of burying all of his prey that he does not at the moment need. . . .

The forest was composed mainly of ridge-pole pines, which grew close together, and did not branch out until the stems were thirty or forty feet from the ground. Beneath these trees we walked over a carpet of pine needles, upon which our moccasined feet made no sound. The woods seemed vast and lonely, and their silence was broken now and then by the strange noises always to be heard in the great forests, and which seem to mark the sad and everlasting unrest of the wilderness. We climbed up along the trunk of a dead tree which had toppled over until its upper branches stuck in the limb crotch of another that thus supported it at an angle halfway in its fall. When above the ground far enough to prevent the bear's smelling us, we sat still to wait for his approach; until, in the gathering gloom, we could no longer see the sights of our rifles, and could but dimly make out the carcass of the elk. As it was useless to wait longer, we clambered down and stole out to the edge of the woods. . . . Once out from under the trees there was still plenty of light although the sun had set . . . and we crouched down under a bush to see if perchance some animal might not also leave the cover. To our right the ravine sloped downward toward the valley of the Big-horn River, and far on its other side we could catch a glimpse of the great main chain of the Rockies, their snow peaks glinting crimson in the light of the set sun. Once again we waited quietly in the growing dusk until the pine trees in our front blended into one dark, frowning mass. We saw nothing:—but the wild creatures of the forest had begun to stir abroad. The owls hooted dismally from the tops of the tall trees, and two or three times a harsh wailing cry, probably the voice of a lynx or wolverine, arose from the depths of the woods. At last, as we were rising to leave, we heard the sound of the breaking of a dead stick from the spot where we knew the carcass lay. It was a sharp, sudden noise, perfectly distinct from the natural creaking and snapping of the branches; just such a sound as would be made by the tread of some heavy creature. "Old Ephraim" had come back to the carcass. . . . It was entirely too dark to go in after him, but we made up our minds that on the morrow he should be ours.

Early next morning we were at the elk carcass and, as we expected, we found that the bear had eaten his fill during the night. His tracks showed him to be an immense fellow. We doubted if he had left long before we arrived and we made up our minds to follow him up and try to find his lair. . . .

My companion was a skillful tracker, and we took up the trail at once. For some distance it led over the soft, yielding carpet of moss and pine needles and the footprints were quite easily made out. . . . We made no sound ourselves, and every little sudden noise sent a thrill through me as I peered about with each sense on the alert. Two or three ravens that we had scared from the carcass flew overhead, croaking hoarsely. The pine tops moaned and sighed in the slight breeze. . . .

After going a few hundred yards the tracks turned off on a well-beaten path made by elk. . . . The beast's footprints were perfectly plain in the dust. He had lumbered along up the path until near the middle of the hillside, where the ground broke away and there were hollows and boulders. Here the trail turned off into a tangled thicket within which it was almost certain we would find our quarry. We could still follow the tracks by the slight scrapes of the claws on the bark, or by the bent and broken twigs. ... When in the middle of the thicket we crossed a breastwork of fallen logs and Merrifield, who was leading, passed by the upright stem of a great pine. As soon as he was past it he sank suddenly on one knee, turning half around, his face fairly flaming with excitement. As I strode past him, with my rifle at the ready, there, not ten steps off, was the great bear, slowly rising from his bed among the young spruces. He had heard us, but hardly knew exactly where or what we were, for he reared up on his haunches sideways to us. Then he saw us and dropped down again on all fours, the shaggy hair on his neck and shoulders seeming to bristle as he turned toward us. As he sank down on his forefeet I raised the rifle; his head was bent slightly down, and when I saw the top of the white bead fairly between his small, glittering, evil eyes, I pulled trigger. Half-rising up, the huge beast fell over on his side in the death throes, the ball having gone into his brain, striking as fairly between the eyes as if the distance had been measured by a carpenter's rule.

The whole thing was over in twenty seconds from the time I caught sight of the game. Indeed, it was over so quickly that the grizzly did not have time to show fight at all or come a step toward us. It was the first I had ever seen and I felt not a little proud, as I stood over the great brindled bulk, which lay stretched out at length in the cool shade of the evergreens. He was a monstrous fellow, much larger than any I have seen since, whether alive or brought in dead by the hunters. As near as we could estimate he must have weighed about twelve hundred pounds. (Of course, we had nothing with which to weigh more than very small portions.) He must have been very old, his teeth and claws being all worn down and blunted; but nevertheless he had been living in plenty, for he was as fat as a prize hog. ... He was still in the summer coat, his hair being short, and in color a curious brindled brown, somewhat like that of certain bulldogs.

18

GRIZZLY BEAR
Colonel Richard Irving Dodge

Colonel Richard Irving Dodge was one of comparatively few men who, having lived through stirring times, possessed the combination of ability and perseverance requisite for the chronicling of these events in an absorbing manner. Graduating from the United States Military Academy in 1848, he was assigned to the Eighth Infantry, serving at various western posts before the Civil War. After the cessation of that conflict he engaged in the campaigns against the Plains Indians during the 1870's, serving as colonel of the Eleventh Infantry until his death in 1895.

His book, *The Plains of the Great West*, one of several detailing his observations of early days in the West, was originally published in 1877. It was later translated into German and published in Vienna in 1884, and it was largely responsible for the "Wild West" enthusiasm of European writers and readers of that time. The book provides a graphic record of army and civilian life on the Plains during the latter part of the nineteenth century which is both readable and authoritative, mostly a firsthand account of Colonel Dodge's life and times.

Colonel Dodge's observations on grizzly bears, reprinted below, are taken from *The Plains of the Great West and Their Inhabitants, Being a Description of the Plains, Game, Indians &c. of the Great North American Desert*, published in New York by G. P. Putnam's Sons, 1877, pages 213–16. Archer House, Inc., of New York, reprinted the book in 1959, to the great benefit of present-day readers.

MY PERSONAL KNOWLEDGE OF THIS ANIMAL is of the slightest. In many years of plains and mountain experience I have never encountered but one grizzly. He ran like a deer. I pursued on horseback; but, after an exciting chase, he escaped into a beaver dam thicket, from which it was impossible to dislodge him.

I have known several men to be killed by grizzlies; and one of the most complete wrecks of humanity I ever saw was a man whom a grizzly, in the last moments of his life, had gotten into his embrace. The man told me his story. He was huntsman for a party of miners in California. One day, when out alone, he ascended a steep and high mountain, and, just as he arrived at the top, met face to face a huge grizzly just starting down the trail by which the man went up. Neither could retreat without giving great advantage to the other. The bear raised himself on his hind legs, and, thus erect, approached the man, who, presenting his rifle and getting his knife ready, awaited the attack. The bear slowly advanced and took the muzzle of the rifle in his mouth. Depressing the butt of the piece so as to direct the ball through the bear's brain, the man fired. Before he had time to use his knife, or even to think, he found himself in the bear's clutches. "It was all over in a second," said he. "I didn't feel pain, and I remember thinking I was about like a mouse in a cat's jaws, and what a fool I was to think I might hurt a grizzly with my knife, when everything went away, and I didn't know any more 'til I come to the next day in camp."

His companions had found him and the grizzly apparently dead in a heap together. The bear was dead, shot through the brain. The man showed signs of life and was taken to camp, restoratives were applied, and his wounds examined and dressed. The bear in his last throes had apparently given but one rake with each of his terribly armed paws. One fore claw passed over the man's right shoulder, had hooked under the right shoulderblade and torn it out entirely. The other fore claw had torn all the flesh from the right side. One hind claw had torn open the lower abdomen, letting out the bowels and badly scarifying the left leg, while the other hind claw had torn every particle of muscle from the right thigh from groin to knee. In spite of these terrible injuries, the man, after many months, recovered. When I saw him he was apparently in good health, but could not use or even move his right arm or either leg. He gave me the particulars of his fight, and described his wounds with great animation and gusto, smoking his pipe the while, and wound up with the remark, "Anybody can fight bear that wants to; I've had enough grizzly in mine." I thought he had.

A year or two ago two soldiers from Fort Wingate foolishly attacked a grizzly on foot. Both were terribly torn, and I believe both died. Only a year ago a soldier of the 3rd Cavalry died from injuries received from a wounded bear, which he rashly followed into a thicket.

In 1870 a small party of citizens were going up the Chaquaque cañon. The trail led along a bench high above the bottom, in which were trees and thickets. The piping of young turkeys was heard in the thicket, and one of the citizens who carried a shotgun proposed to go down and kill some for supper. The party waited for him. He had hardly disappeared in the thicket before he reappeared in full flight, while close at his heels followed a huge she-grizzly with two cubs. In a few seconds she overtook and struck him a powerful blow with her fore paw, knocking him senseless. She then deliberately smelt over the prostrate body, and, apparently satisfied that he was dead, went slowly back to the thicket. The party above had been unable to do anything. As soon as the bear left they hastily consulted together, and some of the boldest were about to go down when the body sprang to its feet, and made the best possible time to the top of the hill. An examination disclosed the fact that the bear's claws had struck the man's body behind just below the waistband of his trousers; and though every particle of clothing, upper and under, had been torn from that part of the person, the skin was not broken nor the man injured beyond some slight bruises. He explained that the blow, throwing him forward on his stomach, had knocked the breath and consciousness out of him. When he recovered his senses the bear was smelling at him, and, knowing the consequence of moving, he laid still. I have never heard of a more striking instance of presence of mind and nerve.

19

VARMINTS AND SUCH

Courtney Ryley Cooper

The long-standing belief that bears hug their victims to death is pure fiction. Many men who have lived through a "hand-to-hand" fight with an enraged grizzly probably would have preferred such bloodless offensive tactics. Courtney Ryley Cooper's epic account of Bill Poronteau's struggle with a mama silvertip borders on the macabre but ends with a fillip. When a she-bear clamps a man's head between her fang-studded jaws, he's never very handsome again, it goes without saying. The story is taken from *High Country*[1] and is reprinted here by the kind permission of Mrs. Courtney Ryley Cooper.

HE'S A FIGHTER, is the bear—the fiercest fighter that the hills know, once he swings into action. Enough of a fighter, in fact, to make history in the mountains; the man who survives a hand-to-hand struggle with a bear is far more famed than the wildest two-gun man that the West could offer. Bill Poronteau, for instance.

We rode the trail last summer, the one where Bill Poronteau fought it out with the silvertip, more than thirty years ago, myself and Jack Nankervis, who, a decade later, put a bullet between the eyes of one of the cubs which caused one of the greatest battles in mountain history. From the heights of the ancient trail leading down from Yankee Doodle Lake, we saw the slight clearing where it all had occurred, and like the boys in a waxworks, we halted and looked at it; we who were fortunate enough to see the place "where Bill Poronteau fought the bear!" That

---

[1] Courtney Ryley Cooper, *High Country: The Rockies Yesterday and Today* (Boston, Little Brown and Company, 1926).

means something, out here in the hills; that was one of those struggles generally described as epic.

Not that Bill had intended it. That morning he had saddled his horse, ridden over the hill from Central City down bubbling Jenny Lind Creek and up into South Boulder Park on the shoulder of the Continental Divide, on a search for a deer. He tied his horse and started forth, suddenly to halt at a noise in the brush and to kneel that he might investigate.

Two silvertip cubs were there; Poronteau gazed for a second, then whirled in a frenzy of fear. Rising to the right, and hurtling toward him with the speed of a tackling football player, was the gigantic mother!

There was no time for the rifle. An instant and the tremendous form had launched upon him, to knock him far to one side and bring him breathless against a sapling, to which he clung with grim desperation. It was a law of hunting, as Poronteau knew it—to struggle with every atom of strength against the possibility of being pulled into a bear's grasp and he intended to stay there as long as his muscles lasted. The bear came on.

But not to seize him. She rose, growling, and put her paws on his shoulders, as though resting herself. And there they stood, a rifleless man, an angry she bear, while the seconds passed like hours. Poronteau's right hand began to move ever so slowly for his hunting knife. An inch, two inches. Then the action was noticed, and with a spasm of speed, the bear seemed to attack at a dozen places at once. She caught his arm, tearing it like the slashing of knives. She pulled him down, and then, her great mouth opening, took his head in it, as though to crush his skull. But something intervened—a blow from Poronteau's knife, driven with all the force that a desperate man could know, and ripping a gash in the silvertip's vitals for more than a foot, while the enemy, crazed by pain, sought to loosen her hold on his head. But her teeth had dug deep by now, and as she pulled back, the scalp of the man loosened, to be dragged farther, farther—until at last it was brought over his eyes, like a horrible ghastly mask. But he continued to fight, sightless, bleeding from a dozen tooth and claw marks; still slashing and driving with his knife.

They tumbled together to the ground. Then, with a great groan, the bear rolled, caught him up and threw him a dozen feet against a tree where he sank, a knee dislocated from the impact. After that quiet, for minutes, for a half-hour. At last a dazed man crawled to his horse, and in some herculean fashion managed, in spite of that dislocated knee, to mount it. Three hours later, the men at a little sawmill saw a ghastly thing rolling in the saddle as a horse, following the homing instinct, moved slowly up Jenny Lind Creek. It was the semi-conscious Poronteau, and they took him in, to dress his wounds, care for him, and finally take him to Central City.

We passed that sawmill last summer. It is only so much rotting wood now; the mill itself long has disappeared. But the story of Poronteau's bear lives on in the hunting annals of the hills.

"Things like that scare a fellow," said Jack, as our pack train plodded slowly by the mill. "Now when I saw that silvertip—the one that'd been a cub when Poronteau got mauled—it sort of sent a shiver down my back. I just had to plug him between the eyes."

"But how did you know it was the cub?" I asked.

"Oh, Bill identified him," said Jack. "You see Poronteau lived. All tore up, but he lived just the same. One place, at least, where a man was tougher 'n a bear because they found the old she-brute deader 'n a doornail. Yep, Bill just took one look at that bear of mine and said, 'It's a picture of his mother,' he said. And he ought to know. He was close enough to that old she-devil!"

20

BUGLE AND TRAILER IN A BATTLE ROYAL
John B. Griffith[1]

Although there isn't a single silvertip left in the state of Oregon today, innumerable Grizzly Peaks, Bear Creeks, etc., witness the fact that the bears once were there. Unfortunately, grizzly-bear days in this state had few chroniclers. We are indebted to the Oregon State Game Commission for the saga of a nineteenth-century bear hunt used here. The story was one of three written by Mr. Griffith and published in the Game Department magazine following a request for hunting stories from readers. It appeared in the January, 1918, issue of *Oregon Sportsman*, Vol. VI, No. 1, pages 34–37, and is a well-written account of pioneer days in the famed Rogue River Valley.

FRED BARNEBURG was one of the good old pioneers of the Rogue River Valley and was one of the first settlers and secured valuable land near Bear Creek. In those days he and Captain John S. Miller used to kill deer where Medford [Oregon] now stands. Fred was known far and wide and loved to hunt better than anybody. . . . I used to hunt a great deal with Fred and Dave Miller and it kept me pretty busy sometimes listening to them both talking at the same time, telling how they came to miss an old buck or managed to bag him.

Fred was several years older than I and used to tell around the

---

[1] John B. Griffith was born in Jacksonville, Oregon, in 1853 while his parents were "forted up" there during an Indian uprising. In 1878 he married Nettie Naylor, whose father built the first sawmill in Jackson County, and they later took a homestead in the Dead Indian country where they ran a dairy and Griffith hunted for the Ashland market. In those days there were lots of deer, elk, bears, wildcats, and cougars in the country. Griffith had one hunting dog which treed more than one hundred bears in the Cascade Mountains. When the dog died, Griffith had a notice of his death printed in the local paper.

campfire of his early hunting days and his hunts in Dead Indian and around Grizzly Peak.

I remember of him telling me of seeing two large grizzlies in mortal combat. He and his brother Aaron were camped near Hoxie Prairie . . . and went out one morning armed with muzzle loading rifles. Upon coming out of the timber to the edge of the prairie they were astonished to see two large grizzlies fighting savagely. It was immense to hear Fred describe the fight. How they would rear upon their haunches and claw each other, bite and growl and roll over and over on the ground oblivious to everything around them.

Fred was so absorbed in the fight that he could only stand and look without a thought of danger, but finally upon looking around, he discovered that he was alone, his brother Aaron having turned and ran for camp as fast as he could go without even calling to Fred to come. This brought him to a realization of his danger and the folly of trying to kill them, and he too turned and fled and found his brother in camp.

Grizzlies in those days were dangerous. As they were plentiful and were not hunted much it took a man with plenty of nerve to tackle one with the old muzzle loading rifles. Sometimes a man had to have considerable nerve to tackle one with a Winchester after those firearms began to come into use. I know this by experience—having met one in the Siskiyou Mountains once while going around the side of a hill in a fog.

We were within forty steps of each other and he looked at me and I at him (like Davy Crockett and the jay bird) but only for a few seconds for he doubled himself up and rolling his hair the wrong way commenced coming, a little sideways at first, with his head down and champing his teeth. I was in open ground and realized that I had to fight. I jerked the gun to my shoulder and caught a bead. The bullet hit him back of the shoulder and ranged quarteringly but didn't get the heart. He then threw his head around and bit at the place and I sent another bullet just as he straightened around again and this time caught him in the fleshy part of the neck, and then he came. Gee, but he was a big one, raw boned and poor. Then the lever began to work up and

133

down and send a stream of lead right at his breast—but he got within twenty feet.

As good luck would have it I struck him in the left shoulder which caused him to fall down and as the hillside was steep, he rolled over and over down through the brush.

I lost no time in getting out of there without waiting to see if my hat was on or not. I went back the next day and took Trailer. He took the scent and followed it for about a hundred yards and found him piled up against a bush, dead. I know that Trailer was disappointed, for after smelling him over he raised his head and looked around as much as to say, "What did you want me for?" I kept him with me all of the time on that hunt, for to tell the truth, my nervous system had received a shock that it took some little time to get over.

I remember another story Fred used to tell about himself and John Miller, the gunsmith of Jacksonville, shooting a big buck out near Hiatt Prairie. The buck fell near a bluff or rim rock with thick brush all along the edge. They walked to where he lay and leaning on the muzzle of their guns stood looking down at him and Miller counted the points on his horns and said to Fred, "He is a seven pointer." Just then the deer began to struggle and before they had time to think was over the bluff and gone, leaving two sadly disappointed men to mourn his loss. They had only creased him.

Another time Fred chased a big buck and going up to him, thinking him dead, set his gun down against a tree, took out his knife and just as he took hold of a horn with his left hand the deer began to struggle. Fred grabbed the other horn with the right hand and still held the knife. He was a stout man, but that buck came near doing him, but Fred finally threw him and cut his throat.

On the hunt I started to tell of, we were camped at the Walker place at Dead Indian. It was the first of November. We had hunted four or five days and killed but four or five deer, Fred especially having had very poor luck which was new to him as he was a splendid hunter and number one shot.

I killed a deer on the east side of Dead Indian Creek the fourth

day and next morning took a horse and went after it, taking Trailer with me. Fred went out across the Prairie and through Sarvis
Glade and then down on the benches on the west side of the
creek. The canyon is deep here and rough, only now and then
a place where a man can get across. When I got down to where
the deer had been hung up he had been eaten slick and clean by
a bear. Trailer immediately took trail and started. I tied my horse
and followed, but in a short distance overtook him. He had struck
a very rough and rocky place and it had not left a scent. I sat
down on a rock and waited awhile and concluded to call Fred
and get Bugle, knowing that he—being a full blooded hound and
Trailer only half—could track it. I called at the top of my voice
and sure enough he answered me. I told him to turn old Bugle
loose and blew the horn, and heard him start, bellowing at every
jump. Sometimes he would stop to listen and I would give the
horn a toot and he would come again. When he got to Dead Indian
Creek he had quite a time getting across, but made it and came
on up the hill. In the meantime Trailer had worked it off the rocks
and was going on. As soon as Bugle got there he took the track
and away they went, down across Dead Indian Creek and out
of hearing. Talk about music, they fairly made the woods ring.
I followed and found a place to cross [the creek] and kept down
on the west side for three or four miles and finally heard them
barking up a tree—still a long way off. I blew the horn to let old
Trailer know I heard him and was coming. When he heard the
horn he commenced to bark steadily and kept at it until I was
close to the tree. When he saw me he wagged his tail as much
as to say, "I've got him."

The tree was an ordinary sized fir and there was thick high
brush all around it, which made it difficult to see him, and while
I was backing around trying to locate him he discovered me and
gave a big snort and commenced to snap his teeth. I saw him then,
next to the body of the tree, partially hidden by the heavy boughs.
I had to move around a little to get a good place to shoot from
and he commenced changing his position and snorted and
champed his teeth continually,—I knew he was on the fight and
a hard customer.

135

I waited a few seconds and when he got still and turned his head down to look at me, caught a bead and fired full in the face, expecting to hit him square between the eyes, but failing on account of shooting in too big a hurry. The bullet caught him square in the side of the head and running around the skull went out in the back of the neck. I saw instantly it was a bad shot and had another load in quick as a flash, as it was a sure bet he would come down now.

He came hand over fist and as good luck would have it on the side next to me. I shot again and hit him in the shoulder. He stopped now and threw his head around and bit at the place where the bullet struck him, which gave me time to load and fire again, hitting him this time behind the shoulder. This shot caused him to let go and come tumbling down to the ground with a crash, but he was up again in a second just as the dogs piled on him. As bad luck would have it, Trailer was at the head and before the bear was up had him by the side of the head, something he seldom did. I am sure he thought the bear was as good as dead or he wouldn't have done it this time.

Quicker than a flash the bear had both paws around him and crushed him down to the ground and would have crushed the life out of him in no time if it had not been for Bugle, who showed his blood right then and there, for he sprang forward with a bellow without the least sign of fear, brave old dog that he was, seized him by the side of the head and the bear went over backwards, letting go of Trailer and throwing Bugle entirely loose. By the time the dogs were up the bear was up and backing against a bush. He stood them off.

I waited for a good chance now and shot him in the head at the butt of the ear and he rolled over. I let Bugle and Trailer go after him now to their heart's content. He was too big to hang up, so I dressed him and straightened him around so he would drain, then started up the hill to look out a way to get the horse down to where he was. I had proceeded about three hundred yards and was going through some open timber when I noticed the dogs raise their heads and sniff like they'd caught the scent of some kind of game. I kept them back, however—thinking it might be deer—

as old Bugle liked to run deer pretty well. I kept moving along up the hill and after awhile came to the edge of a thick patch of brush and studied a minute whether to go around it or through it. I decided to go through it, and hadn't got more than twenty steps when the brush cracked in front of me, and both dogs went by me like a shot and, after running three or four hundred yards, began to bay up a tree.

I went on up to where I heard the brush crack and there on a big log saw where an immense cougar had been lying. As there was a little snow on I could see his track plain. I went on around the sidehill and came in on the upper side of the tree and there he was. He was standing up on the limbs looking down at the dogs just like he would just as soon spring down right among them as not. I kept behind a tree until ready to shoot and then stepped out where he could see me. He had his side to me and turned his head and looked, but not for long—a bullet went crashing through his brain and he rolled out of there dead.

I knew Fred would be delighted at the part Bugle had taken in the two chases as he had been waiting to get him after a bear for a long time. . . . I went on to camp now and got there early, but Fred did not get in until after dark. I had supper ready for him. I asked him if he had killed anything. He said he had killed two deer. I told him then about the bear eating the deer and he got interested right away and wanted to know how Bugle performed.

It fairly took his breath away as I told him about the dogs treeing the cougar and that it was one of the largest I ever saw. Fred had seen a great many and he thought that part of it was a mistake. I told him we would go get them [bear and cougar carcasses] in the morning and he would see.

WITH THE NATURALISTS

21

AMONG THE ANIMALS OF YOSEMITE

John Muir

John Muir's poetic prose takes the reader into the forest primeval, over flower-carpeted plains and among luscious berry
patches which once were the Sierra bruin's own. As a novice
among grizzly bears, Muir came very near not living to tell the
story of his first meeting with one of the big Yosemite bears.
The grizzly was so confused by the naturalist's unorthodox antics
that Muir's life was not endangered, but he never tried to frighten
a bear again.

Muir also tells about bear killers of yesteryear and grizzlies
who raided mountain-pastured sheep in the following delightful
and eventful excerpt from his book, *Our National Parks,* published
by Houghton Mifflin Company in Boston and New York in 1901,
pages 172–88.

John Muir came to the United States from Scotland in 1849
but did not settle in California until 1868. He was a crusader for
the establishment of national parks and was largely responsible for
the creation of Yosemite National Park in the beautiful mountains
of central California. Muir Woods National Monument was
named for him in recognition of his efforts to save portions of the
Western wilderness for future generations. Muir Glacier in
Alaska, which he discovered, also bears his name.

THE SIERRA BEAR, brown or gray, the sequoia of the animals,
tramps over all the park, though few travelers have the pleasure
of seeing him. On he fares through the majestic forests and cañons,
facing all sorts of weather, rejoicing in his strength, everywhere at
home, harmonizing with the trees and rocks and shaggy chaparral.
Happy fellow! his lines have fallen in pleasant places,—lily gardens in silver-fir forests, miles of bushes in endless variety and

exuberance of bloom over hill-waves and valleys and along the banks of streams, cañons full of music and waterfalls, parks fair as Eden,—places in which one might expect to meet angels rather than bears.

In this happy land no famine comes nigh him. All the year round his bread is sure, for some of the thousand kinds that he likes are always in season and accessible, ranged on the shelves of the mountains like stores in a pantry. From one to another, from climate to climate, up and down he climbs, feasting on each in turn,—enjoying as great variety as if he traveled to far-off countries north and south. To him almost every thing is food except granite. Every tree helps to feed him, every bush and herb, with fruits and flowers, leaves and bark; and all the animals he can catch,—badgers, gophers, ground squirrels, lizards, snakes, etc., and ants, bees, wasps, old and young, together with their eggs and larvae and nests. Craunched and hashed, down all go to his marvelous stomach, and vanish as if cast into a fire. What digestion! A sheep or a wounded deer or a pig he eats warm, about as quickly as a boy eats a buttered muffin; or should the meat be a month old, it still is welcomed with tremendous relish. After so gross a meal as this, perhaps the next will be strawberries and clover, or raspberries with mushrooms and nuts, or puckery acorns and chokecherries. And as if fearing that anything eatable in all his dominion should escape being eaten, he breaks into cabins to look after sugar, dried apples, bacon, etc. Occasionally he eats the mountaineer's bed; but when he has had a full meal of more tempting dainties he usually leaves it undisturbed, though he has been known to drag it up through a hole in the roof, carry it to the foot of a tree, and lie down on it to enjoy a siesta. Eating everything, never is he himself eaten except by man, and only man is an enemy to be feared. "B'ar meat," said a hunter from whom I was seeking information, "b'ar meat is the best meat in the mountains; their skins make the best beds, and their grease the best butter. Biscuits shortened with b'ar grease goes as far as beans; a man will walk all day on a couple of them biscuit."

In my first interview with a Sierra bear we were frightened and embarrassed, both of us, but the bear's behavior was better than mine. When I discovered him, he was standing in a narrow strip of meadow, and I was concealed behind a tree on the side of it. After studying his appearance as he stood at rest, I rushed toward him to frighten him, that I might study his gait in running. But, contrary to all I had heard about the shyness of bears, he did not run at all; and when I stopped short within a few steps from him, as he held his ground in a fighting attitude, my mistake was monstrously plain. I was then put on my good behavior, and never afterwards forgot the right manners of the wilderness.

This happened on my first Sierra excursion in the forest to the north of Yosemite Valley. I was eager to meet the animals, and many of them came to me as if willing to show themselves and make my acquaintance; but the bears kept out of my way.

An old mountaineer, in reply to my questions, told me that bears were very shy, all save grim old grizzlies, and that I might travel the mountains for years without seeing one, unless I gave my mind to them and practiced the stealthy ways of hunters. Nevertheless, it was only a few weeks after I had received this information that I met the one mentioned above, and obtained instructions at firsthand.

I was encamped in the woods about a mile back of the rim of Yosemite, beside a stream that falls into the valley by way of Indian Cañon. Nearly every day for weeks I went to the top of the North Dome to sketch; for it commands a general view of the valley, and I was anxious to draw every tree and rock and waterfall. Carlo, a St. Bernard dog, was my companion,—a fine intelligent fellow that belonged to a hunter who was compelled to remain all summer on the hot plains, and who loaned him to me for the season for the sake of having him in the mountains, where he would be so much better off. Carlo knew bears through long experience, and he it was who led me to my first interview, though he seemed as much surprised as the bear at my unhunter-like behavior. One morning in June, just as the sunbeams began to stream through the trees, I set out for a day's sketching on the dome; and before we had gone half a mile from camp Carlo snuffed the air and looked cautiously ahead, lowered his bushy tail, drooped his ears, and began to step softly like a cat, turning every few yards and looking me in the face with a telling expression, saying plainly enough, "There is a bear a little way ahead." I walked carefully in the indicated direction, until I approached a small flowery meadow that I was familiar with, then crawled to the foot of a tree on its margin, bearing in mind what I had been told about the shyness of bears. Looking out cautiously over the instep of the tree, I saw a big, burly cinnamon bear[1] about thirty yards off, half erect, his paws resting on the trunk of a fir that had fallen into the meadow, his hips almost buried in grass and flowers. He was listening attentively and trying to catch the scent, showing that in some way he was aware of our approach. I watched his gestures, and tried to make the most of my opportunity to learn what I could about him, fearing he would not stay long. He made a fine picture, standing alert in the sunny garden walled in by the most beautiful firs in the world.

After examining him at leisure, noting the sharp muzzle thrust inquiringly forward, the long shaggy hair on his broad chest, the stiff ears nearly buried in the hair, and the slow, heavy way in which he moved his head, I foolishly made a rush on him, throwing up my arms and shouting to frighten him, to see him run. He did not mind the demonstration much; only pushed his head farther forward, and looked at me sharply as if asking, "What now? If you want to fight, I'm ready." Then I began to fear that on me would fall the work of running. But I was afraid to run, lest he should be encouraged to pursue me; therefore I held my ground, staring him in the face within a dozen yards or so, putting on as bold a look as I could, and hoping the influence of the human eye would be as great as it is said to be. Under these strained relations the interview seemed to last a long time. Finally, the bear, seeing how still I was, calmly withdrew his huge paw from the log, gave me a piercing look, as if warning me not to follow him, turned, and walked slowly up the middle of the meadow into the forest; stopping every few steps and looking back to make sure that I was not trying to take him at a disadvantage in a rear attack. I was glad to part with him, and greatly enjoyed the vanishing view as he waded through the lilies and columbines.

[1] There is no separate species designated as the cinnamon bear.

Thenceforth I always tried to give bears respectful notice of my approach, and they usually kept well out of my way. Though they often came around my camp in the night, only once afterward, as far as I know, was I very near one of them in daylight. This time it was a grizzly I met; and as luck would have it, I was even nearer to him that I had been to the big cinnamon. Though not a large specimen, he seemed formidable enough at a distance of less than a dozen yards. His shaggy coat was well grizzled, his head almost white. When I first caught sight of him he was eating acorns under a Kellog oak, at a distance of perhaps seventy-five yards, and I tried to slip past without disturbing him. But he had either heard my steps on the gravel or caught my scent, for he came straight toward me, stopping every rod or so to look and listen: and as I was afraid to be seen running, I crawled on my hands and knees a little way to one side and hid behind a libocedrus, hoping he would pass me unnoticed. He soon came up opposite me, and stood looking ahead, while I looked at him, peering past the bulging trunk of the tree. At last, turning his head, he caught sight of mine, stared sharply a minute or two, and then, with fine dignity, disappeared in a manzanita-covered earthquake talus.

Considering how heavy and broad-footed bears are, it is wonderful how little harm they do in the wilderness. Even in the well-watered gardens of the middle region, where the flowers grow tallest, and where during warm weather the bears wallow and roll, no evidence of destruction is visible. On the contrary, under nature's direction, the massive beasts act as gardeners. On the forest floor, carpeted with needles and brush, and on the tough sod of glacier meadows, bears make no mark; but around the sandy margin of lakes their magnificent tracks form grand lines of embroidery. Their well-worn trails extend along the main cañons on either side, and though dusty in some places make no scar on the landscape. They bite and break off the branches of some of the pines and oaks to get the nuts, but this pruning is so light that few mountaineers ever notice it; and though they interfere with the orderly lichen-veiled decay of fallen trees, tearing them to pieces to reach the colonies of ants that inhabit them, the scattered ruins are quickly pressed back into harmony by snow and rain and over-leaning vegetation.

The number of bears that make the Park their home may be guessed by the number that have been killed by the two best hunters, Duncan and old David Brown. Duncan began to be known as a bear-killer about the year 1865. He was then roaming the woods, hunting and prospecting on the south fork of the Merced. A friend told me that he killed his first bear near his cabin at Wawona; that after mustering courage to fire he fled, without waiting to learn the effect of his shot. Going back in a few hours he found poor Bruin dead, and gained courage to try again. Duncan confessed to me, when we made an excursion together in 1875, that he was at first mortally afraid of bears, but after killing a half dozen he began to keep count of his victims, and became ambitious to be known as a great bear-hunter. In nine years he had killed forty-nine, keeping count by notches cut on one of the timbers of his cabin on the shore of Crescent Lake, near the south boundary of the Park. He said the more he knew about bears, the more he respected them and the less he feared them. But at the same time he grew more and more cautious, and never fired until he had every advantage, no matter how long he had to wait and how far he had to go before he got the bear just right as to the direction of the wind, the distance, and the way of escape in case of accident; making allowance for the character of the animal, old or young, cinnamon or grizzly. For old grizzlies, he said, he had no use whatever; and he was mighty careful to avoid their acquaintance. He wanted to kill an even hundred; then he was going to confine himself to safer game. There was not much money in bears, anyhow, and a round hundred was enough for glory.

I have not seen or heard of him lately, and do not know how his bloody count stands. On my excursions, I occasionally passed his cabin. It was full of meat and skins hung in bundles from the rafters, and the ground about it was strewn with bones and hair,—infinitely less tidy than a bear's den. He went as hunter and guide with a geological survey party for a year or two, and was very proud of the scientific knowledge he picked up. His admiring fellow mountaineers, he said, gave him credit for knowing not only the botanical names of all the trees and bushes, but also the "botanical names of the bears."

The most famous hunter of the region was David Brown, an old pioneer, who early in the gold period established his main camp in a little forest glade on the north fork of the Merced, which is still called "Brown's Flat." No finer solitude for a hunter and prospector could be found; the climate is delightful all the year, and the scenery of both earth and sky is a perpetual feast. Though he was not much of a "scenery fellow," his friends say that he knew a pretty place when he saw it as well as any one, and liked mightily to get up on the top of a commanding ridge to "look off."

When out of provisions, he would take down his old-fashioned long-barreled rifle from its deerhorn rest over the fireplace and set out in search of game. Seldom did he have to go far for venison, because the deer liked the wooded slopes of Pilot Peak ridge, with its open spots where they could rest and look about them, and enjoy the breeze from the sea in warm weather, free from troublesome flies, while they found hiding-places and fine aromatic food in the deer-brush chaparral. A small, wise dog was his only companion, and well the little mountaineer understood the object of every hunt, whether deer or bears, or only grouse hidden in the fir-tops. In deer-hunting Sandy had little to do, trotting behind his master as he walked noiselessly through the fragrant woods, careful not to step heavily on dry twigs, scanning open spots in the chaparral where the deer feed in the early morning and toward sunset, peering over ridges and swells as new outlooks were reached, and along alder and willow fringed flats and streams, until he found a young buck, killed it, tied its legs together, threw it on his shoulder, and so back to camp. But when bears were hunted, Sandy played an important part as leader, and several times saved his master's life; and it was as a bear-hunter that David Brown became famous. His method, as I had it from a friend who had passed many an evening in his cabin listening to his long stories of adventure, was simply to take a few pounds of flour and his rifle, and go slowly and silently over hill and valley in the loneliest part of the wilderness, until little Sandy came upon the fresh track of a bear, then follow it to the death, paying no heed to time. Wherever the bear went he went, however rough the ground, led by Sandy, who looked back from time to time to see how his master was coming on, and regulated his pace accordingly, never growing weary or allowing any other track to divert him. When high ground was reached a halt was made, to scan the openings in every direction, and perchance Bruin would be discovered sitting upright on his haunches, eating manzanita berries; pulling down the fruit-laden branches with his paws and pressing them together, so as to get substantial mouthfuls, however mixed with leaves and twigs. The time of year enabled the hunter to determine approximately where the game would be found: in spring and early summer, in lush grass and clover meadows and in berry tangles along the banks of streams, or on pea-vine and lupine clad slopes; in late summer and autumn, beneath the pines, eating the cones cut off by the squirrels, and in oak groves at the bottom of cañons, munching acorns, manzanita berries, and cherries; and after snow had fallen, in alluvial bottoms, feeding on ants and yellow-jacket wasps. These food places were always cautiously approached, so as to avoid the chance of sudden encounters.

"Whenever," said the hunter, "I saw a bear before he saw me, I had no trouble in killing him. I just took lots of time to learn what he was up to and how long he would be likely to stay, and to study the direction of the wind and the lay of the land. Then I worked round to leeward of him, no matter how far I had to go; crawled and dodged to within a hundred yards, near the foot of a tree that I could climb, but which was too small for a bear to climb. There I looked to the priming of my rifle, took off my boots so as to climb quickly if necessary, and, with my rifle in rest and Sandy behind me, waited until my bear stood right, when I made a sure, or at least a good shot back of the fore leg. In case he showed fight, I got up the tree I had in mind, before he could reach me. But bears are slow and awkward with their eyes, and being to windward they could not scent me, and often I got in a second shot before they saw the smoke. Usually, however, they tried to get away when they were hurt, and I let them go a good safe [way] before I ventured into the brush after them. Then Sandy was pretty sure to find them dead; if not, he barked bold as a lion to draw attention, or rushed in and nipped them behind, enabling me to get to a safe distance and watch a chance for a finishing shot.

"Oh yes, bear-hunting is a mighty interesting business, and safe enough if followed just right, though, like every other business, especially the wild kind, it has its accidents, and Sandy and I have had close calls at times. Bears are nobody's fools, and they know enough to let men alone as a general thing, unless they are wounded, or cornered, or have cubs. In my opinion, a hungry old mother would catch and eat a man, if she could; which is only fair play, anyhow, for we eat them. But nobody, as far as I know has been eaten up in these rich mountains. Why they never tackle a fellow when he is lying asleep I never could understand. They could gobble us mighty handy, but I suppose it's nature to respect a sleeping man."

Sheep-owners and their shepherds have killed a great many bears, mostly by poison and traps of various sorts. Bears are fond of mutton, and levy heavy toll on every flock driven into the mountains. They usually come to the corral at night, climb in, kill a sheep with a stroke of the paw, carry it off for a little distance, eat about half of it, and return the next night for the other half; and so on all summer, or until they are themselves killed. It is not, however, by direct killing, but by suffocation through crowding against the corral wall in fright, that the greatest losses are incurred. From ten to fifteen sheep are found dead, smothered in the corral, after every attack; or the walls are broken, and the flock is scattered far and wide. A flock may escape the attention of these marauders for a week or two in the spring; but after their first taste of the fine mountain-fed meat the visits are persistently kept up, in spite of all precautions. Once I spent a night with two Portuguese shepherds, who were greatly troubled with bears, from two to four or five visiting them almost every night. Their camp was near the middle of the Park, and the wicked bears, they said, were getting worse and worse. Not waiting now until dark, they came out of the brush in broad daylight, and boldly carried off as many sheep as they liked. One evening, before sundown, a bear, followed by two cubs, came for an early supper, as the flock was being slowly driven toward the camp. Joe, the elder of the shepherds, warned by many exciting experiences, promptly climbed a tall tamarack pine, and left the freebooters to help themselves; while Antone, calling him a coward, and declaring that he was not going to let bears eat up his sheep before his face, set the dogs on them, and rushed toward them with a great noise and a stick. The frightened cubs ran up a tree, and the mother ran to meet the shepherd and the dogs. Antone stood astonished for a moment, eying the oncoming bear; then fled faster than Joe had, closely pursued. He scrambled to the roof of their little cabin, the only refuge quickly available; and fortunately, the bear, anxious about her young, did not climb after him,—only held him in mortal terror a few minutes, glaring and threatening, then hastened back to her cubs, called them down, went to the frightened, huddled flock, killed a sheep, and feasted in peace. Antone piteously entreated cautious Joe to show him a good safe tree, up which he climbed like a sailor climbing a mast, and held on as long as he could with legs crossed, the slim pine recommended by Joe being nearly branchless. "So you, too, are a bear coward as well as Joe," I said, hearing the story. "Oh, I tell you," he replied, with grand solemnity, "bear face close by look awful; she just as soon eat me as not. She do so as eef all my sheeps b'long every one to her own self. I run to bear no more. I take tree every time."

After this the shepherds corraled the flock about an hour before sundown, chopped large quantities of dry wood and made a circle of fires around the corral every night, and one with a gun kept watch on a stage built in a pine by the side of the cabin, while the other slept. But after the first night or two this fire fence did no good, for the robbers seemed to regard the light as an advantage, after becoming used to it.

On the night I spent at their camp the show made by the wall of fire when it was blazing in its prime was magnificent,—the illumined trees round about relieved against solid darkness, and the two thousand sheep lying down in one gray mass, sprinkled with gloriously brilliant gems, the effect of the firelight in their eyes. It was nearly midnight when a pair of the freebooters arrived. They walked boldly through a gap in the fire circle, killed two sheep, carried them out, and vanished in the dark woods, leaving ten dead in a pile, trampled down and smothered against the corral fence; while the scared watcher in the trees did not fire a single shot, saying he was afraid he would hit some of the sheep, as the bears got among them before he could get a good sight.

In the morning I asked the shepherds why they did not move the flock to a new pasture. "Oh, no use!" cried Antone. "Look my dead sheeps. We move three four times before, all the same bear come by the track. No use. To-morrow we go home below. Look my dead sheeps. Soon all dead."

Thus were they driven out of the mountains more than a month before the usual time. After Uncle Sam's soldiers, bears are the most effective forest police, but some of the shepherds are very successful in killing them. Altogether, by hunters, mountaineers, Indians, and sheepmen, probably five or six hundred have been killed within the bounds of the Park, during the last thirty years. But they are not in danger of extinction. Now that the Park is guarded by soldiers, not only has the vegetation in great part come back to the desolate ground, but all the wild animals are increasing in numbers. No guns are allowed in the Park except under certain restrictions, and after a permit has been obtained from the officer in charge. This has stopped the barbarous slaughter of bears, and especially of deer, by shepherds, hunters, and hunting tourists, who it would seem, can find no pleasure without blood.

22

ROOSEVELT, RANCHER-NATURALIST
Theodore Roosevelt

Because of Theodore Roosevelt's fervid interest in all aspects of nature he has left us some of the most percipient observations ever published on the animals of North and South America and Africa. Although there can be no doubt that he keenly enjoyed hunting as a sport, it was more than that to him. Many of the prize trophies he killed in the West were given to museums. Immediately after leaving the White House he sailed for Africa to collect specimens for the Smithsonian Institution, and on his last expedition (to Brazil in 1913-14), he collected for the American Museum of Natural History. He was rated the foremost authority of his time on North American mammals; John Burroughs said Roosevelt knew as much about birds as he did.

In the following sketch, taken from *The Works of Theodore Roosevelt*, Elkhorn Edition, Volume XVI, pages 46, 50-51, 53-56, 60-62, 64, 67, and 69-70, published by G. P. Putnam's Sons in New York in 1893, Roosevelt describes the grizzly's life pattern intimately and even makes a case for cattle-killing silvertips.

THE KING OF GAME BEASTS of temperate North America, because he is the most dangerous to the hunter, is the grisly bear; known to the few remaining old-time trappers of the Rockies and the great plains sometimes as "Old Ephraim" and sometimes as "Moccasin Joe"—the last in allusion to his queer, half-human footprints which look as if made by some misshapen giant, walking in moccasins. . . .

A full-grown grisly will usually weigh from five to seven hundred pounds; but exceptional individuals undoubtedly reach more than twelve hundredweight. The California bears are said to be much the largest. This I think is so, but I cannot say it with certainty. I have examined several skins of full-grown California bears which were no larger than those of many I have seen from the northern Rockies. The Alaskan bears, particularly those of the peninsula, are even bigger. . . . Bears vary wonderfully in weight, even to the extent of becoming half as heavy again, according as they are fat or lean. In this respect they are more like hogs than like any other animals.

The grisly is now chiefly a beast of the high hills and heavy timber; but this is merely because he has learned that he must rely on cover to guard him from man, and has forsaken the open country accordingly. In the old days, and in one or two very out-of-the-way places almost at the present time, he wandered at will over the plains. It is only the wariness born of fear which nowadays causes him to cling to the thick brush of the large river bottoms throughout the plains country. When there were no rifle-bearing hunters in the land, to harass him and make him afraid, he roved hither and thither at will, in burly self-confidence. Then he cared little for cover, unless as a weather-break, or because it happened to contain food he liked. If the humor seized him he would roam for days on the rolling prairie, searching for roots, digging up gophers, or perhaps following the great buffalo herds either to prey on some unwary straggler which he was able to catch at a disadvantage in a washout, or else to feast on the carcasses of those which died by accident. . . .

However, the grisly is a shrewd beast and shows the unusual bear-like capacity for adapting himself to changed conditions. He has in most places become a cover-haunting animal, sly in his ways, wary to a degree, and clinging to the shelter of the deepest forests in the mountains and of the most tangled thickets in the plains. Hence he has held his own far better than such game as the bison and elk. He is much less common than formerly, but he is still to be found throughout most of his former range; save of course in the immediate neighborhood of the large towns.

In most places the grisly hibernates, or, as old hunters say, "holes up," during the cold season, precisely as does the black bear; but, as with the latter species, those animals which live farthest south spend the whole year abroad in mild seasons. The grisly rarely chooses that favorite den of his little black brother, a hollow tree or log, seeking or making some cavernous hole in the ground instead. The hole is sometimes in a slight hillock in a river bottom, but more often on a hillside, and may be either shallow or deep. In the mountains it is generally a natural cave in the rock, but among the foothills and on the plains the bear usually has to take some hollow or opening, and then fashion it into a burrow to his liking with his big digging claws.

Before the cold weather sets in the bear begins to grow restless, and to roam about seeking for a good place in which to hole up. One will often try and abandon several caves or partially dug out burrows in succession before finding a place to its taste. It always endeavors to choose a spot where there is little chance of discovery or molestation, taking great care to avoid leaving too evident trace of its work. Hence it is not often that the dens are found.

Once in its den the bear passes the cold months in lethargic sleep; yet, in all but the coldest weather, and sometimes even then, its slumber is but slight, and if disturbed it will promptly leave its den, prepared for fight or flight as the occasion may require. Many times when a hunter has stumbled on the winter resting-place of a bear and has left it, as he thought, without his presence being discovered, he has returned only to find the crafty old fellow was aware of the danger all the time, and sneaked off as soon as the coast was clear. But in very cold weather hibernating bears can hardly be awakened from the torpid lethargy.

The length of time a bear stays in its den depends of course upon the severity of the season and the latitude and altitude of the country. In the northernmost and coldest regions all the bears hole up, and spend half the year in a state of lethargy; whereas in the south only the shes with young and the fat he-bears retire for the sleep, and these but for a few weeks, and only if the season is severe.

When the bear first leaves its den the fur is in very fine order, but it speedily becomes thin and poor, and does not recover its condition until the fall. Sometimes the bear does not betray its great hunger for a few days after its appearance; but in a short while it becomes ravenous. During the early spring, when the woods are still entirely barren and lifeless, while the snow yet lies in deep drifts, the lean, hungry brute, both maddened and weakened by long fasting, is more of a flesh-eater than at any other time. It is at this period that it is most apt to turn true beast of prey, and show its prowess either at the expense of the wild game, or of the flocks of the settler and the herds of the ranchman. Bears are very capricious in this respect, however. Some are confirmed game- and cattle-killers; others are not; while yet others either are or are not, accordingly as the freak seizes them, and their ravages vary almost unaccountably, both with the season and the locality.

Throughout 1889, for instance, no cattle, so far as I heard were killed by bears anywhere near my range on the Little Missouri in western Dakota; yet I happened to know that during that same season the ravages of the bears among the herds of the cowmen in the Big Hole Basin, in western Montana, were very destructive.

In the spring and early summer of 1888, the bears killed no cattle near my ranch; but in the late summer and early fall of that year a big bear, which we well knew by its tracks, suddenly took to cattle-killing. This was a brute which had its headquarters on some very large brush bottoms a dozen miles below my ranchhouse, and which ranged to and fro across the broken country flanking the river on each side. It began just before berry-time, but continued its career of destruction long after the wild plums and even buffalo berries had ripened. I think that what started it was a feast on a cow which had mired and died in the bed of the creek; at least it was not until after we found that it had been feeding at the carcass and had eaten every scrap, that we discovered traces of its ravages among the livestock. It seemed to attack the animals wholly regardless of their size and strength; its victims including a large bull and a beef steer, as well as cows, yearlings, and gaunt, weak trail "doughies," which had been brought in very late by a Texas cow-outfit—for that year several herds were driven up from the overstocked, eaten-out, and

drought-stricken ranges of the far South. Judging from the signs, the crafty old grisly, as cunning as he was ferocious, usually lay in wait for the cattle when they came down to water, choosing some thicket of dense underbrush and twisted cottonwoods through which they had to pass before reaching the sand banks on the river's brink. Sometimes he pounced on them as they fed through the thick, low cover of the bottoms, where an assailant could either lie in ambush by one of the numerous cattle trails, or else, creep unobserved toward some browsing beast. When within a few feet a quick rush carried him fairly on the terrified quarry; and though but a clumsy animal compared to the great cats, the grisly is far quicker than one would imagine from viewing his ordinary lumbering gate. In one or two instances the bear had apparently grappled with his victim by seizing it near the loins and striking a disabling blow over the small of the back; in at least one instance he had jumped on the animal's head, grasping it with his fore paws, while with his fangs he tore open the throat or crunched the neck bone. Some of his victims were slain far from the river, in winding, brushy coulees of the Bad Lands, where the broken nature of the ground rendered stalking easy. Several of the ranchmen, angered at their losses, hunted their foe eagerly, but always with ill success; until one of them put poison in a carcass, and thus at last, in ignoble fashion, slew the cattle killer. . . .

In the old days when the innumerable bison grazed free on the prairie, the grisly sometimes harassed their bands as it now does the herds of the ranchmen. The bison was the most easily approached of all game, and the great bear could often get near some out-lying straggler, in its quest after stray cows, yearlings, or calves. In default of a favorable chance to make a prey of one of these weaker members of the herds, it did not hesitate to attack the mighty bulls themselves; and perhaps the grandest sight which it was ever the good fortune of the early hunters to witness was one of these rare battles between a hungry grisly and a powerful buffalo bull. Nowadays, however, the few last survivals of the bison are vanishing even from the inaccessible mountain fastnesses in which they sought a final refuge from their destroyers. At present the wapiti is of all the wild game . . . most likely to fall victim to the grisly, when the big bear is in the mood to turn hunter. Wapiti are found in the same places as the grisly, and in some spots they are yet very plentiful. They are less shy and active than a deer, while not powerful enough to beat off so ponderous a foe; and they live in cover where there is always a good chance either to stalk or to stumble on them. At almost any season bear will come and feast on [an] elk carcass; and if the food supply runs short, in early spring, or in a fall when the berry crop fails, they sometimes have to do a little of their own killing. Twice I have come across the remains of elk, which had seemingly been slain and devoured by bears. I have never heard of elk making a fight against a bear; yet, at close quarters and at bay, a bull elk in rutting season is an ugly foe.

A bull moose is even more formidable, being able to strike the most lightning-like blows with his terrible forefeet, his true weapons of defense. . . . Nevertheless, the moose sometimes fall victims to the uncouth prowess of the grisly, in the thick wet forests of the high northern Rockies, where both beasts dwell. . . .

. . . the grisly is only occasionally, not normally, a formidable predatory beast, a killer of cattle and of large game. Although capable of far swifter movement than is promised by his frame of seemingly clumsy strength, and in spite of his power of charging with astonishing suddenness and speed, he yet lacks altogether the supple agility of such finished destroyers as the cougar and the wolf; and for the absence of the agility no amount of mere huge muscle can atone. He is more apt to feast on animals which have met their death by accident, or which have been killed by other beasts or man, than to do his own killing. He is a very foul feeder, with strong relish for carrion and possesses a gruesome and cannibal fondness for the flesh of his own kind; a bear carcass will toll a brother bear to the ambushed hunter better than most any other bait, unless it is the carcass of a horse. . . .

Grislies are fond of fish; and on the Pacific slope, where the salmon run, they, like so many other beasts, travel many scores of miles and crowd down to the rivers to gorge themselves upon the fish which are thrown up on the banks. Wading into the water, a bear will knock out the salmon right and left when they are running thick.

Flesh and fish do not constitute the grisly's ordinary diet. At most times the big bear is a grubber in the ground, an eater of insects, roots, nuts, and berries. Its dangerous fore claws are normally used to overturn stones and knock rotten logs to pieces, that it may lap up the small tribes of darkness which swarm under the one and in the other. It digs up the camas roots, wild onions, and an occasional luckless woodchuck or gopher. If food is very plentiful bears are lazy, but commonly they are obliged to be very industrious, it being no light task to gather enough ants, beetles, crickets, tumble-bugs, roots, and nuts to satisfy the cravings of so huge a bulk. The sign of a bear's work is, of course, evident to the most unpractised eye; and in no way can one get a better idea of the brute's power than by watching it busily working for its breakfast, shattering big logs and upsetting boulders by sheer strength. There is always a touch of the comic, as well as a touch of the strong and terrible, in a bear's look and actions. It will tug and pull, now with one paw, now with two, now on all fours, now on its hind legs, in the effort to turn over a large log or stone; and when it succeeds it jumps round to thrust its muzzle into the damp hollow and lap up the affrighted mice or beetles while they are still paralyzed by the sudden exposure.

The true time of plenty for bears is the berry season. Then they feast ravenously on huckleberries, blueberries, kinnikinic berries, buffalo berries, wild plums, elderberries, and scores of other fruits. They often smash all the bushes in a berry patch, gathering the fruit with half-luxurious, half-laborious greed, sitting on their haunches, and sweeping the berries into their mouths with dexterous paws. So absorbed do they become in their feasts on the luscious fruit that they grow reckless of their safety, and feed in broad daylight, almost at midday; while in some of the thickets, especially those of the mountain haws, they make so much noise in smashing the branches that it is a comparatively easy matter to approach them unheard. . . .

Like most other wild animals, bears which have known the

neighborhood of man are beasts of the darkness, or at least of the dusk and the gloaming. But they are by no means such true night-lovers as the big cats and the wolves. In regions where they know little of hunters they roam about freely in the daylight, and in cool weather are even apt to take their noontide slumbers basking in the sun. Where they are much hunted they finally almost reverse their natural habits and sleep throughout the hours of light, only venturing abroad after nightfall and before sunrise; but even yet this is not the habit of those bears which exist in the wilder localities where they are still plentiful. In these places they sleep, or at least rest, during the hours of greatest heat, and again in the middle part of the night, unless there is a full moon. They start their rambles for food about mid-afternoon, and end their morning roaming soon after the sun is above the horizon. If the moon is full, they may feed all night long, and then wander but little in the daytime.

Aside from man, the full-grown grisly has hardly any foe to fear. Nevertheless, in the early spring, when weakened by the hunger that succeeds the winter sleep, it behooves even the grisly, if he dwells in the mountain vastnesses of the far Northwest, to beware of a famished troop of great timber wolves. These northern Rocky Mountain wolves are the most formidable beasts, and when many of them band together in the time of famine they do not hesitate to pounce on the black bear and cougar; and even a full-grown grisly is not safe from their attacks, unless he can back up against some rock which will prevent them from assailing him from behind. . . .

The grisly occasionally makes its den in a cave and spends there the midday hours. But this is rare. Usually it lies in the dense shelter of the most tangled piece of woods in the neighborhood, choosing by preference some bit where the young growth is thick and the ground strewn with boulders and fallen logs. Often, especially if in a restless mood and roaming much over the country, it merely makes a temporary bed, in which it lies but once or twice; and again it may make a more permanent lair or series of lairs, spending many consecutive nights in each. Usually the lair or bed is made some distance from the feeding-grounds; but bold bears, in very mild localities, may lie close by a carcass, or in the middle of a berry-ground. . . .

Bears are very fond of wallowing in the water, whether in the sand, on the edge of a rapid plains river, on the muddy margins of a pond, or in the oozy moss of a clear, cold mountain spring. One hot August afternoon, as I was climbing down a steep mountain-side near Pend Oreille Lake, I heard a crash some distance below, which showed that a large beast was afoot. On making my way towards the spot, I found I had disturbed a big bear as it was lolling at ease in its bath; the discolored water showed where it had scrambled hastily out and galloped off as I approached. The spring welled out at the base of a high granite rock, forming a small pool of shimmering, broken crystal. The soaked moss lay in a deep wet cushion round about and jutted over the edges of the pool like a floating shelf. Graceful, water-loving ferns swayed to and fro. Above, the great conifers spread their murmuring branches, dimming the light, and keeping out the heat; their brown boles sprang from the ground like buttressed columns. On the barren mountainside beyond, the heat was oppressive. It was small wonder that Bruin should have sought the spot to cool his gross carcass in the fresh spring water.

The bear is a solitary beast, and although many may assemble together, in what looks like a drove, on some favorite feeding ground—usually where the berries are thick, or by the banks of a salmon-thronged river—the association is never more than momentary, each going his own way as soon as its hunger is satisfied. The males always live alone by choice, save in the rutting season, when they seek their females. Then two or three may come together in the course of their pursuit and rough courtship of the female; and if the rivals are well-matched, savage battles follow, so that many of the old males have their heads seamed with scars made by their fellow's teeth. At such times they are evil tempered and prone to attack man or beast upon the slightest provocation.

The she brings forth her cubs, one, two or three in number, in her winter den. They are very small and helpless things, and it is some time after she leaves her winter home before they can follow her for any distance. They stay with her throughout the summer and the fall, leaving her when the cold weather sets in. By this time they are wellgrown; and hence, especially if an old male has joined the she, the family may number three or four individuals, so as to make what seems like quite a little troop of bears. . . .

23

CHARACTERISTICS AND HABITS OF A GRIZZLY
William H. Wright

William H. Wright had a passion for bears and was dedicated to their preservation in the Rocky Mountains and elsewhere in the West. He came West, as a young man, in charge of a trainload of immigrants and settled in Spokane. Shortly after his arrival there, in 1883, he went on a weekend excursion into the wilds adjacent to Spokane, possibly in the vicinity of Coeur d'Alene. Unbelievable as it will seem to present-day Washingtonians, he writes of having seen about one dozen grizzlies on this foray. The trip, using horse transportation, could not have extended too far from the outskirts of Washington's third-largest city. There are still supposed to be five or six grizzly bears left in Washington State, all reported to be in the mountains northeast of Spokane.

The two chapters reproduced here are from *The Grizzly Bear*, by W. H. Wright and J. B. Kenfoot (Charles Scribner's Sons, 1909), pages 201–16 and 256–64). This book is considered by many naturalists and conservationists as the most reliable, the richest, and most just book on the grizzly. Readers with preconceived ideas about the habits of these bears have some surprises in store in the following fascinating excerpts.

GRIZZLY CUBS are born with their eyes closed, and do not open them for about the same period as puppies and kittens. There is very little hair on their bodies at birth, and what there is is so short that they have every appearance of being naked. They are born without teeth, or, rather, their teeth are so little developed that they can barely be felt by pressing one's finger down on their gums. These teeth, however, grow very rapidly, and are early replaced by a new set as sharp as needles.

The dam and her family leave the den anywhere between the

first of April and the middle of May, according to the locality. I have never found the fresh track of a grizzly in the Kootenai country earlier than the 5th of May, while in the southern part of central Idaho I have seen where a grizzly had left his den as early as the middle of March. The male bears leave their dens from one to three weeks before the female and her cubs come out; yet in any one locality, nearly all of each class leave their dens about the same time.

How the brutes can tell just when to come out is one of their own secrets. In the Selkirks they den so high up among the peaks that when they emerge there are from four to six (and in some cases even ten) feet of snow still lying over the country like a great white blanket. Only on the slides, which have been swept by the tremendous avalanches that usually come down in March, is the ground clear. Yet on one of our trips to this region we saw where thirteen grizzlies came down the mountain side in a single night. They all came down an open place not over half a mile across, and it was in following their trails back up the mountain that I found the six dens hereafter mentioned. These were all natural caves among the cliffs, their mouths well concealed by thick firs and juniper brush, and the animals, in coming out, had broken through some five feet of snow. As it is, therefore, not the melting snow that arouses them, it would seem that there must be some kind of nature's alarm clock, known to the bears, that informs them when it is time to get up.

It is some months before the young cubs begin to forage for themselves, even in part. Dr. Hornaday, speaking of bears in captivity, writes me: "I think the average age at which a grizzly cub begins to feed independently of his mother's milk is about four months. Of course, the beginning on solid food is made very slowly, and the youngsters nurse vigorously all summer."

I am, however, sure that this weaning process begins later in the wild state. I have many times seen a mother grizzly digging roots and feeding on grasses in August while her cubs were running about or lying in the sun, and seemed to take no interest whatever in the food that she was so busy in getting. Yet a bear cub, when the time comes, knows just as much about the proper food of the bears in the locality where it was born as does the oldest bear on the range.

I have caught them when they first came from the den, and when the earth was covered with a thick mantle of snow, and have then taken them from their mothers, and for weeks fed them milk and such soft foods as I could make them eat; and then found that, when they were old enough, they would go out and, wholly untaught, select the food that the old bears were eating at the time. One black bear cub that I took in this way I kept with me all through the summer and fall hunting, having caught him early in June, in the Bitter Root Mountains, when the ground was covered with snow and when he first came from the den. He was then a little fellow not larger than a common house cat, and cried for his mother the greater part of the time for a couple of weeks.

This cub I took about with me all over the mountains for more than four months, and I learned many a thing about bears from him. Whenever, as he grew older, we were in camp and he wished to get loose, as he would show by pulling at his chain and bawling, I would free him, and then follow to see what he was after. He invariably made for some bottom land and dug for roots, or nipped off the grass where it grew young and tender. I have seen him dig more than a foot down into the ground for some root that had not yet sent up its shoot, and—although how the young rascal could tell just where to dig was beyond me—he always found his tidbit. Moreover, he knew the berry bushes from the others by the same inherited knowledge. He would reach up and pull down the branches of these to examine them, although there might not be any berries on them at the time, and he never, that I saw, made a single mistake. He soon came to pay no attention to my presence, and whenever he dug up anything from the earth that I did not recognize, I would open his mouth, take it away from him, and keep it while I examined it.

When the cubs first come from their dens at from two to three months of age, they are about the size of a house cat, and will weigh from ten to fifteen pounds. At from five to six months of age, that is to say, in July or August, they will probably weigh about thirty pounds. Late in the fall, when ready to den up again, they will tip the scales at from fifty to seventy-five pounds. When a grizzly is nearly two years old, that is, in the second fall, when he is ready to den up for the winter, he will ordinarily weigh anywhere from one hundred and fifty to two hundred pounds.

In their wild state the cubs den up with the mother for the winter following their birth, and follow her during the second summer, after which they are cast aside to shift for themselves, and the old lady will again den up alone, bringing out another litter of cubs the following spring. Naturalists, who have studied these bears in captivity, claim that they then breed every year, but I am satisfied that this is not true of them in a state of nature. In the open, one sees as many she grizzlies with yearling cubs as one sees with little spring cubs.

When a litter of young grizzlies come to leave their mother they do not, as a rule, separate, but travel in company for at least a year; and it is, I imagine, this habit of theirs that has given rise to the idea that the full-grown animals are gregarious. I know that in some cases, and I believe in most, if not all, the cubs den up together for their second winter, and it is (or used to be, alas!) a common sight to see them, during their third summer, working together under the undisputed command of the one to whom they had yielded the leadership. I incline to the belief that they do not separate and breed until the following spring.

When not feeding, grizzlies lie up in some dense thicket near a stream, or, if in a region where they are apt to be disturbed, far back in some high cañon. I have seen many of their beds. In the Selkirks, these sleeping places are far above timber line, dug out from the side of steep mountains where there is not a shrub or a bush to screen them, and where they have an unobstructed view of miles of country. Here, as the signs indicate, they return to sleep day after day.

I have sometimes almost thought that these bears, in a way, enjoy the grand view to be had from these heights. Not only have I found their bedrooms high up among the crags and overlooking range upon range of highest mountain, with restful, wide-spreading valleys below; but it has been no unusual experience, while

166

hunting in these high regions, to see an old bear, after feeding for an hour or more far out of reach of my rifle, stroll deliberately out to the edge of some high cliff overlooking all creation, and sit there on his haunches like a dog, swinging his massive head slowly and dignifiedly from side to side. . . .

Grown grizzlies do not climb trees. And this for a simple reason. They are not built that way. Once in a while I have seen a grizzly cub go up a tree whose branches started at the very ground and grew in such a way as to allow him to step from one to another; but they never climb smooth and straight-bodied trees as do black bears of all ages, and they never encircle the tree with their arms, as such an animal must, in order to climb a smooth trunk. Grown grizzlies will walk out on a leaning tree such as a man might walk out on with rubber-soled shoes, and they are very expert walkers on fallen logs and timber, and often take to them when trailed. But they not only do not, but cannot, climb.

The grizzly is not, as many hunters and sportsmen suppose, a gregarious animal. One may, and, indeed, often does, see several of them feeding at the same time in the same bottom, or among the bushes of a single berry patch. But, except in the case of a she bear with cubs, or of a litter of cubs that have left their mother, but have not yet disbanded, they will always be found to come singly, and to depart in like manner. Indeed, the etiquette that appears to govern these chance meetings is one of the most amusing things about these animals. An old bear will emerge from the bushes surrounding an open glade where several others are already feeding; he will pause and look critically about as though examining the lay of the land and the distribution of the trees and bushes; but he will show in no way that he is conscious of the presence of the other bears; and these, in their turn, will go on about their business, and by not so much as a batted eyelid show any recognition of his arrival. Sometimes, later on, if two of them meet, or clash over some tidbit, their first movement is always one of surprise at the other's presence, and this enforced dropping of their incognito is more likely than not to be followed by the retreat of the smaller of them from the feeding ground.

I have seen as many as nine grizzlies in one berry patch, and as many as five fishing on one riffle of a salmon stream; but they not only came and went singly, but, while there, they gave no outward sign of mutual recognition or even of mutual consciousness.

It is even open to doubt as to whether the males and females travel together during the mating season, and I have never seen full-grown grizzlies living or travelling in company.

The mating time of the grizzly throughout the Northwest extends, according to locality, from about the middle of June until about the first of August. I have been unable to determine whether individual males and females deliberately seek each other out during this time, pair off, and stay together for a month or more, or whether they meet by chance and again separate. I am inclined to believe the latter, as I have never seen the two together at any time of the year. That they do not stay together during the winter I am absolutely convinced, and I do not believe that they remain in company for any material part of the summer.

This opinion . . . is based on many observations, no one of which was conclusive, but all of which, taken together, were not to be ignored. I may, for example, cite the following instance: On one occasion, while on a bear-hunting expedition in May and June, I was camped in a part of the Bitter Root range near an old trapper who was trapping bear. It was near the end of the trapping season, and this old fellow was about to take up his traps, as fur was becoming poor. Near where he had one of his traps set we had, on several occasions, seen the tracks of a large grizzly, and he had left this trap to the very last in hopes of catching him.

It was now the mating season, and although there were bear tracks all over the country, we could never find where more than one large bear had gone at a time.

The last morning that he went to look at the trap near where we had seen the large tracks, I went with him, thinking that, as the bears were so much on the move, I might, perhaps, get a shot. There were also some large snow-banks near by, upon which these bears are very fond of lying when the weather is warm, and as I had already shot several bears there, I thought it likely that I might catch the old fellow cooling himself on the snow.

As we came near the pen in which the trap was set we saw the old grizzly rise up just outside of it, but, as we both supposed that he was fast in the trap, we did not shoot. To our surprise, however, after taking a look at us, he bolted for a thicket and disappeared in a twinkling. It was all so sudden and unexpected that we simply stood agape, and as the bear had only to make a couple of jumps to get out of sight, he was safe before we had any chance of shooting him.

But a greater surprise than this awaited us. On coming up to the pen we found a large female grizzly caught in the trap, and chewed, mauled, and pounded to death. From the looks of things there had been a hot old fight. Of course we had seen from a distance that the logs forming the pen had been thrown down, but we had assumed that the bear that ran away had done this before we knew that he was not fast in the trap. The head of the dead bear was chewed to such an extent that her most intimate friends would not have recognized her, and, upon taking off her skin, we found great masses of clotted blood under the hide that showed how fearfully she had been mauled.

Why the male had killed her can, of course, only be surmised; but the facts seemed to point to only one conclusion. The two had come to the pen, as the tracks showed, from different directions. The female had, of course, come first, as she had been caught in the trap, but the male must have arrived at about the same time, or the one in the trap would have dragged it from the pen. Probably, being exasperated by her predicament, the female had been unable or unwilling to reciprocate in love-making, and the male had become enraged and killed her.

This is one of the experiences that lead me to believe that these bears do not travel together during the mating season. It also leads me to doubt the claim sometimes made that they are more pugnacious at this season than any other; else this one, already enraged and disappointed, would surely have attacked us as we approached him.

I have never yet seen a whole family of grizzlies together; that is, the male, female, and cubs; and I do not believe that they consort together in this way. I am, indeed, inclined to the opinion

169

that the male will kill the young when they are under four or five months of age. I have noticed that a mother bear, when with her young cubs, takes every means to avoid meeting any male bear, and is always cranky and ready to scrap with any other grizzly, be it male or female, that chances to put in an appearance.

On two occasions, I have known an old male grizzly to kill and eat a small cub that was tied up with a chain, and once, while hunting bears in the spring, I witnessed the following incident, or, rather, found the evidences of it. A trapper had caught in one of his traps a female grizzly that was accompanied by her two cubs. She had dragged the trap and clog for several hundred yards, where the clog had finally caught in a clump of brush and stopped her. And while thus held fast, an old male grizzly had come along, and had not only killed her, but had killed and eaten the cubs. When we arrived, he was sitting under a tree close by, and we shot him through the head. We found a few scraps of the cubs lying about, and part of one of them was buried near where he had been sitting.

All my observations, as I say, have led me to believe that a free male grizzly will, if he gets a chance, kill his young cubs; but as the matter is not susceptible of proof, I consulted Dr. Hornaday as to what his observations had been on this point, in the matter of bears in captivity, and I give herewith what he says of the matter: "Of course, male bears in captivity would be likely to destroy young cubs during their first six months—if they got the opportunity. It is absolutely necessary to sequestrate [sic] the males and give each female a den wholly to herself and her cubs. We had great trouble in keeping our young cubs from getting their paws into adjoining dens and having them bitten off by older bears."

The grizzly does not den up for the winter at as low an altitude as does the black bear, but seeks the higher hills, where he usually goes into his winter quarters some time in November, or perhaps a little later, according to the locality and the weather conditions.

The den is usually in some natural cave, although occasionally it may be made by the bear himself. I have found a number of the winter homes of the grizzly, and he usually selects a dryer and warmer shelter than does the black bear. Black bears will den in almost any place, and while they usually dig a hole under an upturned root, or under a fallen tree, I have seen where they have used natural caves, into which they have scraped a bed of grass or leaves; but the grizzly seldom, if ever, takes his long nap under fallen timber. He usually seeks the higher altitudes along the timber line, and sometimes even goes higher yet. Here, in the cañons among the cliffs, natural caves are found, and into these a grizzly will scrape and drag anything that can be converted into a bed, and, thus hidden and protected, will pass away the several months of winter undisturbed by snow and storm.

Under certain conditions they will dig large holes under big rocks, in which to make their beds. I have examined several such places, and in two instances found where the bears had dug clean through to the other side. I have also seen where, the elements having in the course of time caved in the earth close to the rocks, the bears had pulled old logs and brush over the breaks, and thus repaired the damage. These were evidently favorite places for dens, and the bears, loath to give them up, had done this in order to retain their old bedrooms. My friend, Mr. A. L. A. Himmel-wright, of New York, found a den of exactly this sort a few years ago in the mountains west of the Big Hole country, in Montana. It was rather late in the fall, with a veneer of snow on the ground, and he found the den by trailing the bears, an old female and two cubs.

It is sometimes claimed that when the denning time comes, the male and female go into the same den; but this, I think, is a false notion. Not only do I believe that the male bear would kill and eat the cubs after they were born, but I have never discovered a den that showed evidences of having been occupied by more than the old female bear. In the case of a barren she bear, a partnership arrangement as to winter quarters may possibly be made, now and then; but I cling to the belief that no two full-grown grizzlies go into the same den for the winter. In the Selkirks, where the bears den along the high mountain tops, and in the spring come down from their winter homes over the deep snows, it is an easy matter to back-track them and find where they have wintered. I have often done this and, having gone into the mountains two or three weeks before a bear track could be found, have, when the first track appeared, taken the trail and followed it back to the den.

I have seen as many as four grizzlies come from one den. But they were of about the same size, and were youngsters not over two years old, and presumably all of one litter that had not yet been broken up.

James Capen Adams, in describing his capture of Ben Franklin in the den whence the cub's mother had just issued to her death, says that, before going into the dark den to look for young bears, "I trembled for the moment at the thought of another old bear in the den; but on second thought I assured myself of the folly of such an idea; for an occurrence of this kind would have been against all experience."

I once found six of these dens in a single day in the Selkirks, and not more than one bear had come from any of them, although, while some of the dens were only large enough for one to lie in, others were of a size sufficient to hold several bears had they wished to sleep together. In the smaller caves, because of restricted quarters, I found much hair that had been rubbed off the animal by contact with the sharp rock, as each had changed his position from time to time during his long period of slumber. Now, were it a common practice for bears to den together in the same cave, it seems that they would have done so here; for all six caves were in the same ridge, and the two extreme caves were less than half a mile apart. I thought, at the time, that I would visit these caves in the fall and see if the same den was occupied year after year, but the opportunity to do so never presented itself.

The grizzly is rather a restless fellow just before denning up. The bed is usually prepared beforehand and made ready for occupancy at a moment's notice. After which, long excursions in search of food are often made about the country, some of them to points as far as ten or twenty miles away.

To what age the grizzly lives in the wild state is entirely a matter of conjecture. I am of the opinion, however, that, under favorable circumstances, they live to be from twenty-five to forty years old. I have come to this conclusion from the fact that I once, for twelve successive years, kept track of one identical bear that was full grown when I first met him, and that showed no evidence of old age when I lost sight of him. This was in the Bitter Root range in Idaho. Every fall, for these twelve years, we saw where this old grizzly had made his way up to the main range to den up for the winter; and each succeeding spring we saw his track as he again sought the lower country to spend the summer among the berries and the salmon. That it was the same bear I am certain, for not only was his track a huge one, and not likely to be duplicated, but I have seen the bear himself many times, and on several occasions could have shot him. He was, as I say, full grown the first time I saw him, and there was during all these years no appreciable difference in the size of his track, which measured nearly fifteen inches. Each fall, as we came from these hunting grounds, and made our way out into Montana, we looked for the track of this old monarch, and invariably saw his footprints. Where he kept himself during the summer and early fall I was never able to learn, as I could not, during these times, find even his track.

Dr. Hornaday, in speaking of bears in captivity, says: "The bears of North America generally reach full maturity between the ages of six and seven years. Some are full grown at six years—others not until seven."

I am inclined to believe that in the wild state grizzlies do not usually reach full maturity until somewhat later. I have watched several that inhabited certain localities, and they, I am sure, did not reach their full growth under eight years. Allowing, then, for the time it must have taken this grizzly to attain his growth, and adding to this the time he roamed the hills under my observation, his age when I last saw him would have been beyond the twenty-year limit. Of course, bears in captivity may, on an average, live longer than those exposed to the dangers and vicissitudes of the open. Yet they have not the inducements to live so long, nor do they, I believe, grow so large as those in the wild state. Those in captivity have neither the fields to roam in, nor the streams to plunge into, nor the sunlight that a bear loves, nor the exercise that all bears take so freely in the wilds. All these things work together for the health and vigor of the bears in far places. On the other hand, those confined in man-made dens and pits have the certainty of food, security from enemies, and the vegetating chances of a life of sloth. Nevertheless, something of the allotted age of free bears may be inferred from the known life span of those in captivity. On March 22, 1909, a grizzly was chloroformed in the Central Park Menagerie, in New York, that had been purchased from Barnum's Circus in 1884, and had, during these twenty-five years, been confined in the pits in New York.

That many bears in the open live to what, for a bear, constitutes a ripe old age, I am able to testify. I have seen them so decrepit that they walked like octogenarians, and I have killed those that showed unmistakable evidences of being full of years. Strangely enough, I have never yet seen or found dead a grizzly bear that had died a natural death. In no one of the caves where they hibernate have I ever found a solitary bone, and, although I have more than once seen an aged bear in a certain locality one season, and found the next year that he had disappeared, I have never, even after careful search, found trace of his remains or hint of the manner of his end.

Probably in some hidden cave, in some remote and lonely spot, the old hero of a hundred fierce contests had passed, all unconsciously, perhaps, from his winter slumber into his unwaking sleep.

24

FACT VERSUS FICTION
William H. Wright

WHEN I FIRST BEGAN actually to hunt the grizzly I found that much of what I had read about him and most of what I had heard was fiction.

From childhood I had read every book that I could lay hands on that treated of these bears, and later I had listened (I dare say with open mouth and eyes) to those I met who claimed to have had experience. I had come to look upon the old-time hunters as heroes and demigods, and was inclined to accept their successors, when I ran across them, as teachers at whose feet I was glad to sit and learn. When, therefore, my early experience began to tumble my supposed knowledge about my ears, I hastily said in my heart, like the Psalmist, that all men were liars.

But since then I have seen more both of men and of bears, and have come to realize that if the men who have written nonsense about grizzlies were technically liars, most of them were quite unconscious of the fact; and that if grizzlies are not altogether as they have been represented, they are sufficiently variable and individual in their actions and habits to have, in most cases, supplied some nucleus of fact for the fictions to form on.

I have come, for instance, to see how inevitable it was that, with the exception of here and there a really scientific naturalist, hardly any of those who have written about the grizzly have written from personal experience. And I have come to understand how naturally, under these circumstances, more romance than truth has found its way into print, and why it is that so very little of what is set down actually touches the real character of the animal. And I have thought in this chapter to speak of a few

175

of the more widely current of these misconceptions, and to cite a few amusing instances of their method of growth.

And first let us quite candidly face the simple truth that, as a rule, the old hunters and trappers, however well meaning they may be, are not to be relied upon for information that is worth much from a scientific standpoint. I well remember the first one I ever saw. He was an old, grizzled fellow, all covered with scars, which he claimed were the results of his encounters with grizzly bears, mountain lions, and Indian arrows. This old chap had heard that there was a man in town that was going bear hunting, and he took occasion to seek me out and have a talk with me about the trip.

He said that as sure as I went hunting grizzlies with the gun I then had (it was my old .44 Winchester) I would be killed, as it was not powerful enough to kill a bear. He declared emphatically that no bear could be killed with one shot, and that the animals would attack a person at sight. He maintained that he had shot grizzlies that had gone a mile or more after receiving several mortal wounds, and that, when finally overtaken, they were found to have plugged up the bullet holes with moss to stop the flow of blood.

When I returned I hunted the old fellow up, and told him that the bears were too wild to hunt with any show of success; but he merely looked me up and down, remarking that this was my first hunt, and intimated that if I had kept on hunting and remained of the same opinion, people would not be bothered long with my presence above ground.

And I dare say that up to a certain point he was honest with me. These old fellows are as full of superstition as an egg is of meat. There are a hundred bits of wood-lore and animal legend that they have taken on faith, and that, not being at all vital to the conduct of their own affairs, they have never even questioned and would never think to question. They are quite devoid of what might be called scientific curiosity. The one thing about a bear that interests them is his hide. The only facts they ever learn about him are how to lure him into traps. If this old man had ever really shot a grizzly, had ever come into closer quarters with

one than to set a deadfall for him, I have no doubt that he looked
back upon the adventure much as St. George may have looked
upon his set-to with the dragon; and the tale of his prowess
had grown in the telling until he believed in the revised version
himself. I have heard many of these old fellows declare that the
mountain lion of California has a mane like the African lion, and
that they had killed these animals that would measure from twelve
to thirteen feet from tip to tip.

And, of course, we must not mix up the entirely distinct acts
of lying and "stuffing the tenderfoot." When a man can neither
read nor write and lives most of his life alone on fresh venison
and flapjacks, he is entitled to some amusement.

One of the most widely disseminated legends about the grizzly
is the alleged fact that they bite and scratch trees as a sort of challenge to would-be-rivals. It has even been asserted that these
marks are purposely made and duly heeded as a sort of "warning
against trespassers," and mark the limits of the range claimed by
the bear that makes them. The laws that govern the matter have
almost been codified. We are told that the grizzly that posts one
of these notices holds a good title to the posted territory until
another bear comes along that can put his own mark above it.
That the bear with the longest reach is "boss" of that ward. We
are told how an ambitious young grizzly on the lookout for a
location will wander from one part of the hills to another, measuring up the various marks, until he finds one that he can overtop
by an inch or so, when he puts his sign-manual above it and enters
then and there into possession while the old owner slinks off to
look for a new job.

One writer has even told of an especially clever but dishonest
young bear that rolled a stump up to the notice tree, and by standing on it placed his mark so far out of reach of ordinary property
owners that it struck terror to a whole neighborhood.

Now there is just one grain of truth in this entire mass of
imagination—grizzlies do, occasionally, bite chunks out of trees.
Why they do it the Lord that made them may know, but I am
certain that no one else does; and, so far from ever having seen
it claimed that the writers of these phantasies ever saw a grizzly

examine one of these "challenges" and heed it, I have never seen an eye-witness's account of the making of these marks; and only three times in all the years that I have watched these animals have I stumbled on a sight of the operation.

The first time was many years ago while sitting one evening on the side of a mountain watching five grizzlies that were out feeding. It was August, and their hides were worthless, and I was studying them with no idea of shooting. The bears all came out of a thickly timbered cañon through which ran an old game trail made by deer and elk. I had often travelled this trail, and noticed that here and there large pieces had been ripped out of the trees, apparently by some animal with long, sharp teeth. Inspection indicated two teeth had been sunk into the wood an inch or more, and then, by a sharp twist, a slab of wood had been torn off, and I had supposed the animal that did it was a bear, for I could plainly see the mark of a bear's claws in the bark.

The evening in question, while watching the mouth of this cañon, I saw, first, an old she bear and her two yearling cubs appear and start feeding on the ripe berries. Later an old male came out and also started feasting; and these four bears were making great inroads on the berries when a fifth appeared. He was smaller than the older male, but he came out of the cañon slowly and sedately, and seemed to be very lazy and not more than half awake. He came to the edge of the timber and, looking indifferently around, as these animals will under such circumstances, sat down and scratched his ear with his hind foot. He then got up lazily, sniffed up and down the trunk of a small fir-tree, stretched his paws upward and, raising himself on his hind feet to his extreme height, set his teeth into the small trunk and yanked off a chunk similar to those that I had seen scattered along the trail. This was all done in the most unconcerned and bored manner imaginable, without any show of ugliness or temper. There was nothing to indicate in the least that the brute intended the act as a defiance or a challenge to any other bear. He acted as if he had nothing to do and was hard pressed to pass away the time. Afterward he walked out to where the other bears were and joined them at berry picking. The other male bear paid no attention whatever to the action.

On another occasion I saw two three-year-old grizzlies peacefully ambling along a side hill. They were tranquilly inclined and were apparently out for a promenade, with nothing of special importance on their minds. They would walk along for a short distance, stop and sniff at stumps, scratch a little, then move on again. After a time they came to some trees, and one of them stood up with his paws against a trunk, smelled quite around it, turned his head sideways, drove his teeth through an inch or more of wood, and with a twist of his head ripped off a slab. He then sniffed at the open place, lapped it a little with his tongue, dropped down on all-fours, and followed the other bear that had meanwhile moved on. In this instance it was the larger of the two bears that did the "challenging."

On the third occasion I saw a lone bear stop beside a trail and go through practically this same performance. In each instance it was a grizzly bear that did the biting. I have never seen a black bear make these marks on trees.

I would like, myself, to know why the bears do this, but I never expect to. And, after all, the action is so casual, so animal-like, so similar to a cat's stretching itself against a tree, that it is probably quite without hidden meaning. It seems to me that we are much given to overworking our imaginations.

Another notion commonly current is that a grizzly will throw his fore legs around an antagonist and "hug" him to death. There is no truth whatever in this idea, beyond the fact that a grizzly, in attacking a large animal like a steer, will sometimes hold it with one paw while he strikes it or rips it open with the other. Indeed, I imagine that this supposed habit has been attributed to the grizzly merely because it has long been credited to bears in general.

Again, contrary to the usual belief, I have never yet seen a charging grizzly stand on his hind legs and thus walk up to his antagonist. I do not believe that this is their mode of attack. All that I have seen fight went at things with a rush on all-fours; sometimes with a bawl and a snort and with champing of jaws, but never with open mouth. They will, however, bite and rend with their teeth, sometimes holding down the object of their wrath with their fore paws while they tear and bite. I have seen them rear up on their hind feet to deliver a blow, but have never known them to do this until they were near enough to strike. The idea that a grizzly deliberately stands up and walks up to his antagonist, like one of the principals in a prize-ring, is a mistaken one. A grizzly will, upon any pretext whatever, stand up and look about him. Whenever he sees, or thinks he is going to see, anything, up he goes to his full height on his hind feet; but I have never seen one start to make a charge from this position.

Again, it is often supposed that some of the oddly colored bears of the Rocky Mountain region are crosses between the black and the grizzly bears. Any one who has seen the agility with which a black bear will take to a tree if a grizzly happens along, or has marvelled at the refinement of scent or hearing that enables one to detect the approach of a grizzly (and beat a silent retreat in consequence) long minutes before a human watcher becomes aware of a grizzly's presence in the neighborhood, would not need the denial of science to help him discredit this bit of genea-logical speculation.

But it would be an endless task to run down all these flourish-ing misconceptions. Just to give an idea of how they spread, I quote a few extracts from various articles that have, from time to time, been solemnly put forth as authoritative and even scientific.

One writer blandly remarks that "all grizzlies interbreed, and this obliterates some characteristic marks of the several species. On the southern Pacific Coast the two gray species—the light and the mud grays—are closely allied." And, again, that "the original silver-tips sprang from grizzly and brown bears, and they com-bine all the ferocity and prowess of the former, with the agility and stubbornness of the latter."

In summing up the food habits of the animals the same writer says: "He has a fondness for horse and mule meat, and he will climb trees, rob birds' nests, and eat the eggs there." Also, that "he will climb a fruit-tree strip whole branches of ripe fruit with his huge paws and claws, and then on the way home will finish off the meal with a toad or a lizard." This gentleman also says that "a grizzly loves to feed on ants." But then, perhaps startled over finding himself so well within the bounds of fact, adds that "he knocks the top off an ant hill, buries his nose in the interior, and by a few inward breaths like a suction pump, draws every vestige of life from the greatest hill."

Another writer, a State Senator by the way, tells of shooting a grizzly four times through the heart and having it still chase him over down timber and bad going, and only fall dead as it was about to fell him. And he goes on to tell of a grizzly bear in the San Bernadino Mountains that used to come once a week, climb a live-oak tree, walk out along a horizontal branch over a high-fenced pigpen, drop in, steal a little pig, push the gate open (it opened out), and go home.

One frequently, in the mountains, sees a great fir-tree growing among the rocks with only a thimbleful of earth within reach. If one follows up the published literature on the grizzly bear, one is likely to see that misinformation has the knack of flourishing upon an equally small store of fact.

25

TRAILING WITHOUT A GUN
Enos Abija Mills

The colorful observations of Enos Abija Mills provide an important record of the now almost extinct Rocky Mountain grizzly bear. Although one or two of Mills's contemporaries have taken exception to some incidents recorded by this writer, nevertheless he "enlarges and refreshes mountain life . . . he saw much and wrote vividly."[1]

Mills, known as "the Father of the Rocky Mountain National Park," spent most of his adult life as a hunter, guide, and Rocky Mountain snow gauger. In later years he abandoned his rifle to trail bears and other wild animals with his camera and to study their curious ways.

The following chapter from *The Grizzly, Our Greatest Wild Animal*, published in Boston by Houghton Mifflin Company in 1919, pages 119–35, is used with the most gracious consent of the late Mrs. Enos A. Mills and the administrators of her estate.

I HAD GONE INTO WILD BASIN, hoping to see and to trail a grizzly. It was early November and the sun shone brightly on four inches of newly fallen snow; trailing conditions were excellent. If possible I wanted to get close to a bear and watch his ways for a day or two.

Just as I climbed above the last trees on the eastern slope of the Continental Divide, I saw a grizzly ambling along the other side of a narrow cañon, boldly outlined against the sky-line. I was so near that with my field-glasses I recognized him as "Old Timberline," a bear with two right front toes missing. He was

[1] J. Frank Dobie, *A Guide to Life and Literature of the Southwest* (Dallas, Southern Methodist University Press, 1952), 163.

a silver-tip,—a nearly white old bear. For three days I followed Old Timberline through his home territory and camped on his trail at night. I had with me a hatchet, kodak, field-glasses, and a package of food, but no gun.

The grizzly had disappeared by the time I crossed the cañon, but a clear line of tracks led westward. I followed them over the Divide and down into the woods on the other side. In a scattered tree-growth the tracks turned abruptly to the right, then led back eastward, close to the first line of tracks, as though Old Timberline had turned to meet any one who might be following him.

The most impressive thing I had early learned in trailing and studying the grizzly was that a wounded bear if trailed and harassed will sometimes conceal himself and lie in an ambush in wait for his pursuer. I never took a chance of walking into such danger. Whenever the trail passed by a log, bowlder [sic], or bushes that might conceal a bear, I turned aside and scouted the ambush for a side view before advancing further.

Old Timberline's tracks showed that he had now and then risen on hind feet, listened, and turned to look back. He acted as though he knew I was following him, but this he had not yet discovered. All grizzlies are scouts of the first order; they are ever on guard. When at rest their senses do continuous sentinel duty, and when traveling they act exactly as though they believed some man was in pursuit.

Following along the trail and wondering what turn the grizzly would make next, I found where he had climbed upon a ledge in the edge of an opening, and had evidently stood for some seconds, looking and listening. From the ledge he had faced about and continued his course westward, heading for a spur on the summit of the Divide.

We were in what is now the southern end of the Rocky Mountain National Park. The big bear and myself were on one of the high sky-lines of the earth. We traversed a territory ten thousand to twelve thousand feet above sea-level, much of it above the limits of tree growth. There were long stretches of

moorland, an occasional peak towering above us, and ridges long
and short thrusting east and west, and cañons of varying width
and depth were to be seen below us from the summit heights.

Crossing this spur of the Divide, the grizzly entered the woods.
Here he spent so much time rolling logs about and tearing them
open for grubs and ants that I nearly caught up with him. I
watched him through the scattered trees from a rocky ledge until
he moved on. This after a few minutes he did. As he came to an
opening in the woods, I wondered whether he would go around it
to the right or to the left. To my astonishment, without the least
hesitation he sauntered across the opening, his head held low and
swinging easily from side to side. But the instant he was screened
by trees beyond, rising up, with fore paws resting against a tree,
he peered cautiously out to see if he was being followed. When
the next opening in the woods was reached, he went discreetly
round it. You never know what a grizzly's next move will be nor
how to anticipate his actions.

Old Timberline started down into a cañon as though to descend a gully diagonally to the bottom. I hastily made a short cut
and was ready to take his picture when he should come out at the
lower end. But he never came. After waiting some time, I back-

tracked and found he had gone only a few hundred feet down the gully, then returned to the top of the cañon and followed along the rim for a mile. He had then descended directly to the bottom of the cañon and gone straight up to the top on the other side.

Autumn is the time when bears most search the heights for food. Old Timberline's trail headed again for the heights. When I next caught sight of him, he was digging above the tree-line, but as it was now nearly night, I went back a short distance into the woods and built a fire by the base of a cliff. Here all through the clear night I had a glorious view of the high peaks up among the cold stars.

Before daylight I left camp and climbed to the top of a treeless ridge, thinking that the bear might come along that way. In the course of time he appeared, about a quarter of a mile east of me. After standing and looking about for a few minutes, he started along the ridge, evidently planning to recross the Continental Divide near where he had crossed the day before. As I could not get close to him from this point, I concluded to follow his trail of the preceding night and if possible find out what he had been doing.

A short distance below him I found his trail and back-tracked to a place which showed that he had spent the night near the entrance of a recently dug den. I learned some weeks later that this den was where he hibernated that winter. A short distance farther on I came to where he had been digging when I saw him the evening before. Evidently he had been successful. A few drops of some blood on the snow showed that he had captured some small animal, probably a cony. From this point I trailed Old Timberline forward and eastward, and near noon I caught a glimpse of him on the summit of the Divide.

While roaming above timber-line he did not take the precaution to travel with his face in the wind. He could see toward every point of the compass. He was ambling easily along, but I knew that his senses were wide awake—that his sentinel nose never slept and that his ears never ceased to hear. Climbing to the very summit of a snow-covered ridge, he lay down with his back to the wind. Evidently he depended upon the wind to carry the warning scent of any danger behind him, while he was on the lookout for anything in front of him. Nothing could approach nearer than half a mile without his knowing it. He looked this way and that. After only a short rest he arose and started on again.

I hoped that some time I should be able to photograph Old Timberline at twenty-five or thirty feet. But at all times, too, I was more eager to watch him, to see what he was eating, where he went, and what he did. . . .

Usually I followed in the bear's trail, but sometimes I made short cuts. So long as Old Timberline remained on the moorland summit of this treeless ridge, I could not get close to him. But when he arose and started down the ridge, I hurried down the slope, hoping to get ahead and hide in a place of concealment near which he might pass. I kept out of sight in the woods and hastened forward for two miles, then climbed up and hid in a rock-slide on the rim of the ridge.

By and by I saw Old Timberline coming. When within five hundred feet of me he stopped and dug energetically. Buckets of earth flew behind, and occasionally a huge stone was torn out and hurled with one paw to the right or left. Once he stopped digging, rose on hind feet, and looked all around as though he felt that some one was slipping up on him. He dug for a few minutes longer and then again stood up and sniffed the air. Not satisfied, he walked quickly to a ledge from which he could see down the slope to the woods. Discovering nothing suspicious, he returned to his digging, stepping in his former footprints. He un- covered something in its nest, and through my glasses I saw him strike right and left and then rush out in pursuit of it. After nosing about in the hole where he had been digging, he started off again. He went directly to the ledge, walking in his former well-tracked trail, then descended the steep eastern slope of the Divide toward the woods. I hurried to the ledge from which he had surveyed the surroundings and watched him.

Arriving at a steep incline on the snowy slope, Old Timberline sat down on his haunches and coasted. A grizzly bear coasting on the Continental Divide! How merrily he went, leaning forward with his paws on his knees! At one place he plunged over a snowy

ledge and dropped four or five feet. He threw up both fore paws with sheer joy. Soon he found himself exceeding the speed-limit. Looking back over one shoulder, and reaching out his paw behind him, he put on brakes; but as this did not check him sufficiently, he whirled about and slid flat on his stomach, digging in with both fingers and toes until he slowed down.

Then, sitting up on his haunches again, he set himself in motion by pushing along with rapid backward strokes of both fore paws. He coasted on toward the bottom. In going down a steep pitch of one hundred feet or more he either quite lost control of himself or let go from sheer enthusiasm. He rolled, tumbled, and slid recklessly along. Reaching the bottom, he rose on hind feet, looked about him for a few seconds, and then climbed halfway up the course for another coast. At the end of this merry sliding he landed on an open flat in the edge of the woods.

As it was nearly dark and I should not be able to see or follow the bear much longer, I concluded to roll a rock from the ledge down near him. Twice I had noticed that he had paid no attention to rocks that broke loose above and rolled near him. But he heard this rock start and rose up to look at it. It stopped a few yards from him. He sniffed the air with nose pointing toward it then went up and smelled it. Rearing up instantly, he looked intently toward the mountain-top where I was hidden. After two or three seconds of thought he turned and ran. Evidently the stone had carried my scent to him. It was useless to follow him in the night.

The next morning I left camp and followed Old Timberline's trail through the woods. He had run for nearly ten miles almost straight south until coming to a small stream. Then for some distance he concealed, involved, and confused his trail with a cleverness that I have never seen equaled. Most animals realize that they leave a scent which enables other animals to follow them, but the grizzly is the only animal that I know who appears to be fully aware that he is leaving telltale tracks. He will make unthought-of turns and doublings to walk where his tracks will not show, and also tramples about to leave a confusion of tracks where they do show.

Arriving at the stream, the bear crossed on a fallen log and from the end of this leaped into a bushy growth beyond. I made a detour, thinking to find his tracks on the other side of the bushes, and I threw stones into the bushes, not caring to go into them. Both tracks and grizzly seemed to have vanished. I went down stream just outside the bushes bordering it, expecting every instant to find the grizzly's tracks, but not finding them. Then I returned to the log on which he had crossed the stream, and from which he had leaped into the bushes.

Examining the tracks carefully, I now discovered what I had before overlooked. After leaping into the bushes the bear had faced about and leaped back to the log, stepping carefully into his former tracks. From the log he had entered the water and waded up stream for a quarter of a mile. Of course not a track showed. At a good place for concealing his trail he had leaped out of the water into a clump of willows on the north bank. From the willows he made another long leap into the snow and then started back northward, alongside his ten-mile trail and one hundred feet from it, as though intending to return to the place where I had rolled the stone down the slope near him.

I did not discover all this at once, however. In my search for his trail I went up stream on the north side and passed, without noticing, the crushed willows into which he had leaped. Crossing to where the bank was higher, I started back down stream on the other side, and in doing so chanced to look across and see the crushed clump of willows. But it took me hours to untangle this involved trail.

When I had followed the tracks northward for more than a mile, the trail vanished in a snowless place. Apparently the grizzly had planned in advance to use this bare place, because the moves he made in it were those most likely to bewilder the pursuer. He did three things which are always more or less confusing and even bewildering to the pursuer, be he man or dog. He changed his direction, he left no tracks, and he crossed his former trail, thereby mixing the scents of the two. He confused the nose, left no record for the eye, and broke the general direction.

Unable to determine the course the bear had taken across

this trackless place, I walked round it, keeping all the time in the snow. When more than halfway round I came upon his tracks leaving the bare place. Here he had changed his direction of travel abruptly from north to east, crossed his former trail, gone on a few yards farther, and then abruptly changed from east to north.

I hurried along his tracks. After a few miles I saw where perhaps the night before he had eaten part of the carcass of a bighorn. To judge from tooth marks, the sheep had been killed by wolves. The trail continued in general northward, parallel to the summit and a little below it. As I followed, the tracks approached timberline, the trees being scattered and the country quite open.

Suddenly the trail broke off to the right for five or six hundred feet into the woods, as though Old Timberline had remembered an acquaintance whom he must see again. He had hustled along straight for a much-clawed Engelmann spruce, a tree with bear-claw and tooth marks of many dates, though none were recent. Old Timberline, apparently, had smelled the base of the tree and then risen up and sniffed the bark as high as his nose could reach. He had neither bitten nor clawed. Then he had gone to two near-by trees, each of which had had chunks bitten or torn out, and here smelled about.

Retracing his tracks to where the trail had turned off abruptly, the bear resumed his general direction northward. When he stopped on a ridge and began digging, I hurried across a narrow neck of woods and crept up as close as I dared. A wagonload of dirt and stones had been piled up. While I watched the digging, a woodchuck rushed out, only to be overtaken and seized by the bear, who, having finished his meal, shuffled on out of sight.

I followed the trail through woods, groves, and openings. After an hour or more without seeing the grizzly, I climbed a cliff, hoping to get a glimpse of him on some ridge ahead. I could see his line of tracks crossing a low ridge beyond and felt that he might still be an hour or so in the lead. But, in descending from the cliff, I chanced to look back along my trail. Just at that moment the bear came out of the woods behind me. He was trailing me!

I do not know how he discovered that I was following him.

He may have seen or scented me. Anyway, instead of coming directly back and thus exposing himself, he had very nearly carried out his well-planned surprise when I discovered him. I found out afterwards that he had left his trail far ahead, turning and walking back in his own footprints for a distance, and trampling this stretch a number of times, and that he had then leaped into scrubby timber and made off on the side where his tracks did not show in passing along the trampled trail. He had confused his trail where he started to circle back, so as not to be noticed, and slipped in around behind me.

But after discovering the grizzly on my trail I went slowly along as though I was unaware of his near presence, turning in screened places to look back. He followed within three hundred feet of me. When I stopped he stopped. He occasionally watched me from behind bushes, a tree, or a bowlder. It gave me a strange feeling to have this big beast following and watching me so closely and cautiously. But I was not alarmed.

I concluded to turn tables on him. On crossing a ridge where I was out of sight, I turned to the right and ran for nearly a mile. Then, circling back into our old trail behind the bear, I traveled serenely along, imagining that he was far ahead. I was suddenly startled to see a movement of the grizzly's shadow from behind a bowlder near the trail, only three hundred feet ahead. He was in ambush, waiting for me! At the place where I had left the trail to circle behind him, he had stopped and evidently surmised my movements. Turning in his tracks, he had come a short distance back on the trail and lain down behind the boulder to wait for me.

I went on a few steps after discovering the grizzly, and he moved to keep out of sight. I edged toward a tall spruce, which I planned to climb if he charged, feeling safe in the knowledge that grizzlies cannot climb trees. Pausing by the spruce, I could see his silver-gray fur as he peered at me from behind the bowlder, and as I moved farther away I heard him snapping his jaws and snarling as though in anger at being outwitted.

Just what he would have done had I walked into his ambush can only be guessed. Hunters trailing a wounded grizzly have been ambushed and killed. But this grizzly had not even been shot at nor harassed.

Generally, when a grizzly discovers that he is followed, or even if he only thinks himself followed, he at once hurries off to some other part of his territory, as this one did after I rolled the stone. But Old Timberline, on finding himself followed, slipped around to follow me. Often a grizzly, if he feels he is not yet seen,—that his move is unsuspected,—will slip around to follow those who are trailing him. But in no other case that I know of has a bear lingered after he realized that he was seen. After Old Timberline discovered that I had circled behind him, he knew that I knew where he was and what he was doing.

But instead of running way he came back along the trail to await my coming. What were his intentions? Did he intend to assault me, or was he overcome with curiosity because of my unusual actions and trying to discover what they were all about? I do not know. I concluded it best not to follow him farther, nor did I wish to travel that night with this crafty, soft-footed fellow in the woods. Going a short distance down among the trees, I built a rousing fire. Between it and a cliff I spent the night, satisfied that I had had adventure enough for one outing.

26

THE BIOGRAPHY OF A GRIZZLY
Ernest Thompson Seton

Since Ernest Thompson Seton was one of the founders of the Boy
Scouts of America and active in other youth organizations, it is
understandable that most of his writing was in the form of nature-
lore for young people. His books, delightfully illustrated with his
own drawings, are still popular with boys and girls nearly three-
quarters of a century after they first appeared. The following
excerpt from Seton's sensitive story of an orphaned grizzly cub,
although intended for juvenile readers, can be enjoyed by adult
readers because this fictionalized biography reveals a keen knowledge of both bears and human beings. The selection is taken from
The Biography of a Grizzly Bear, first published by The Century
Company in 1900 in New York (Chapters I and II).

HE WAS BORN over a score of years ago, away up in the wildest
part of the wild West, on the head of the Little Piney, above
where the Palette Ranch is now.

His mother was just an ordinary Silvertip, living the quiet life
that all Bears prefer, minding her own business and doing her
duty by her family, asking no favors of any one excepting to
let her alone.

It was July before she took her remarkable family down the
Little Piney to the Graybull, and showed them what strawberries
were, and where to find them.

Notwithstanding their Mother's deep conviction, the cubs
were not remarkably big or bright; yet they were a remarkable
family, for there were four of them, and it is not often a Grizzly
Mother can boast of more than two.

The wooly-coated little creatures were having a fine time,

and reveled in the lovely mountain summer and the abundance of good things. Their Mother turned over each log and flat stone they came to, and the moment it was lifted they all rushed under it like a lot of little pigs to lick up the ants and grubs there hidden.

It never once occurred to them that Mammy's strength might fail sometime, and let the great rock drop just as they got under it; nor would any one have thought so that might have chanced to see that huge arm and that shoulder sliding about under the great yellow robe she wore. No, no; that arm could never fail. The little ones were quite right. So they hustled and tumbled one another at each fresh log in their haste to be first, and sqealed little squeals and growled little growls, as if each was a pig, a pup, and a kitten all rolled into one.

They were well acquainted with the common little brown ants that harbor under logs in the uplands, but now they came for the first time on one of the hills of the great, fat, luscious Wood-ant, and they all crowded around to lick up those that ran out. But they soon found that they were licking up more cactus-prickles and sand than ants, till their Mother said in Grizzly, "Let me show you how."

She knocked off the top of the hill, then laid her great paw flat on it for a few moments, and as the angry ants swarmed on to it she licked them up with one lick, and got a good rich mouthful to crunch, without a grain of sand or a cactus-stinger in it. The cubs soon learned. Each put up both his little brown paws, so that there was a ring of paws all around the ant-hill, and there they sat, like children playing 'hands,' and each licked first the right and then the left paw, or one cuffed his brother's ears for licking a paw that was not his own, till the ant-hill was cleared out and they were ready for a change.

Ants are sour food and made the Bears thirsty, so the old one led down to the river. After they had drunk as much as they wanted, and dabbled their feet, they walked down the bank to a pool, where the old one's keen eye caught sight of a number of Buffalo-fish basking on the bottom. The water was very low, mere pebbly rapids between these deep holes, so Mammy said to the little ones:

194

"Now you all sit there on the bank and learn something new."
First she went to the lower end of the pool and stirred up a
cloud of mud which hung in the still water, and sent a long tail
floating like a curtain over the rapids just below. Then she went
quietly round by land, and sprang into the upper end of the pool
with all the noise she could. The fish had crowded to that
end, but this sudden attack sent them off in a panic, and they
dashed blindly into the mud-cloud. Out of fifty fish there is
always a good chance of some being fools, and half a dozen of
these dashed through the darkened water into the current, and
before they knew it they were struggling over the shingly shallow. The old Grizzly jerked them out to the bank, and the little
ones rushed noisily on these funny, short snakes that could not get
away, and gobbled and gorged till their little bellies looked like
balloons.

They had eaten so much now, and the sun was so hot, that
all were quite sleepy. So the Mother-bear led them to a quiet little
nook, and as soon as she lay down, though they were puffing
with heat, they all snuggled around her and went to sleep, with
their little brown noses tucked into their wool as though it were a
very cold day.

After an hour or two they began to yawn and stretch themselves, except little Fuzz, the smallest; she poked out her sharp
nose for a moment, then snuggled back between her Mother's
great arms, for she was a gentle, petted little thing. The largest,
the one afterward known as Wahb, sprawled over on his back
and began to worry a root that stuck up, grumbling to himself
as he chewed it, or slapped it with his paw for not staying where
he wanted it. Presently Mooney, the mischief, began tugging at
Frizzle's ears, and got his own well boxed. They clenched for a
tussle; then, locked in a tight, little grizzly yellow ball, they
sprawled over and over on the grass, and before they knew it,
down a bank, and away out of sight toward the river.

Almost immediately there was an outcry of yells for help
from the little wrestlers. There could be no mistaking the real
terror in their voices. Some dreadful danger was threatening.

Up jumped the gentle Mother, changed into a perfect demon,

and over the bank in time to see a huge Range-bull make a deadly charge at what he doubtless took for a yellow dog. In a moment all would have been over with Frizzle, for he had missed his footing on the bank; but there was a thumping of heavy feet, a roar that startled even the great Bull, and, like a huge bounding ball of yellow fur, Mother grizzly was upon him. Him! the monarch of the herd, the master of all these plains, what had he to fear? He bellowed his deep war-cry, and charged to pin the old one to the bank; but as he bent to tear her with his shining horns, she dealt him a stunning blow, and before he could recover she was on his shoulders, raking the flesh from his ribs with sweep after sweep of the her terrific claws.

The Bull roared with rage, and plunged and reared, dragging Mother Grizzly with him; then, as he hurled heavily off the slope, she let go to save herself, and the Bull rolled down into the river.

This was a lucky thing for him, for the Grizzly did not want to follow him there; so he waded out on the other side, and bellowing with fury and pain, slunk off to join the herd to which he belonged.

II

Old Colonel Pickett, the cattle king, was out riding the range. The night before, he had seen the new moon descending over the white cone of Pickett's Peak.

"I saw the last moon over Frank's Peak," said he, "and the luck was against me for a month; now I reckon it's my turn."

Next morning his luck began. A letter came from Washington granting his request that a postoffice be established at his ranch, and contained the polite inquiry, "What name do you suggest for the new post-office?"

The Colonel took down his new rifle, a 45-90 repeater. "May as well," he said; "this is my month"; and he rode up the Graybull to see how the cattle were doing.

As he passed under the Rimrock Mountain he heard a faraway roaring as of Bulls fighting, but thought nothing of it till he rounded the point and saw on the flat below a lot of his cattle pawing the dust and bellowing as they always do when they smell the blood of one of their number. He soon saw that the great Bull, "the boss of the bunch," was covered with blood. His back and sides were torn as by a Mountain-lion, and his head was battered as by another Bull.

"Grizzly," growled the Colonel, for he knew the mountains. He quickly noted the general direction of the Bull's back trail, then rode toward a high bank that offered a view. This was across the gravelly ford of the Graybull, near the mouth of the Piney. His horse splashed through the cold water and began jerkily to climb the other bank.

As soon as the rider's head rose above the bank his hand grabbed the rifle, for there in full sight were five Grizzly Bears, an old one and four cubs.

"Run for the woods," growled the Mother Grizzly, for she knew that men carried guns. Not that she feared for herself; but the idea of such things among her darlings was too horrible to think of. She set off to guide them to the timber-tangle on the Lower Piney. But an awful, murderous fusillade began.

Bang! and Mother Grizzly felt a deadly pang.

Bang! and poor little Fuzz rolled over with a scream of pain and lay still.

With a roar of hate and fury Mother Grizzly turned to attack the enemy.

Bang! and she fell paralyzed and dying with a high shoulder shot. And the three little cubs, not knowing what to do, ran back to their Mother.

Bang! Bang! and Mooney and Frizzle sank in dying agonies beside her, and Wahb, terrified and stupefied, ran in a circle about them. Then hardly knowing why, he turned and dashed into the timber-tangle, and disappeared as a last *bang* left him with a stinging pain and a useless, broken hind paw.

That is why the post-office was called Four-Bears. The Colonel seemed pleased with what he had done; indeed, he told of it himself.

But away up in the woods of Anderson's Peak that night a little lame Grizzly might have been seen wandering, limping along, leaving a bloody spot each time he tried to set down his hind paw; whining and whimpering, "Mother! Mother! oh mother, where are you?" for he was cold and hungry, and had such a pain in his foot. But there was no Mother to come to him, and he dared not go back where he had left her, so he wandered aimlessly about among the pines.

Then he smelled some strange animal smell and heard heavy footsteps; and not knowing what else to do, he climbed a tree. Presently a band of great, long-necked, slim-legged animals, taller than his Mother, came by under the tree. He had seen such once before and had not been afraid of them then, because he had been with his Mother. But now he kept very quiet in the tree, and the big creatures stopped picking the grass when they were near him, and blowing their noses, ran out of sight.

He stayed in the tree till near morning, and then he was so stiff with cold that he could scarcely get down. But the warm sun came up, and he felt better as he sought about for berries and ants, for he was very hungry. Then he went back to the Piney and put his wounded foot in the ice-cold water.

He wanted to get back to the mountains again, but still he felt he must go to where he had left his Mother and brothers. When the afternoon grew warm, he went limping down the stream through the timber, and down on the banks of the Graybull till he came to the place where yesterday they had had the fish-feast; and he eagerly crunched the heads and remains that he found. But there was an odd and horrid smell on the wind. It frightened him, and as he went down to where he last had seen his Mother the smell grew worse. He peeped out cautiously at the place, and saw there a lot of Coyotes, tearing at something. What it was he did not know; but he saw no Mother, and the smell that sickened and terrified him was worse than ever, so he quietly turned back toward the timber-tangle of the Lower Piney and nevermore came back to look for his lost family. He wanted his Mother as much as ever, but something told him it was no use.

As cold night came down, he missed her more and more again, and he whimpered as he limped along, a miserable, lonely, little, motherless Bear—not lost in the mountains, for he had no home to seek, but so sick and lonely, and with such pain in his foot, and in his stomach a craving for the drink that would nevermore be his. That night he found a hollow log, and crawling in, he tried to dream that his Mother's great, furry arms were around him, and he snuffled himself to sleep.

27

MY GRIZZLY BEAR DAY
William T. Hornaday

William T. Hornaday became the first director of the New York
Zoological Park in 1896, a position he held until his retirement in
1926. He was known particularly for his efforts for the preservation of wild life; his writings on behalf of the American bison
were largely responsible for saving the genus from extinction.
Hornaday initiated the drive which culminated in the creation
of Elk River (Montana) Game Preserve, the Montana Bison
Range, and the Wichita National Bison Range. He was also one
of the backers of the movement that led to passage of laws for-
bidding importation of the plumage of wild birds.

In the following, taken from *Camp-Fires in the Canadian
Rockies,* published in New York in 1906 by Charles Scribner's
Sons, pages 160–71, Hornaday gives an excitement-packed account of killing his first silvertip, with the added interest of the
trained zoologist's observations on the ways of grizzly bears.

WHEN CHARLIE [SMITH] came in on the evening of the 19th of
September and reported a bear at the carcass of my first goat, it
really seemed time to hope for at least a distant view of Old
Ephraim.

. . . Charlie and I took two saddle-horses and set out before
sunrise, intending to visit all the goat carcasses before returning.
We pulled briskly up to the head of Avalanche Creek, climbed
to the top of the pass, then dropped down into the basin on the
north. I dreaded a long climb on foot from that point up to our
old camp on Goat Pass, but was happily disappointed. Thanks to
the good engineering of some Indian trail-maker, the trail led

from the head of the basin, on an easy gradient, up through the green timber of the mountain side, quite to our old camp.

We found fresh grizzly-bear tracks within fifty feet of the ashes of our camp-fire; but our goat skins in the big spruce, and our cache of provisions near it, had not been touched.

With only a few moments delay, we mounted once more and rode on northward toward the scene of the first goat-kill. As we rode up the ridge of Bald Mountain, a biting cold wind, blowing sixty miles an hour, struck us with its full force. It went through our clothing like cold water, and penetrated to the marrow of our bones. At one point it seemed determined to blow the hair off the dog Kaiser's back. While struggling to hold myself together, I saw the dog suddenly whirl head on to the fierce blast, crouch low, and fiercely grip the turf with his claws to keep from being blown away. It was all that our horses could do to hold a straight course, and keep from drifting down to the very edge of the precipice that yawned only twenty-five feet to the leeward. We were glad to get under the lee of Bald Mountain, where the fierce blast that concentrated on that bleak pass could not strike us with its full force.

At last we reached the lake. . . . Dismounting in a grassy hollow that was sheltered from the wind, we quickly stripped the saddles from our horses and picketed the animals so that they could graze. Then, catching up our rifles, cameras, and a very slim parcel of luncheon, we set out past the lake for the ridge that rises beyond it.

The timber on the ridge was very thin, and we could see through it for a hundred yards or more. As we climbed, we looked sharply all about, for it seemed very probable that a grizzly might be lying beside a log in the fitful sunshine that struck the southern face of the hill. Of course, as prudent hunters, we were prepared to see a grizzly that was above us, and big, and dangerous,— three conditions that guarantee an interesting session whenever they come together.

Dog Kaiser was peremptorily ordered to follow us, which he did with a degree of intelligent obedience that would have shamed many a man. He is what is called a "slow trailer," which means that in following big game he either keeps close behind his master, or else goes ahead so slowly that it is possible for the latter to keep up with him, and see the game before the dog disturbs it.

We reached the crest of the ridge, without having seen a bear, and with the utmost caution stalked on down the northern side, toward the spot where the two goat carcasses lay on the slide-rock. The noise we made was reduced to an irreducible minimum.

We trod and straddled like men burglarizing Nature's sky-park. We broke no dead twigs, we scraped against no dead branches, we slid over no fallen logs. Step by step we stole down the hillside, as cautiously as if we had known that a bear was really at the foot of it. At no time would it have surprised us to have seen Old Ephraim spring up from behind a bush or a fallen log, within twenty feet of us.

At last the gray slide-rock began to rise into view. At last we paused, breathing softly and seldom, behind a little clump of spruces. Charlie, who was a step in advance, stretched his neck to its limit, and looked on beyond the edge of the hill, to the very spot where lay the remains of my first mountain goat. My view was cut off by green branches and Charlie.

He turned to me, and whispered in a perfectly colorless way, "He's lying right on the carcass!"

"What? Do you mean to say that a *bear* is *really* there?" I asked, in astonishment.

"Yes! Stand here, and you can see him,—just over the edge."

I stepped forward and looked. Far down, fully one hundred and fifty yards from where we were, there lay a silvery-gray animal, head up, front paws out-stretched. It was indeed a silver-tip; but it looked awfully small and far away. He was out on the clean, light-gray stipple of slide-rock, beside the scanty remains of my goat.

Even as I took my first look, the animal rose on his haunches, and for a moment looked intently toward the north, away from us. The wind waved his long hair, one wave after another. It was a fine chance for a line shot at the spinal column; and at once I made ready to fire.

"Do you think you can kill him from *here?*" asked Charlie, anxiously. "You can get nearer to him if you like."

"Yes; I think I can hit him from here all right." (I had carefully fixed the sights of my rifle, several days previously.)

"Well, if you don't hit him, I'll kick you down this ridge!" said Charlie, solemn as a church owl, with an on-your-own-head-be-it air. To me, it was clearly a moment of great peril.

I greatly desired to watch that animal for half an hour; but when a bear-hunter finds a grizzly bear, the thing for him to do is to kill it first, and watch it afterward. I realized that no amount of bear observations ever could explain . . . the loss of that bear.

As I raised my .303 Savage, the grizzly rose in a business-like way, and started to walk up the slide-rock, due south, and a little quartering from us. This was not half so good for me as when he was sitting down. Aiming to hit his heart and lungs, close behind his foreleg, and allowing a foot for his walking, I let go.

A second or two after the "whang" the bear reared slightly, and sharply wheeled toward his right, away from us; and just then Charlie's rifle roared,— close beside my ear! Without losing an instant, the grizzly started on a mad gallop, down the slide-rock and down the canyon, running squarely across our front.

Heavens!" I thought, aghast. "*Have I missed him?*"

Quickly I threw in another cartridge, and fired again; and "whang" went Charlie, as before. The bear fairly flew, reaching far out with its front feet, its long hair rolling in great waves from head to tail. Even at that distance, its silver-tipped fur proclaimed the species.

Bushes now hid my view, and I ran down a few yards, to get a fair show. At last my chance came. As the bear raced across an opening in my view, I aimed three feet ahead of his nose, and fired my third shot.

Instantly the animal pitched forward on his head, like a stricken rabbit, and lay very still.

"Ye fetched him that time!" yelled Charlie, triumphantly. "He's down! He's down! Go for him, Kaiser! Go for him!"

The dog was ready to burst with superheated eagerness. With two or three whining yelps he dashed away down the ridge, and out of sight. By this time Charlie was well below me, and I ran down to where he stood, beaming up.

"You fixed him, Director! He's down for keeps."

"Where is he?"

"Lying right on that patch of yellow grass, and dead as a wedge. *Shake!*"

We shook. It would have been conceited folly to have done otherwise. To come twelve miles, find our long-lost silver-tip, and down him by eleven o'clock made us feel that we were each of us entitled to a few gloats over the result.

"Woo, yow-yow!" said Kaiser, far below,—about ten seconds after he had disappeared; and there he was, looking very small, and joyously biting the hams of the dead grizzly. Instead of sitting astride a killed animal, and being photographed with one hand upon it, Kaiser gloats over his dead game by biting its hams.

As quickly as possible, we descended the slope and soon stood beside the dead grizzly. Then, as often happens, its sex changed very suddenly. Every grizzly is a "he," until shot! This one was a fat young female, not as big as we had hoped, but in beautiful pelage for September. In remarking upon the length and immaculateness of the furry coat, which still waved in the wind, Charlie said that at this season the female grizzlies have longer hair than the males. I was sorry we could not weigh the animal, but at that moment my scales were twenty miles away. . . .

We made a careful autopsy of the bear, and were able to determine to a certainty the details of our shooting, and its results. By good luck, my first shot went true to the mark aimed for,— the heart region, immediately behind the foreleg. But it did not go through the heart. The animal was quartering to me, sufficiently that my ball passed close behind the heart, tore the lungs and liver to bits, and passed out at the middle of the right side, low down. We thrust a small stick through, in the track of the ball, and left it there.

Charlie Smith fired as the bear was turning to the right. His bullet entered the left thigh, tore a great hole through the flesh between the skin and the femur, passed through the entrails, and lodged against the skin of the right side, well back. His bullets were of a larger calibre than mine, and this one was fully identified. We marked the course of that bullet, also, with a stick. After receiving those two bullets, the bear ran as if unharmed for about a hundred yards, when my third shot broke its neck, and brought it down in a heap, too dead to struggle. It was not touched by any other bullets but the three described. The distance, as nearly as we could estimate, was one hundred and fifty yards, good measure.

My first shot was of course absolutely fatal, and had I but known it, I need not have fired again. It was marvellous that the animal did not fall at the first fire, and equally so that with its lungs torn to pieces, it was able to run a hundred yards at top speed. How much farther could it have gone, had no other shots been fired? Not far, surely, for as it ran, it spattered the clean gray rocks with an awful outpouring of blood. . . .

. . . we sought the carcass of Mr. Phillip's goat, which was rolled over the cliff, and fell immediately above the spot where our silver-tip gave up her ghost. On seeking it, we found a grizzly-bear's cache of a most elaborate and artistic character. On the steep hillside a shallow hole had been dug, the whole carcass rolled into it, and then upon it had been piled nearly a wagon-load of fresh earth, moss and green plants that had been torn up by the roots. Over the highest point of the carcass the mass was twenty-four inches deep. On the ground the cache was elliptical in shape, about seven by nine feet. On the lower side it was four feet high, and on the upper side two feet. The pyramid was built around two small larch saplings, as if to secure their support.

On the uphill side of the cache, the ground was torn up in a space shaped like a half-moon, twenty-eight feet long by nineteen feet wide. From this space every green thing had been torn up, and piled on the pyramid. The outer surface of the cone was a mass of curly, fibrous roots and fresh earth.

In her own clumsy way, the bear had done her best to provide for a rainy day. Her labors would indeed have protected her prize from the eagles, but a wolverine would have laughed in ghoulish glee at that two feet of soft stuff while he laid bare the contents of the cache with about six rakes of his rascally paws.

The bear had been feeding on the body of my goat, which lay far out on the slide-rock, and she had eaten all that her stomach could contain. There being still a good quantity of pickings remaining, she had decided to bury it, but from much feeding was very lazy in carrying out this intention. She had, however, torn up and carried out about twenty mouthfuls of moss, earth and plant-roots, and dropped them, together with half a dozen sticks, upon the remains. It was in an interval of rest from this arduous labor that we first sighted the animal; and she was starting up to fetch down more material when I first fired at her. I photographed the bear's cache, but on the films the cache failed to appear.

At last we finished our work, packed the bear skin and some of the best of the meat upon one of our horses, and started for camp, riding turn about. We rolled in just before sunset, tired, but puffed up.

CATTLEMEN AND BEAR HUNTERS

28

ARIZONA BEAR FIGHTS

Joseph Miller[1]

Newspapers of another era, often aged in an attic or turned yellow on homestead cabin walls, are always fascinatingly quaint or picturesque, replete with the muskiness of nostalgia. Joseph Miller has woven news items from early Arizona papers into a fast-paced trio of books which bring that state's turbulent territorial and early statehood days into sharp focus.

From the "Letters to the Editor" column of the *Clifton Copper Era* Mr. Miller brings us some yarns of the cattlemen's war with Old Ephraim, taken from *Arizona: The Last Frontier*[2] and reprinted here with the permission of the publisher.

ONE SELDOM, *if ever, reads of a bear fight in this day and age, although there are still plenty of bear to be had in the great Mogollon (Mogey-own) country stretching across central Arizona. The inroads of civilization have decimated them, however, and forced them into the more remote areas. . . .*

A citizen of the Blue River country wrote the following letter to the Clifton Copper Era in 1907:

Among your many good articles we never see any bear stories. Now I can see you smile and hear you say, "Bear stories!" Reputable newspapers have long since quit "loading" their readers with bear and fish stories. I am sure this is the attitude of your

---

[1] Joseph Miller has been photographing and writing about Arizona for a quarter of a century. He was on the staff which produced the Arizona guide book, *Arizona: The Grand Canyon State,* which he revised in 1956 (New York, Hastings House); he also revised the New Mexico guide book, *New Mexico: The Colorful State* (New York, Hastings House, 1962) and has a number of other historical and pictorial books to his credit.

[2] Joseph Miller, *Arizona: The Last Frontier* (New York, Hastings House, 1956), 288–94.

worthy papers; were it not, your news gatherers could obtain facts from the Blue River ranchers showing desperate encounters with wounded bears and hair-breadth escapes as wild and thrilling as the adventures of the big game hunters in Darkest Africa.

The bear and cattlemen of the mountains are sworn enemies, and whenever and wherever they chance to meet, the crack of the unerring rifle deals death or brings on a desperate combat. There is no animal in the world more dangerous and hard to kill as an enraged and wounded grizzly bear and woe unto man or horse who permits his embrace or comes within reach of his terrible claws. Many times a bear will put up a stiff fight after being shot through the vitals.

All of the cowmen in this section have killed many bears; many have had narrow escapes and not a few wear marks of bruin's valor. Johnson, Fritz, Cosper, Jones, Thomas, and Forest Hall are all veteran bear hunters, and there is scarcely a time when they came to town but some of them could tell of encounters with bears that are true and would be interesting reading. But they are so modest and little given to boasting of their exploits that the facts can only be obtained after a thorough cross-examination. For example, Jones could tell of crawling into a bear's den and dispatching him, while Fritz could inform you how it feels to be caressed by a wounded, enraged silvertip, and how when he was all but dead, a lucky chance shot broke the bear's jaw, and saved Fritz from a horrible death. (*The Fritz story later.*)

Awakening one night at the barking of his dog, Forest Hall got up and shot a bear from a tree so close to his camp that the bear fell on his bed.

But J. H. T. Cosper, better known as Toll Cosper, bears the reputation of having killed more bears than any other man in the Blue country. His ranch and range lies on and adjacent to the Blue range, a wild and rugged country, with deep canyons and high hills whose slopes are covered with dense thickets of pine and underbrush. Many bears inhabit these canyons and forests, and Cosper's work frequently brings him in contact with them. He seems to have an eye for bears. His luck at finding them is phenomenal, and rarely do the soft-nose bullets from his thirty-forty fail to do deadly work. But even a thirty-forty does not kill every time, and Cosper has had many narrow escapes with enraged and wounded bears.

Some years ago when in a bear fight and while trying to protect a boy from a wounded bear that was pursuing him, Cosper rode too near the bear. The desperate animal unable to stand the fire from behind, suddenly wheeled, charged Cosper, and leaped upon his horse, and in another instant would have torn him to pieces had not a well-directed bullet broken his jaw and sent him reeling to the ground.

Last fall while riding along a lonely trail on the Blue range, a huge silvertip suddenly appeared in the path not over forty yards away, and insisted on the right-of-way. While the bear stood sizing him up, Cosper quietly dismounted, took deliberate aim and began "fogging" him. Although the first bullet dealt him a mortal wound, the bear uttered a savage roar and made for his enemy. His horse took fright and fled, and Cosper thinking discretion the better part of valor, tried to fly up a pine tree, but ere he could climb beyond his reach, the bear was almost upon him and would have caught him had not the snorting and plunging of his horse attracted bruin's attention for a moment. As the bear turned to the horse, the hunter seized the opportunity and while holding to the tree with one hand fired his gun with the other, breaking the bear's neck. When he descended and examined his gun, there was only one cartridge left in the magazine. The bear weighed about seven hundred pounds.

Unless wounded, a bear rarely shows fight, but either runs or stands curiously eyeing the hunter, but occasionally and especially when hungry, a bear will assume the offensive.

Last May, Cosper, his two sons and Charles Chapman were "riming" for cattle in Stray Horse, a deep canyon that heads on the Blue range. When they reached Rose Peak, a high mountain near the head of the canyon, they stopped to rest their horses and while seated on a log Chapman jestingly remarked that he wished seven hundred bears would charge them. The others laughed and expressed their opinions as to how quickly he could ascend a tree in case even one should happen along. Scarcely had

their laughter died away when a hoarse growl told them his wish
had come to pass. They scarcely had time to snatch their guns
from the scabbards, when a huge silvertip appeared in the trail
above them not twenty yards away, making straight for them.
Four rifles spouted forth and sent death-dealing missiles into his
body, but the bear was not checked until he was almost upon
them and a dozen bullets had entered his body, one going down
his windpipe and through his heart. Had it been one man instead of four, nothing but a lucky shot could have saved him from
death. This bear weighed fully eight hundred pounds. He measured eight feet from his nose to tail and the hide when spread out
measured nine feet across from the front paw to the hind paw.

Mr. Editor, if you ever want to go on a bear hunt, go with
Cosper, and there will be "something doing."

Yours very truly,
J. T. MATHEWS

*Fred Fritz, a ranchman of the Blue River country, visited Clifton
in 1905 and gave the Clifton Copper Era the details of a fierce
fight which he had had some time since with an old silvertip
bear which had been a terror to the ranchmen of that section for
many years.*

While riding his range in the neighborhood of Maple Springs
he cut the trail of a bear, which was nothing unusual in that
section. He had four dogs with him and a pistol, hence he did
not hesitate to follow the trail, feeling certain that he would have
little trouble in dispatching bruin. Fritz had killed many bears
previous to this time without an experience worth reporting. But
this bear was different. He was not only big, old and tough, but
also a fighter. He trailed the old fellow only a short distance
when he was overtaken in some piñon timber. Fritz opened fire
with his pistol. The dogs also took an interest in the fight, but
the bear did not apparently take an interest in them, but he
made a break for Fritz, and being on higher ground he jumped
partly onto the horse and grabbed him with his mouth and claws.
Fritz then got another shot which broke the bear's jaw, and

caused him to relax his hold on the horse. He then emptied his revolver at the bear thinking he would settle him, but owing to the fact that the horse was fractious and the bear's hide tough, he was not able to land a fatal shot. He rode off a short distance and reloaded, and then discovered that he had only six cartridges. In the meantime the dogs were following bruin and worrying him greatly. He then took up the trail, and after following it about a mile overtook the bear in a narrow canyon. He dismounted from his horse and followed the bear up into some sharp rocks, and just as he was surmounting one of them the bear jumped onto him and together they rolled down several feet, the bear landing on top. Fritz landed face downward. He was somewhat stunned by the fall, but was quickly brought to his senses by the bear taking the back of his head in its mouth, and had it not been for the fact that the brute's jaw had previously been broken, no doubt the battle would have ended in favor of bruin.

Fritz managed to get his gun into action and firing over his shoulder caught the bear in the mouth, the bullet coming out at the butt of his ear. Ordinarily this should have ended the fight, but not so in this case. The bear apparently realizing that he could not use his mouth effectively proceeded with his claws to tear the leather "chaps" off of the now almost helpless man. This turned him over and he was again able to use his pistol, which he did until every shot had been fired. The dogs again took an interest in the fight, and attracted bruin's attention, but every time Fritz attempted to get up the bear came back and sat upon him while slapping at the dogs. He used the pistol as a club and broke it. He then managed to get out his pocket knife, which was so small and light that it would not penetrate through the tough hide of the bear. Fritz then realized that his only show of escape was through the dogs, and he encouraged them in their attack, and in this manner more dead than alive, with his clothes almost torn off, and bloody from head to foot, he managed to reach his horse. At this time his nephew, who had heard the shooting, arrived on the scene, and the two men followed the bear who was dragging the dogs with him. When they overtook the bear they saw that he was very sick. The nephew took one shot at him, and the bear afterwards died. Fritz was laid up at his ranch for many days, and will carry the scars of the battle with him to the grave. When the bear was skinned seven bullets were found in his body.

The Copper Era carried this story in 1907:

Bear stories usually made their appearance in Clifton about this time of the year when hunting parties begin to return from the mountains. Jack Holman, Reese Webster, Judge Hampton, Sheriff Anderson, Dick Franz, Jack Hagerty, and several others recently returned from the White Mountains. Now it had always been reported that Hagerty was the only bear hunter in the country, but it seems that he got his reputation in the level parts of Kansas, where running is good, and parties who knew him there say they know of several thrilling bear fights in which Jack actually run the bear to death. Bear hunting in the mountains was a new thing to Hagerty and it took him several days to get next. He always had a hobby to do his hunting alone. One day the party started out on a hunt and it was some time before he could conveniently separate himself from the crowd. The rest of the hunters finished their skirmish and returned to camp with empty bags. Hagerty sneaked through the rough places and finally came across the tracks of a monster bear. He trailed the bear for some time and the boys in camp decided that he was lost, when he appeared in a fit of excitement. His flushed face, glaring eyes and short breath convinced the boys that Jack had had another fierce encounter. When he settled down he told his story. Well, he followed the bear until he located him. The bear was above him and the country was so rough that he at once decided not to shoot; as running was poor. About that time another bear appeared and Jack forgot to shoot. Covering a rocky country with a heavy gun was the limit and that is the reason he returned to Clifton without his gun. He says the next time he goes bear hunting it will be in a level country.

29

THE KILLING OF OLD EPHRAIM
Frank Clark

The life and death of Old Ephraim has been more or less immortalized in northern Utah, the story having been written many times (one version was included in *The Best American Short Stories of 1951*[1]). Frank Clark, the man who was responsible for the old bear's undoing, was never satisfied with the publicity his adventure in the moonlight received. To set the record right his version of the incident was published in the *Utah Fish and Game Bulletin*, Vol. 9, No. 8 (September, 1952), on pages 4 and 5. The story is used here with the permission of the Utah Fish and Game Department.

Frank Clark was a Utah sheepherder and range conservationist, born in 1879 in a pioneer's log cabin in Idaho. He didn't do much fishing or hunting, but the chase which resulted in Old Ephraim's demise lasted from 1911 until 1923. In the end Clark's craftiness paid off, but success brought him little pleasure.

I WAS TRANSFERRED to the Cache National Forest from Idaho in 1911. This country was infested with bears at that time. They were of two varieties: the brown and the grizzly bear. Many of them were sheep killers. I know of them killing as many as 150 head of sheep in one summer from one herd.

The men were not used to these killer bears and I had some trouble trying to get men to stay on the job. After we had killed and trapped one or two, however, their feelings toward them changed. I killed 13 in 1912 alone.

One bear had become known as Old Ephraim. He was a grizzly bear. The bear's name was given to him, I think, because of an

[1] Ray B. West, Jr., "The Last of the Grizzly Bears," *Epoch*, Vol. III, No. 2 (Fall, 1950), 67–94.

outlaw bear found in California that had been written up by
P. S. Barnham. Old Ephraim was well known, mainly because
everyone who saw his tracks recognized him. He had one de-
formed toe. Many weird tales were told about him. He was supposed to have ranged all the way from northern Utah to the
Snake River section in Idaho, but I never found his tracks more
than two miles from the range that I was using.

I began in 1914 to trap for him, but it was not until 1923 that
I caught him. He had a large pool scooped out in a little canyon
and at least once a week he would come to wallow in the pool he
had made. I set my trap in this pool thinking I would catch him,
but every time I set it and the bear visited the pool, he would
"pertly" pick it up and set it on the side of the pool. It was not
until 1923 that he changed his plan of enjoying himself in this
wallow. I thought of moving the trap each time. One time I came
back and found the bear had dug another pool just below the
old one. I set my trap in the new location and this proved Old
Ephraim's undoing.

Old Ephraim was not the greedy killer that some bears seem
to be. He would usually kill one sheep, pick it up and carry it
into the more remote sections of the mountains and devour it.
This is in strict contrast to the actions of some killer bears who
may kill as many as 100 sheep in one night. It had become a legend
that Old Ephraim never seemed to pick on the same herd twice
in succession, but roamed around for several miles, in the proximity
of the spring where he bathed and would take only one or two
sheep from each separate camp.

I remember well the night of Old Ephraim's undoing. I had
set the trap in his new pool, stirred up the mud so that it would
set well on the trap. My camp was about one mile down stream
from the site. April 23 was a beautiful cool night and after supper
I lighted my pipe and set my gaze at the stars that seemed to be
trying to get a message of some kind to the people down here.
My nearest company were other herders about four miles away
and my horses on a meadow some distance below my camp.

After bedding down for the night and sleeping for some time
I was suddenly awakened by the most unearthly sound I have

ever heard. Ordinarily my dog would bark at anything unusual; this time he did not. After the first cry, I noticed that the grumbling of this bear stopped and then after a short time, a roar heard again, echoed from canyon wall to canyon wall. I quickly slipped on my shoes, didn't bother to put on pants, grabbed my rifle and started along the trail. Expecting to go only a few yards from camp, was why I did not fully dress. As the sounds kept up I could tell they were in the bottom of the canyon nearing me. I skirted the mountain side above. I finally realized that I had caught either Old Ephraim or another bear and soon heard the noise in the willows along the creek bed below me. After it had passed, I slipped down and along the trail in the bright moon light and I could see the tracks of the big bear as he went down the stream. I followed the noise slowly down the creek until I got near the point where my camp was and there came crashing out of the creek bottom the giant form of Old Ephraim walking on his hind feet. He was carrying on his front foot the large trap that weighed 27 pounds and the 15 feet of log chain neatly wrapped around his right forearm. As he came towards me, it chilled me to the very bone and for several paces I didn't even attempt to shoot. Finally, more out of fear than any other passion, I opened up with my small 25–35 caliber rifle and pumped six shots into him. He fell at my feet dead, and as I looked at the giant form of Old Ephraim I suddenly became sorry that I had killed this giant bear. Retracing the bear's trail from the place where he had been caught I found that for over one mile he had walked on his hind feet holding the trap and chain on his front foot. Also, that he had cut the large 15 foot log that I had the chain tied to in 2 and 3 foot lengths. All the trees as far as the length of the chain would let him go had been cut down. It looked as if the quaking aspen up to six inches in diameter had been cut with a single blow.

Old Ephraim's body was buried near my camp site and remained there until it was unearthed and his skull sent to the Smithsonian Institute where it remains today. A monument has been erected by the Boy Scouts of America of Cache County to the memory of Old Ephraim and hundreds of Boy Scouts have visited my camp and been thrilled to the story I have told hundreds of times of the killing of Old Ephraim.

[Editor's note] Old Ephraim's grave mark reads:

OLD EPHRAIM'S GRAVE (GRIZZLY BEAR)
KILLED BY FRANK CLARK, MALAD, IDAHO
AUGUST 22, 1923—WEIGHT APPROX.
1100 POUNDS—HEIGHT 9 FT. 11 IN.
SMITHSONIAN INSTITUTE HAS EPHRAIM'S SKULL[2]

[2] Information on grave marker furnished by Utah Department of Fish and Game.

30

LEPLEY'S BEAR

Charles M. Russell

At the age of fifteen Charles M. Russell became a wrangler on a cattle ranch in Montana Territory. From that time on he lived the part of a frontiersman, eventually becoming famous as the West's "cowboy artist." All the excitement and wonderful humor of the old range country is "laid on" in Russell's writings, just as all the color and picturesqueness of the Indians, cowboys, and animals of the plains and mountains were brushed onto his canvases and shaped into his bronzes.

The story of Lepley's bear is told in the colloquialism of the range, just as Russell wrote his colorful personal letters, illustrated with humorous or to-the-point pen-and-ink or water-color sketches. The story is taken from Russell's book, *Trails Plowed Under*, published by Doubleday and Company, Inc., Garden City and New York, in 1927, pages 75–76, and is reprinted here with the kind permission of Russell's son, Jack Cooper Russell.

OLD MAN LEPLEY TELLS ME one time about a bear he was near enough to shake hands with but they don't get acquainted. He's been living on hog side till he's near starved. So, one day he saddled up and starts prowling for something fresh. There's lots of black-tail in the country but they have been hunted till they are shy, so after riding a while without seeing nothing he thinks he'll have better luck afoot. So, the first park he hits, he stakes his hoss. It's an old beaver meadow with bluejoint to his cayuse's knees, and about the center (like it's put there for him) is a dead cottonwood snag handy to stake his hoss to.

After leaving the park he ain't gone a quarter of a mile till he notices the taller branches of a chokecherry bush movin'. There's no wind, and Lepley knows that bush don't move without something pushing it, so naturally he's curious. 'Tain't long till he heap savvys. It's a big silvertip and he's sure busy berrying. There's lots of meat there, and bear grease is better than any boughten lard. So, Lepley pulls down on him, aimin' for his heart. Mr. Bear bites where the ball hits. It makes Old Silver damn disagreeable—he starts bawlin' and comin'.

As I said before, there ain't no wind. It's the smoke from his gun hovering over Lepley that tips it off where's he's hiding. He's packing a Sharp's carbine an' he ain't got time to reload, so he turns this bear hunt into a foot race. It's a good one, but it looks like the man'll take second money. When he reaches the park his hoss has grazed to the near end. Lepley don't stop to bridle, but leaps for the saddle.

About this time the hoss sees what's hurrying the rider. One look's enough. In two jumps, he's giving the best he's got. Suddenly something happens. Lepley can't tell whether it's an earthquake or a cyclone, but everything went from under him, and he's sailin' off; but he's flying low, and uses his face for a rough lock, and stops agin some bushes. When he wakes up he don't hear harps nor smell smoke. It ain't till then he remembers he don't untie his rope. The snag snapped off, and his hoss is trying to drag it out of the country, and Mr. Bear, by the sound of breaking brush, is hunting a new range and it won't be anywhere near where they met. When his hoss stops on the end of the rope, that old snag snaps and all her branches scatter over the park. I guess Mr. Bear thinks the hoss has turned on him. Maybe some of them big limbs bounced on him and he thinks the hoss has friends and they're throwing clubs at him. Anyhow, Mr. Bear gives the fight to Lepley and the hoss.

Lepley says that for months he has to walk that old hoss a hundred yards before he can spur him into a lope, and that you could stake him on a hairpin and he'd stay.

31

CHASING AND CATCHING THE RAINBOW
Montague Stevens

Montague Stevens was an Englishman who came to New Mexico and settled there to ranch. He was an enthusiastic hunter and, unlike the proverbial Britisher, was able to see the funny side of a joke and turn the trick on the joker. His book, *Meet Mr. Grizzly*, is rated by a competent judge to be "about the most mature yet published by a ranchman"[1] and is one of the most informative and authentic to be written about grizzly bears. The reader will undoubtedly find this unusual bear story both amusing and enlightening. It appears on pages 32–40 of *Meet Mr. Grizzly: A Saga on the Passing of the Grizzly*, published by the University of New Mexico Press at Albuquerque in 1944, and is reprinted here through the courtesy of the publisher and the author.

WHEN I GOT MY SECOND GRIZZLY, a large party of both invited and uninvited guests was with me. Deer hunting parties would drift through the country during October and November—the game season—and hearing of my being out on a bear hunt with my hounds, would send word to me, asking if they might be allowed to join in the hunt. Of course they were welcome.

On this hunt we caught several black bear during the first week or two. We became very well acquainted, and joking one another became the order of the day. This developed into playing practical jokes, but it was understood that jokes calculated to hurt anyone's feelings or do physical harm would be considered as "hitting below the belt." . . .

I had been getting off a few harmless jokes on some of the

[1] J. Frank Dobie, *A Guide to Life and Literature of the Southwest* (Dallas, Southern Methodist University Press, 1952), 164.

party, for which they were determined to get even with me at first chance, and such an opportunity soon presented itself.

One day, during my absence, one of the men reported that he had found a rattlesnake close to camp, and thereupon, a keg, which had contained horse-shoes, was emptied, a dish-pan was borrowed from the cook, forked sticks were cut from surrounding trees, and thus armed, the whole party advanced on the bush under which the snake had been seen. He was still there, and was promptly ejected and pinned down with the forked sticks, then pushed into the keg, on top of which the dish-pan was placed and secured with a heavy rock, the whole thing being then hidden in the bushes.

The next morning, I was awakened by the cry of "Breakfast ready," so I got up and began to dress. Usually, I was one of the first ones up, but this morning, everybody seemed to be around the campfire eating breakfast, and though it struck me as strange, I thought little of it.

I reached for one of my lace-top boots, which I always wore, and started to draw it on, when to my horror, my foot touched something cold and squirmy. This was a case that called for swift action, and casting dignity to the winds, I threw myself on my back and kicked off the boot, flinging it through the air. And out of the boot flew a wriggling rattlesnake.

At the same moment, a roar of laughter came from the crowd around the campfire, and then I tumbled. It was a practical joke. I got up to retrieve my boot, saying loud enough for them all to hear:

"It seems to me that putting a live rattlesnake in a man's boot is hitting below the belt."

"Before you say that," shouted one of the jokers, "look at the snake."

I did so, and saw that the snake's head had been cut off.

Like eels, snakes wriggle for a long time after they have been killed, so when I touched it with my foot, as this one was still quivering, I thought it was alive. The joke was on me and I returned to my bed and put on my boots.

The evenings around the campfire were spent in telling stories of hunting adventures. On the occasion of this hunt, I had hired two hunters, one a great deal older than the other. The elder man was a good-natured, simple-minded soul, who listened to our tales with great interest. In one story, the word "paradox" was mentioned, and when the old hunter asked the meaning of the word, it was agreed that each one of us should give him a definition. Such time-honored expressions as "not seeing the forest for the trees" were trotted out, and when it came to my turn, I said:

"Common sense is the least common of all the senses."

This was rejected on the ground that it was only a frivolous wise crack, so I gave them:

"If you want to deceive, one of the best ways is to tell the truth." The objection to this was that it wasn't so, but I had occasion to prove it on our next chase.

The following morning, I got word that a cow had just been killed by a silvertip near a spring about twenty miles away. So, amid great excitement, we moved and made camp a few miles from the spring.

At daylight the next day, we sallied forth in high hopes of getting this bear, for he had been eating on the cow during the night, and had left a hot trail for the hounds. As usual, they soon ran out of hearing, and we all got separated. It had been previously arranged that we should meet on the top of the mountain, which was above timber-line and quite bare, where we could see each other at a distance. So we all got together again, and spent the rest of the day listening in vain at the heads of different canyons for the hounds.

Toward late afternoon, it was decided that it was useless to continue with the hunt, and as we were about to start down the mountain, we could see the smoke from our campfire in the valley below some ten miles off. It gave promise of the supper that was cooking, and as everyone was very hungry, an untactful suggestion on my part was promptly over-ruled. I remarked that it was quite possible that the bear, after running hard all day, might go to a little spring on the side of the mountain, about four miles out of our course, for a drink. This proposition was resentfully rejected, with many unkind remarks, so I made up my mind to go it alone, and as I left them, someone shouted out:

"You'd chase a rainbow if you thought a silvertip was tied to one end of it." And another added:

"Hope you catch your rainbow."

As I rode on, I began to suffer from a severe attack of introspection as I quite realized that the chances of running onto this bear were so very remote as to justify my fellow hunters in deeming me obstinate to an asinine degree. But as I started for the spring, I resolved to cast off these depressing thoughts and go on. I reached the canyon where the spring rippled over its rocky bed for about a mile to a ledge of rock, three or four feet high, which crossed the canyon. The stream trickled over this ledge, forming a pool beneath it.

As I drew near the pool, I concluded that my cold-footed companions were right, and then something unexpected happened. A coincidence came about, so extraordinary that I must ask my readers to "believe it or not," depending on their individual predilections.

A steep bank of soft earth butted up against the ledge on the farther side of the canyon, and there, on top of this bank, sat Old Drive, looking below him with a quizzical expression. Without thinking, I called out, "Why, hello, Drive!" and the next instant, the silvertip, who had been lying in the pool below, jumped onto the ledge, shaking himself vigorously and throwing a heavy spray of water around him in all directions. The rays of the setting sun lit up the spray, and there appeared, for a full three seconds, a perfect rainbow, in the center of which was the bear.

He turned and jumped onto the bank, but, as it was of soft earth and very steep, he slid down, his front claws leaving deep furrows. Then he ran down the canyon, and I followed him.

I had two dogs with me, my fox terrier, Twist, and Czar, a wolf hound, kindly lent me by General Miles, who had obtained him from the kennels of the Czar of Russia.

After running a short distance down the canyon, the bear climbed the farther bank, which was not very steep. The dogs took after him, Twist, as usual, running ahead and barking in his face, while Czar, who had had experience in fighting black bear, nipped his heels.

Like a flash, the bear whirled around, and literally pounced on Czar, crushing him to the ground, and biting him through the fleshy part of the thigh.

In the meantime, I had jumped off my horse, and was aiming at the bear. I shot him in the shoulder, just at the moment he took hold of Czar. He snapped viciously at the place where the bullet had struck him, and then, catching sight of me, bolted into the canyon and came towards me.

I ran back of my horse, George, who, unlike most horses, luckily was not in the least afraid of bear. Throwing another cartridge into my rifle I awaited the grizzly's coming. George was standing still, and I was on the upper side of him, looking over the saddle. The bear ran around behind the horse, while I ran around the head, and as he passed George's head, I ran to his tail, getting ready to shoot as soon as I got a good opportunity. But instead of coming round the horse's head, as I had thought, he kept straight on, making several ineffectual attempts to catch Twist, who was still barking in his face. Then he turned, re-crossed the canyon, and started up the other side, going straight away from me. This gave me a line shot on his backbone, and I fired, breaking it. He rolled over, and going up to him, I found him alive, but unable to get on his feet, so I finished him with my six-shooter.

After the unpleasant job of gutting him, I went to the stream to wash my hands, but changed my mind, and returning to the bear, cut off a tuft of hair, showing the silver tips, which I placed in an old envelope I had in my pocket. I then mounted my horse and started for camp.

By this time, it had grown quite dark. There was no moon, and my progress was slow, as I had to travel mostly through thick timber, giving me ample time to think things over.

Here, at last, was my opportunity to get back on the whole party for the rattlesnake joke and others they had played on me, as well as the unkind remarks they had made! One remark was to the effect that when I said anything with an air of injured innocence, I was least to be trusted, but I have to admit that the man who made this remark had good cause for saying it.

As I rode along, I began to form plans, which, if I could carry them out, would enable me to make a grand slam on the whole outfit. My plan was to tell them I had killed the bear, but in such a way that none of them would believe me, proving my repudiated paradox: "The best way to deceive is by telling the truth."

I easily located the camp, as there was a huge fire burning, and as I rode up, there were cries of:

"Did you get lost?" To which I replied:

"No, or I wouldn't be here!"

Some of the party were professional men, whom we regarded as "wise guys," and a "wise guy," as I take it, is a man who knows more than is good for him, and who is, therefore, easily fooled, provided he is approached in the right way.

The younger hunter was of a very suspicious nature, and that kind, also, is not hard to fool, because he generally suspects in the wrong place. But these tactics would not work on the older hunter, because, right or wrong, he would believe anything I told him, whether it was true or not being quite immaterial.

The cook had kept my supper hot, so I turned to him and apologized for being so late, explaining that I had to kill the silvertip on the way in, which delayed me. At this, there was a roar of laughter, and someone shouted:

"You were always good at excuses, but this one takes the cake!" With an air of injured innocence, I held up my hand, with the dried blood on it, in the full light of the fire.

"Look at the blood on my hand," I said, "there's my proof!"

"You can't fool me," yelled the younger hunter. "That blood is from a deer you killed on your way back."

"Very well," I replied, "have it your way."

Then I went off, washed my hands, and returned to eat my supper. While I was eating, I was the target for innumerable sallies of wit at what they deemed my boastful claims as to the killing of the bear. When I had finished my supper, I said:

226

"Well, if you want more proof, I have it here."

I pulled the envelope out of my pocket, and removed the tuft of hair, which I passed around for inspection, and when it reached the old hunter he remarked:

"This is silvertip hair, all right . . . but you cut it off that old silvertip hide you've got at the ranch."

The old hunter asked to see it again, and this time he looked at it more closely. Then he said:

"The hair on an old hide straightens out, but this hair is crinkly, so it must have come from a fresh hide."

This opinion caused a general look of surprise, and to my dismay, the crowd looked as though they might believe it. The only way to save the situation was to create a diversion, so I seized the tuft from the old hunter's hand, and looking at the others, said:

"You remember telling me that I would chase a rainbow if I thought a silvertip was tied to one end of it? Well, I caught that rainbow; that is, I was near enough to hit it with a rock, if I had wanted to. But the funny thing was that the bear was in the center of the rainbow—not tied to one end."

This was too much for the crowd to swallow, and out of the corner of my eye, I observed one of them tap his forehead significantly, while the others slowly nodded their heads in silent approval.

It seemed to me that this was the right moment to retire, so I bade them "Goodnight," and went to bed.

At breakfast next morning, one of the party remarked:

"You seem to have forgotten all about that silvertip you killed yesterday":

I replied that I had and to make good this oversight, I directed Telesfor, who had charge of the saddle horses, to put pack saddles on two of them, and be ready to go with us to fetch the bear. Then, with a bored expression, I said to the others:

"I suppose you want more proof, so I'll give it to you."

At my call, Czar, who was sleeping by my bed, came hobbling along, dragging his injured leg. He had been licking the wound all night, so that the four round holes made by the bear's canine teeth showed up plainly in his silky, white hair.

In an unguarded moment, the younger hunter exclaimed:

"Why, what's the matter with him?"

"Oh, nothing much," I said, "Those four holes were made by the teeth of the deer you said I killed yesterday."

All the crowd, except the younger hunter, laughed at this.

Incidentally, a deer only has front teeth in the lower jaw, and these are flat, not round.

Deer hunting was the order of the day, as the hounds had to have a rest. The horses were all saddled, and at my suggestion, the party agreed to accompany me as far as the spot where I had left the bear. I led the way to the canyon, and pointed out the ledge onto which the bear had jumped from the pool, then from the ledge to the steep bank on the other side, where the claw marks in the soft earth proved he had slid down when he tried to climb it. Then I went to the place where the bear had jumped onto Czar, showing a lot of white hair on the ground, which had been rubbed off in his struggles to escape. Then we went on down to the bear, which the hunters began to skin, while the rest of us sat around and smoked.

The old hunter, very much impressed by what he had seen, thought that I had not been fairly treated by the crowd, and feeling that he should make amends, he raised his skinning knife in the air, and looking at me, proclaimed solemnly:

"From now on, I'll believe anything you say, even if it's a damned lie!"

Then one of the crowd called out, questioningly:

"What's the big idea in trying to fool us all into thinking you hadn't killed a bear, when you had?"

Without repressing a smile, I answered:

"Because you all repudiated my paradox, that one of the best ways to deceive is by telling the truth. I've tried it out on you fellows and it seems to have worked."

There was a moment's silence, and then, being sportsmen, all the hunting party, with the exception of the younger hunter shouted lustily:

"You win!"

And this chivalrous admission permitted me to think that the rattlesnake joke had been repaid in full.

32

THE FIGHTING SILVERTIP OF ALBEMARLE
Frank C. Hibben

Frank C. Hibben shot his first grizzly in Idaho at the age of
fifteen. Before writing *Hunting American Bears*,[1] from which
"The Fighting Silvertip of Albermarle" is taken, he had killed
twenty-nine bears, black and grizzly, for the Cleveland Museum
of Natural History. He holds twenty-four North American big-
game records and is one of the few hunters who have bagged all
species of North American game animals, including all bears and
cats. In addition he has hunted extensively in Mexico, Central
America, the Near East, Africa, and Europe. Nor is his interest
in wild game entirely lethal. He is chairman of the New Mexico
Department of Game and Fish and has been instrumental in the
importation of foreign animals into North America for the benefit
of future hunters.

Hibben's position as professor of anthropology in the University of New Mexico and his vocation of writing dovetail remarkably with his avocation. Anthropological field trips around
the world have carried him into areas from which he has taken
some unusual game trophies. While on a hunting expedition in
the Sudan, Hibben uncovered a piece of bone which was identified as a fragment of the skull of an ax man who lived about
750,000 B.C., now in the Nairobi Museum in Kenya. It goes without saying that Hibben has had many exciting experiences. That
he writes an enthralling story is proved by the following tale of
a grizzly bear who inhabited a New Mexico ghost town, reprinted
here with the kind permission of the University of New Mexico
Press and the author.

[1] Frank C. Hibben, *Hunting American Bears* (Philadelphia and New York,
J. P. Lippincott Company, 1950), © Frank C. Hibben, 1950, pages 70–92.

230

IT ISN'T OFTEN that we have a grizzly in New Mexico at all. But the silvertip which visited us this last season was not only unexpected in our mountains, but actually lived in a town.

Don't picture this monarch in a zoo or a circus, for he was as wild as they come—perhaps wilder—for he fought with all of the snarling fury of a demon of hell when he came to bay. But he did live in a town, curious as that was for a beast that avoided by habit and disposition the tracks and traces of men.

Cass Goodner and I had visited the town of Albemarle on several occasions before. In the time of Teddy Roosevelt, some two thousand miners had made this rugged canyon reverberate with their activity. They followed the veins of silver which were the treasure arteries of the mountainside. Prospect holes and shaft openings scarred the rough canyon walls at all levels, like an infestation of burrowing animals. In the canyon below these diggings, the hardy miners had built a town. Of course there was little left of the place as Cass and I sat our horses for a moment and looked down into Albemarle. Most of the houses along the main street in the bottom of the canyon had collapsed long ago and slithered into nondescript piles of weathered boards in the floor of the wash. The false front of a saloon still stood with an alder tree growing through its warped timbers. There was a house clinging to the steep canyon wall almost beside the horse trail above the main town. The stoping which had once kept this dwelling level was buckled and leaning precariously outward. Any canyon wind would send the whole weather-beaten structure splintering down the rocks into the ghost town below.

As we skirted the hardy house on the hill and rounded the talus pile at the mouth of a shaft opening, we could see the major part of the town, or what was left of it. This had been the cyanide mill and the center of activity of Albemarle in its heydey. Colossal iron wheels and rusted lengths of cable were everywhere. The tower of the mill was racked to one side and showed at its open seams the rough iron of its framework. Pulleys and wheels of inner workings had fallen to the rough ground, or yet hung precariously on rusting shafts.

But the firs and scrub oaks of the forest were even here be-

ginning to obliterate the rough rock piles. The man-made scar
that had been Albemarle was already almost healed over by trees
and time.

We jogged our horses up what had been the main street,
pausing occasionally to stoop from the saddle and peer into the
darkened window of some miner's cabin that still stood. The hoofs
of our mounts clinked against the litter of bottles, purpled into
"desert glass" since the times that some miner had thrown them
into the streets of Albemarle. Everywhere there was the litter
of dirty men and vanished hopes. Assay retorts and broken iron
stoves, miners' picks and broken boxes showed where forgotten
men had lived and worked.

At the upper end of this almost-vanished street we stopped
for a moment to look down into the rough pit that had formed
part of the foundation of the mill. "Look!" Cass said, pointing
past me toward the edge of the pit. "Some horse has skidded down
that bank yonder." Cass was right as usual, although wild horses
were rare in this part of the Jemez. A line of large round prints
marked the passage of a heavy animal that had walked down the
edge of the pit and into a tangle of alders below. We had ridden
only a few yards farther when we saw the tracks again, this time
in front of a tumbled wooden building that must have been a
store of some sort fifty years ago. Cass Goodner was out of the
saddle as though a hornet had stung him. There was something
suggestive about those tracks. Certainly no wild horse had made
the round imprints that led through the sagging door of that old
building. Cass grinned up at me as I slid to the ground beside him.
He parted a few sparse blades of grass with his hands so that we
could see the imprint better.

Some mountain torrent long ago had washed down the steep
canyon walls and burst through the back of this old building,
carrying a flood of sand and mud which had covered the floor
and flowed in a fan out through the old doorway where we stood.
Deep in this soft stuff was the print of a bear's paw and he was
a monster. "He'd weigh six or seven hundred pounds," Cass was
saying, as he outlined with his finger the mark of the front paw.
"And look at those claw marks out in front of the toes!" There

were indeed the marks of long, arched claws that made a deep imprint in front of each flattened toe of the monster bear.

"Cass. It's a grizzly!" I said with rising excitement as I stepped past him inside the old building.

"Can't be," he commented with little conviction. "We haven't had a grizzly in the Jemez Mountains for years." Both of us knew, however, that black bear do not show claw marks in front of their toes, and never attain this size.

As we explored the inside of the old mining building where the huge bear tracks were, Cass insisted repeatedly that it couldn't be a grizzly. I noticed, however, that he had slipped his short-barreled .30-30 from the scabbard beneath his saddle fender, and now used the gun barrel to point at the tracks, or to gesticulate in defense of his weak arguments. After my own first burst of enthusiasm, I had become dubious. Perhaps it was some super-colossal black bear who hadn't trimmed his toenails. A five hundred pound black bear in these regions is a near record. Perhaps some paragon of this species had grown prodigiously in the remote loneliness of this canyon ghost town.

While our horses grazed in the sparseness of the street, Cass and I explored the several buildings that had once been upper Albemarle. We found the tracks of the huge bear in several places. The lumbering animal had wandered aimlessly around the old mill and past and through several of the old mining shacks. Certainly there were no traces of food in these old places. The rusted tin cans of the miners had long ago been licked clean by the coyotes and bears of former years. The big bear of Albemarle seemed as interested in the town as we were. We found one place where he had torn open a rotten timber with one sweep of a mighty paw and had licked the ants and bugs from the interior. At another spot the bear had garnered several mouthfuls of lush grass that grew in a dampish corner among the fallen houses. As we found old tracks, and other marks of those tremendous feet that were more recent, it became evident that this particular bear lived here. The ghost town of Albemarle was not quite un-inhabited.

Cass Goodner and I were looking for mountain lions when

we found the inhabitant of Albemarle. With the lions we had no luck on that particular occasion. We had found a good place to come for dusky grouse and we had found some other bear sign, both of which promised good hunting when the season rolled around. On the fifteenth of September, this was the place we intended to hunt with a hound pack. We had a hunch that Albemarle canyon would reverberate again with an activity of a different sort.

In the short weeks that passed until we could ride again through the ghost town in the canyon, we talked much of the gigantic bear tracks with the claw marks. At a distance, however, and away from the bewitching atmosphere of the deserted town, the possibility seemed fantastic, and we became as incredulous as the friends to whom we told the story. But there was one firm conviction in the whole mysterious business and that was that we would revisit the ghost town of Albemarle, and that very soon.

It was with mixed feelings that we led our dog pack in the briskness of a September morning, up over the ridge out of Bland Canyon, heading for the ghost town of Albemarle. We followed an old mining road that wound precariously up the face of the cliff. Here in the solid rock the iron wagon tires of lumbering freight wagons of former years had worn grooves eight inches deep. Now the old road was overgrown and broken away in places, all but impassable even to horses.

Cass' hunting hounds were a tried and dependable lot. The lead dog, Drive, had over eighty mountain lions and bear to his credit. Sissy, a red bitch, was a veteran of many a bear chase. Pancho, a heavy-bodied Airedale, whimpered and rubbed against my leg with the expectation of excitement to come. I don't think any of us realized just what excitement that was to be.

A two-hour ride up over the divide would take us to the old ghost town where our dogs could pick up the track. We had not ridden for half an hour on that frosty morning until there was a cry ahead. Drive, the tan and white veteran, had caught a scent beneath a clump of oaks. From the tone of the long-drawn bark that the dog gave, it must be bear. Even as we listened, Sissy gave tongue, then some of the younger dogs joined in. The track was burning fresh. We urged our sweating horses in to a hacking gallop up the steep grade. The mining road which we had been following, although rutted and washed beyond any practical usefulness, served as a comparatively easy ascent of the steep canyon wall. Even with a flapping of legs and the inhuman application of the end of the bridle reins, the horses' pace seemed inadequate.

Above the roar of the dogs I could hear the labored breathing of my own animal as he sturdily breasted the slope to try to get us to the dogs in time. Pumice and fragments of lava rock rolled beneath his gouging hoofs as he lunged upward. A wicked-looking snag from a dead pine tree caught beneath the camera tripod that I had foolishly tied on the saddle at my left leg. The whole aluminum business came away with a ripping of saddle strings as the horse threw his weight against the obstacle. A piece of my leg was left behind with the tripod, forgotten and unnoticed in the excitement of the chase. With both arms before my face, I fended off the whipping branches, even as I urged my horse forward. Once again, the tip of the rifle-boot caught behind the trunk of a small pine tree as we swept past. There was a frantic clawing and kicking, as I strove to keep the scabbard from breaking away, the same as the camera tripod of a moment ago. But we swept on, enthusiastic, with certain scratches and lacerations that would have to be attended to in some calmer moment.

Cass was ahead as we topped out on the ridge above Bland Canyon. The dogs, too, sounded remote as though they had already dropped into Coya Canyon on the far side. Cass was sitting his heaving horse on the rim of the canyon, looking down at some sprays of fresh dirt on the ground below him. I trotted my horse alongside, at the same time pulling my equipment together and taking stock of wounds and casualties.

"It's a black bear. He was down to water this morning at Bland Creek, and we must have bumped right into him. Listen to that," and Cass cocked his head to one side, like a pheasant looking at a hawk.

The roaring cry of the dogs had taken on an insistent note.

THE GRIZZLY BEAR

I could distinguish in the melange of sound, the voice of old Drive, barking in a series of ecstatic yelps. The dogs were looking up at the bear. The beast had climbed a tree. There was little cause for hurry. The lip of the canyon gave way to a gently drooping swale of lush grass, aspens and large oak trees. As we rode more slowly, we looked around us and saw that the oaks had been freshly torn and broken, as though by a high wind. A few yards farther, the devastation increased. Whole trees, the size of a man's leg, had been bent and splintered to the ground. Limbs and twigs dangled by threads of bark, or were scattered underneath, completely broken away. Most of the leaves of these broken oaks were hardly wilted, though the night had been frosty. This was fresh work, and the devastation had been caused by no wind or hail of any angry nature. We did not need to look at the bear sign which was everywhere beneath the oaks, to tell who were the authors of this impressive business. Acorns had been scarce in the Jemez that year and it looked as though every bear in the whole mountain range had been feeding on Bland ridge. With their heavy bodies, the rascals had ridden down the oak trees to crop the luscious acorns from the tree tips in a way that we had seen before. These bears were laying up fat for their winter's hibernation, and there must have been a dozen or so of them, judging from the destruction. Cass and I remarked to each other on each particularly large tree that was broken, or place where some feeding bruin had sat among the branches and broken off all within reach. But these were the signs where bears had been, although recently. Our dogs called insistently to us of a place where a bear was, and right at the moment.

We could see the bear now, several limbs up in a big Douglas fir. The beast was as black as the ace of spades, and of no great size. It looked like a female as we rode beneath the tree, and she panted and looked down at us with her little eyes. A red tongue flicked out and licked a brown-colored muzzle in a questioning manner. We had a bear, and in the excitement of the moment we forgot that we had been heading for the Albemarle Canyon beyond.

At this bear tree the story was the same as many times before.

236

A few pictures first, then the crack of a single rifle shot echoed in the morning stillness from the canyon walls. The black bear slumped, head first, down and out of the tree and hit limply among the snarling dogs. It was just a quarter to eight when Cass and I shook hands across the black carcass of the first victim.

With the bear draped across the saddle, we started down the mining road back into Bland Canyon and our camp. As we walked, we talked. "Do you know anybody that wants to catch a quick bear?" Cass was saying. "I'll bet there's a dozen of them up there in that oak patch. Drive could catch one an hour in those acorns."

"I sure do," I replied. "Bill Burk, my architect friend, is crazy to get a bear. Say," I said with sudden inspiration, "there's a Forest Service telephone at Bland. I can call him and get him out here before noon." Of such sudden whims are later regrets born.

The mining town of Bland was a ghost town too, but the venerable postmaster of the place had stayed on these many years to act as a caretaker. Mr. Arnold and his gracious wife yet keep alive the hopes and traditions of this once-busy mining camp. Their link with an outside world that had all but forgotten the once-wealthy Bland strike, is the thin telephone wire that swings from tree to tree down the Bland Canyon road. Over this same wire that morning went my enthusiastic greeting to Bill Burk. "Get in your jeep and get up here quick. We have a bear, guaranteed and all tied up."

Cass and I breakfasted again at about the same time that most people in town were just getting up and going about their business task. We already had one black bear stretched by the heels in the shed across from the Arnold's house.

My friend Burk arrived just before noon, which was a tribute to the enthusiasm of my call, and we started out immediately. Bill had brought a friend, a fellow from the East who had never hunted a bear and had never been in a chase of any sort. It promised to be high excitement for both of them. Inasmuch as we were short of horses, the two newcomers rode their jeep up the side of the canyon, following the old mining road. It is a compli-

237

ment to the designers of this vehicle that the grinding mechanism never paused once in the ascent. Cass and I on our horses were hard put to it to keep up with the jeep and reach the oak grove, where the bears were feeding, at the same time.

I was just suffering my first misgivings of over-enthusiasm when the dogs opened up in the oak brush at the side of the overgrown road. Again there was the barking of hound voices as they circled for the track. Then a concerted chorus of barks and yelps burst out as they found it together and started off through the trees. We were on a chase again and this track was as hot as the last one.

It was an actual advantage to be on foot among those awful oaks. They leaned at all angles from the ground with unresisting stems. The ironlike twigs interlaced in a pattern which seemed to refuse admittance to man or horse. It was sheer punishment to gallop through that awful stuff. The dogs running underneath or a man crouching low could get through the oaks as easily as a bear. Cass and I fell far behind.

This animal ran in the opposite direction to our previous bear and suddenly the noise of the dogs ahead died away as the chase dropped over the edge of a rocky rim into Coya Canyon. But this bruin had laid up too much of his winter's fat already. The chase was short and furious. As the dogs dropped down the slopes of Coya Canyon, the bear was in sight and they closed on the fleeing animal rapidly. When we slipped from our saddles to look down that slope, the chase was done. Even at that distance we could see the dark form of the bear in a large tree that jutted from a rock slide. The bear dogs danced excitedly beneath, and their howls and yelps reverberated up to us from the volcanic pinnacles that rose from the slope. Cass grinned at Bill Burk in an offhandish manner and he didn't really need to add: "There's your bear."

The four of us slipped and slid together down the almost-straight slope toward the tree below. Bill kept his rifle ready in case the bear should jump and run. But the animal sat quiescent, close to the bole of the tree, and dripped saliva from distended jaws. This was a brownish-colored bear, with a wash of yellow across the shoulders, a really beautiful skin. But this animal was no monster. I doubt if the yellow bear weighed three hundred pounds, although it was full grown. Even at the crack of Bill's long-barreled rifle, I thought of the big bear of Albemarle ghost town—the real one we had come to get. From where we held ourselves with difficulty on the steep slope, I could see the mouth of Albemarle Canyon and almost imagine in the hazy distance that I also could make out some of the weathered buildings of the old town. But the yellow bear of Bill Burk tumbled limp and lifeless almost at my feet and for the next few minutes there was excited talk and the cleaning of the animal to offer distractions. At one-thirty of that memorable day, we had already carried the yellow bear to the bottom of the canyon and Cass had gone for the horses to bring it in.

I walked ahead on foot and our lead dog, Drive, snuffled the bushes in a satisfied manner a few yards to one side. All the other dogs had gone back with Cass to the horses on the top of the ridge. Two bears in one day wasn't a record, but it would do. Bill Burk's eastern friend accompanied me but he walked over the rough ground on the side of the canyon with considerable difficulty. I glanced at the man a time or two with curiosity. He was a well-built fellow with the shoulders of a fullback and the legs of a soccer player. But the breath whistled through his distended lips with an asthmatic vibration. His cheeks were flabby and were an unhealthy fish-belly color. We had not had much of a chase after the yellow bear. Perhaps it was the excitement that made the man's eyes so dull-looking. I motioned to him to keep up and slowed my own pace even more. It would not do to lose this stranger in these rough canyons.

After Cass and Bill had lugged the beautiful yellow bear back to the jeep, Cass was to rejoin me with the horses to follow out our original plan. Meanwhile the easterner and I would drop down the slope of Coya Canyon and head for the ghost town of Albemarle on foot. We didn't get far.

Drive, my canine friend, displayed the same self-satisfied air as myself. He circled lazily through the sparse vegetation on the slope as we dropped down into Coya Canyon. He momentarily pricked up his drooping ears as a herd of big, gray mule deer bounded off among the frostbitten oaks with a crashing of dead limbs. Suddenly Drive thrust his nose into the air and waved it against the gentle breeze that came up the canyon wall. When this veteran of a hundred hunts handled his nostrils in that manner it meant game. Usually when a hunting dog smells the wind it means he has scented a kill. On a dozen previous occasions Drive had led us in this way to the mangled carcass of a deer that some mountain lion had killed and carefully covered up. Sometimes a less reliable dog will smell in this manner the hot body scent of venison as a trembling doe crouches close in the brush upwind. Could Drive be scenting the forbidden smell of the deer we had just seen? This valuable dog had been deer-broken since the time he was a puppy, but I would keep close to the old rascal just the same. I turned once and flailed my arm to get my eastern friend up abreast of me in case we had to turn quickly in a new direction. Drive was trotting ahead with his nose still in the air as though that sensitive organ were leading him on an invisible string directly to the origin of some exciting smell. The old hound's tail had stiffened in an upward curve and he had the attitude of a dog pointing at something which he could not see. Unconsciously I broke into a trot and then a dead run over the rough ground. But without effort, Drive pulled ahead and disappeared in the mountain mahogany brush of a small ravine on the side of the canyon.

I stopped for a moment panting, and looked around for my eastern friend. Cass would never forgive me if I lost this new addition to our hunting party. His name was Talbot and he seemed to be sickly to say the least. Turning, I retraced my steps to the point of a small rise. There was Talbot, across the slope below me, practically where I had seen him last, and he was sitting down. I cupped my hands for a mighty shout that would echo on those eastern ears like a clap of New Jersey thunder. But the noise never came. Even as I filled my lungs for an angry bellow, there was another noise instead. It was a snarl and a bark all blended together. The savageness of the noise whirled me half around. Drive had attacked something in that brushy ravine. Or something had attacked him. There was a furious swirl of vicious sound.

I thought even at that distance I could distinguish the mouthed growls of some other animal. The yelps and shrieks of Drive seemed smothered as though his mouth were full of hostile fur. Whatever Drive had found, it was not dead meat.

I waved a rifle in a wide arc toward my fellow hunter on the rock below. He had half-started up and was staring at me stupidly like a bewildered owl. I yelled with all the force I could muster, the two words "Keep up!"; then whirled to join the excitement in the little ravine. The noise of the fighting was moving upward but was still hidden from view. If only I had a horse, even on that steep slope I might have gotten there in time. The human legs are dreadfully inadequate organs of locomotion in times of crisis. I galloped through the heavy brush, clawing at the restricting branches with rifle and gloved hand. By sheer weight and desperation I forced my way through the thickets and down the slope toward the roar of sound of the battling animals. But it was no use. The noise moved away and above me.

As I stopped for a second to spit out some broken twigs and gulp in a lungful of unadulterated air, I could hear Drive's bark above me. It was a long rolling howl of a hound hot on the trail. Whatever the dog's antagonist was, it was running now and Drive was close behind. If I was ever to be in any part of this chase I would have to mount that awful slope and fast. But my eastern friend—there was the insistent barking of Drive on the hot track, and yet my responsibility clearly called me in another direction. "Why wouldn't the damned dude keep up?" I muttered, unreasoning, to myself. I milled around with two or three half turns of indecision. After all, if we did catch another bear, this was the guy who was supposed to shoot it. I had already killed one. "Well," I commented again to myself in a moment of sad decision, "I'll have to get the guy up here, even if I must carry him."

It was only a few hundred yards back to where I found him, but every one was a yard in the wrong direction. The poor fellow was panting like a bereaved porpoise and was holding both hands over his heart. For the first time I had a touch of apprehension. "Something wrong?" I asked.

"No, going fine," he wheezed. He had spunk, that one. I looked back up the slope toward the now-faint sound of Drive's insistent barking. I had at the same time a rare inspiration.

"Do you see that ridge over there, Talbot?" I asked, pointing toward a spur which descended the canyon perhaps a mile distant. "The main trail into Albemarle goes down that ridge. GET ON THAT TRAIL. Cass is coming down there with the horses. Meet him, then find me. I'll see what Drive is after."

The poor fellow said, "Glug," or something else unintelligible which I did not stop to hear. I was already slanting toward those very distant dog sounds.

About halfway up, I crossed the trail of Drive and his adversary. The prints in the rock and dirt looked like those of a horse or of an animal just as heavy. Could it be? I thought to myself. And yet we were three or four miles from Albemarle. But those prints—it must be just another black bear. The country was crawling with them. But no! There were the claw marks out ahead of the toes. The outlines of the pads of those mighty feet told of a body far larger than that of any black bear that the Jemez supports. My heart was already pounding from the climb, but there was a sudden thrill and exhilaration. Drive had jumped the monarch of Albemarle Canyon. That wily hound must have smelled the bear as he passed unseeing in the brush. But Drive was alone. "That grizzly will kill him," I said aloud, although there was no one to hear. I started up the slope again with redoubled energy. I had a fleeting thought, too, that I would probably die from an enlarged heart at some time in the future, but I would certainly have some excitement before I did.

The side of Coya Canyon was rugged as any in this wild country. Patches of oak brush and mountain mahogany gave way to higher slopes so steep that there was no vegetation on them at all. I thought, too, as I clawed my way over one of these treacherous stretches, of what Cass has often said: "It all looks level to a bear." I passed patches of slide rock and worked my way up through clefts in sheer ledges and cliffs. Still the chase was above me. We climbed for half an hour, I think, although in the excitement I had scarcely noticed the passage of minutes.

The fleeing bear above had apparently come to the foot of one of those vertical lava cliffs that make the walls of these canyons straight-sided and impossible in places. It was not that this venerable bear was lost or confused. He seemed to know every gully, every crack in these interlaced canyons. But now he began to slant along the foot of the cliff and actually drop down toward the head of the canyon.

In a few more minutes I was parallel with the sound of Drive's barking and then by climbing on a jutting spur of rock at the foot of the lava escarpment, I was actually above the noise. I pulled myself to the edge of this precarious perch by grasping a gnarled pinyon tree that grew in a crack in the rock. As I raised my head level with the top, there was a burst of noise from the far side. Drive was fighting the bear again. The beast had come to bay. I squirmed quickly through the resinous branches of the pinyon and stuck my head over the edge of the lava spur. There they were, some two or three hundred yards from me, and slightly below. I could pick out easily the brown-and-white spotted body of Drive as he circled and darted at his antagonist.

In an almost level spot at the foot of the cliff was a gnarled fir, one of those mighty trees that had found a pocket of rich volcanic soil in that austere place. Backed against the bole of this tree, and as dark as the bark itself, was a bear. Even at that distance I was struck by his size and ferocity, by the mighty sweeps of his paws as he lunged at the dancing dog before him. I could catch the flash of red from his jaws as he surged forward to try to sweep the wary hound into the arc of those gleaming teeth.

Each time, as the dog snarled and jumped backward, the bear would rear again with his back against the tree trunk, swinging his mighty paws in front of him as though daring Drive to come within reach of those hooked claws. Fortunately our lead dog was imbued with a caution which is not always common in his kind. The hound leaped in with lightning swiftness to snap within inches of the soft belly of the bear at bay. As quickly he jumped away each time as the swinging sledge hammers of the bear's paws swept down from above. Drive leaped to the right and left, trying to come in behind the bear's quarter, behind the swinging of

those awful forepaws and their death-dealing blows. As the bear turned to meet these onslaughts from the side and back, he dropped to all fours for a moment, and bit savagely at the dog that sought to close with him.

I could see then that the sides of this monster were streaked with gray that showed slightly against the dark bark of the tree behind. The animal had a hump over his shoulders where the gray color showed the lightest, and the nose and snout of the bear were long and tapering. "It's a grizzly!" I said aloud, slapping my knee. "It's a grizzly!" as though there had been some doubt about it before. I raised the rifle and even half-pulled back the hammer. When the monster bear again reared up against the bole of the tree I could hit him in the chest. But wait! The easterner Talbot was to shoot this bear, and besides at that distance with a short saddle gun, I might hit Drive, just at the time when he leaped in at the bear's middle.

The easterner! For a moment I had forgotten. I looked back for the first time since I had left my friend. "Frank—Frank" drifted to me faintly from the depths of the canyon. It was Cass with the horses. Good! I thrilled to the anticipation of showing Cass this grizzly bear at bay.

"Cass! Up here! Bear! Bring more dogs!"

I heard in answer the exultant whoop below that meant that Cass had understood. I turned to watch the grizzly again. He was gone. There was only the dark trunk of a giant fir that jutted from the slope at the foot of the cliff

Moments later I had a glimpse of the grizzly and the white dot that was Drive, close behind. The dark form of the bear was rounding the ridges and gullies, and appearing and disappearing among the brush in the direction of the head of the canyon. We were going to lose him. Again I turned to bawl in the direction of the trail: "Cass, for God's sake hurry! Cass" I screamed again. "Yeah!" he called, his voice now much nearer. I slid with reckless abandon off the side of the pinnacle on which I had been perched. To one side of this towering monument was a rock slide of that same loose and treacherous stuff that we usually avoided. Down this declivity I climbed recklessly toward the form of Cass and the several horses below. He undoubtedly thought I had a bad case of mountain madness or something equally serious. The horses started and reared as I slid toward them in a shower of rocks. "Whoa! Hold on there!" Cass growled. Then turning to me: "You've got a bear treed, so what?" He clipped the words off in a most abrupt manner.

"Yeah, we got a bear, but we haven't got him," I explained descriptively in my most lucid manner. "It's a grizzly, Cass! A great big gray grizzly with a black belly! It's the same one we saw the track of!" At the word "grizzly" Cass' eyes gleamed as though the canyon wind had fanned a fire within them. Then he too thought of the inevitable. "Where's Talbot?"

"He's on the Albemarle trail." Cass slipped off his horse and flipped the reins in my face. "Take these horses and get Talbot. I'll get the rest of the dogs up to help Drive." And then as an afterthought he added: "Bring the horses along the Albemarle ridge. I'll meet you someplace there," and then he was gone, running along the canyon slope urging the other hounds ahead of him.

I mounted one of the horses slowly, cursing my luck as I did so. As an afterthought I turned and yelled after Cass: "If you get to him again, you'd better shoot him." I then turned to the uninspiring task of working the horses back along the lower slopes of the canyon to Albemarle trail.

My eastern friend was, as usual, sitting down when I found him. My explanations were short and to the point. "Get on a horse," I said, flinging the reins at him. "We've got a grizzly chase up the canyon, and you're supposed to shoot the bear." I must not have sounded particularly inviting, but the word "grizzly" seemed to infuse the breath of life even into this would-be hunter. Now that we were mounted, my only thought was to get back in the chase again. If we could work our way back toward the head of Coya Canyon we might yet be in on the excitement. I had hit upon the brilliant plan of putting Talbot on his horse ahead of me and leading Cass' horse behind. In this way I could drag one and drive the other.

246

The bottom of Coya Canyon was not a race track. As a matter of fact, along this awesome stretch, a sober man would walk and lead a horse, or better yet, not take a horse at all. But we trotted in places and urged our reluctant horses to a fast walk in others. We splashed through pools of water surrounded by impenetrable clumps of willows. We pranced and lunged over jumbled piles of boulders where any slight mischance would mean a broken horse's leg and a nasty fall. But on we went. Talbot hung low to one side of the saddle, and I have no doubt he prayed. It was a terrifying ride, but I soon could hear the sound of dogs barking up the canyon.

I paused for a moment where the canyon made a bend. Talbot's horse ahead stopped automatically when the urging from behind ceased. The muscles on the haunches of the poor animal quivered and jerked from the exertion. The roar of the dogs was quite close. I could distinguish the high insistent yap of the female, Sissy. There was the harsh bark of the Airedale, Pancho, and others in the hound chorus. Drive had help. By the noise, the chase had turned back from the head of Coya Canyon and had crossed to the ridge toward Albemarle. We might yet be in time.

I abandoned Cass' horse which had hampered my efforts, and concentrated on whipping the other horse ahead of me to a greater burst of speed. I turned the two animals up a rocky spur toward Albemarle ridge. By circling and lunging around the basaltic columns that jutted from this slope, we could work our way upward. These horses were made of stern stuff or they could have taken little of this punishment. In ten minutes, foam-flecked and with the sides of the animals heaving between our legs, we were high on the Albemarle slope amidst a riot of rocks, rock slides and scattered trees. I slipped off my mount to stand a few yards away so that his labored breathing would not deaden my attempts to hear. The sound of the dogs was remarkably close. They were barking wildly in a clump of trees in a rincon on the side of the slope. I ran to the horse and jerked the rifle from the scabbard. "Come on!" I yelled, looking at my companion for the first time in several minutes. He was hanging from the saddle like a bag of wet mush. I helped him to the ground where he lay flat, white as a sheet. I shrugged my shoulders and ran toward the sound of the fighting dogs.

There was a riot of noise, the yaps and yelps of a hound pack fighting an animal on the ground. I knew that animal; I had seen that gray-sided monster not so long ago.

The ground was rough and my legs were shaking from the exertion in the saddle. I stumbled once and tore open my knee on a wicked fragment of lava. I brushed the triangular piece of flesh back into place with my hand and went on. I could hear the high-pitched voice of Cass among the dogs, shouting encouragement. The welter of sound rose to a crescendo and by the mouthed noises, I could tell that some of the dogs at least, had their teeth full of grizzly meat and fur. Even before I could see the bear, I could imagine the downward flail of those awful paws, ripping among the unwary dogs. There were young hounds in that pack, unaccustomed to the deadly action of an enraged bear. There would be dog blood as well as grizzly blood on this mountainside.

I struggled through some intervening bushes and among the small trees where the fight was taking place. I could see the bear's head now. It was a gigantic head with pinpoint eyes of fiery red, and a mouth that flashed open and shut with a snap of jaws that I could hear plainly many yards away. I could see, too, the top of Cass' hat as he darted among the dogs. His head reached no higher on the bear than in the middle of that mighty chest as the animal stood erect. I clawed at the bushes that barred my way, with no thought of the pain in my knee; that would come later. I raised my head to look again and a form hurtled end over end out of the welter of sounds and shapes ahead. It was a dog that crashed into the brush at one side; a dog's body that had been as lightly tossed through the air as though it were a leaf on some wilful air current.

I broke through the last mountain mahogany brush to a small hollow on the canyon slope where the bear had come to bay again against the trunk of a tree. I could see the white form of Drive, dancing as before under the arcs of the grizzly's striking paws.

248

One of the younger dogs was stretched on the dirt in front, apparently lifeless. Pancho, the faithful Airedale, had disappeared. As I rushed up breathless, Cass closed in for the coup de grace. He pulled the dogs aside and yelled loudly at Drive who was leaping in the face of the bear. He thrust his short-barreled rifle almost within reach of the long curved claws that struck from both sides so desperately. If the grizzly lunged forward he would gather Cass in and bite his head to a bloody pulp as he had the hound on the ground.

The rifle seemed to recoil against Cass' shoulder and I waited for the report, but there was none. Cass pumped frantically at the lever action and raised the rifle again. Again nothing happened. There was only the mouthed growls of the grizzly. Cass jerked open the lever again and an unused shell arched out and fell in the leaves beside the bleeding hound. I rushed forward, extending my own rifle toward him. But it was enough. The huge grizzly, seeing two humans closing in with the dogs around them, dropped to one side. With a final sweep of his paw at Drive, he was off among the trees and rocks as swiftly as before. I half-raised the the gun in a futile effort for a fleeing shot past the bounding dogs and Cass himself.

Cass threw his useless rifle in the dirt and picked up the form of the limp hound. "Get Pancho," he barked at me, jerking his thumb toward the bushes at one side. Sure enough, there was the faithful Pancho, the veteran of a dozen fights such as this. The dog lay still, with his tongue out in the dirt, and a trickle of blood over his white teeth. I carefully brought him back and laid him with the other casualty. Pancho had a broad brass collar, heavy with pointed studs, such as bulldogs wear. This brass was crushed in a flattened oval around the dog's neck, as though it had been pounded in this position with a hammer.

"Cass! Pancho's still breathing," I said quickly as I knelt over the dog's limp form. "Help me fix this collar." There were deep indentations where the bear's teeth had closed upon the metal. Between the two of us we pulled the major part of the crimp out of Pancho's collar. Even as we did so, the dog sucked in gulps of air and his eyes flickered open. His bloody lips rolled back into a snarl, and I thought for a moment he was going to bite our hands. Then he recognized us and his warm tongue licked out over his blood-stained teeth. The other hound, too, was living, and apparently only stunned by a chance sweep of the bear's paw. A direct blow would have broken every bone in this foolish dog's body.

We looked to Cass' rifle. A bullet at some time past had been torn from the shell casing and lodged in the chamber. A new shell pumped into the breach hit this obstacle and would not seat completely. If a shell had been fired in the weapon, the rifle undoubtedly would have blown up and there would have been more than wounded dogs on the canyon slope.

Cass had recovered himself somewhat. Whenever anything happened to his dogs, it hurt him as much as though it had happened to himself. With one good rifle, we encouraged the remaining hounds to follow. Sissy and Drive were already ahead. In a few moments even Pancho had recovered enough from his near strangulation to join the others. It was but a short distance to the top of the ridge. The grizzly with the dogs pursuing had already topped over.

In a few minutes more a battered and bloody crew of men and dogs stood on the ridge above Albemarle. Drive and Sissy were already below us. The bear was heading for the old mining town in the canyon. As we stood on the rim of the ridge, we caught a momentary glimpse of a comical drama below. The gray form of the grizzly was lumbering down the ridge, at the edge of the outermost buildings of the ghost town. Drive was walking parallel with the bear, a few yards to one side. Both of them were apparently so exhausted that they had declared an enforced truce for the moment, and from that distance it looked as though they were strolling along side by side and the best of friends. Only the long-drawn bark of the faithful hound gave evidence that it was still a case of the hunter and the hunted.

As the hulking form of the gray grizzly disappeared far below among the tumbled ruins of Albemarle, we knew he had reached his home. Would he come to bay again among these ruins? Sissy was at this time far behind in the chase and Drive was again single-handed in the pursuit of the monster. Could we hope to win? I turned to Cass for a decision.

"You'd better go get him," he said, jerking his head backward.

I felt a sudden wave of dejection and fatigue pass over me. If I went back now, I was definitely out of the chase. "You'd better drop back and bring him around by the trail," Cass was saying. "You'll never get the horses over this ridge."

"And you?" I asked, as I looked in the direction of the ghost town.

"I'm going to get that bear." Cass said this with fierce determination, but he didn't say when. Cass just started down the slope with giant strides along the tracks that the grizzly had taken into the town of Albemarle.

That night, about eleven o'clock, I found Cass seven or eight miles on the other side of Albemarle on a lonely ridge. It was a wonder I found him at all, for his voice was weak and he could scarcely talk above a whisper. I had left Talbot far behind by a fire and told him to stay there. Leading Cass' horse I had gone up through the town of Albemarle and had searched the evening and most of the night for a trace of the combatants. Never again on that momentous day did I hear a dog bark. As it grew late I lighted a fire on a high point. It was to this that Cass came, exhausted and almost speechless. The dogs with him were beaten warriors, scarred, tired and voiceless. "We lost him in Peralta Canyon," Cass croaked between his parched lips. "He just kept running and fighting, running and fighting." His voice trailed off to a whisper. I have never seen a man so exhausted.

"Well, Cass, we've got something," I reminded him in a pleasant tone. "We have an eastern fellow sitting back there waiting for us."

Cass raised himself on one elbow by the fire, as though he didn't hear. "I'm going to give up bear hunting or any kind of dog hunting," he said with fierce finality. "But," and he emphasized each word with his cracked voice, "I'm going to catch that grizzly first."

33

ARIZONA GRIZZLIES
Gaston Burridge

In early days grizzlies were common in eastern Arizona's White Mountains and along the upper branches of the Blue River in that same area. Although there are occasional reports of individuals having seen the big bears in the state, none of these reports have been verified for many years. In 1936 a grizzly was reported killed, but Gaston Burridge concluded that it was "a light-colored brown bear." Burridge spent considerable time and effort in trying to learn who killed the last of the Arizona grizzlies, but with inconclusive results. He says it may have been Ben Lilly, but he isn't sure of that. Burridge started from California in 1928 to visit the legendary hunter, but when he was caught in a cloudburst and had to turn back he lost his last opportunity to rendezvous with Lilly before the old hunter's death. So he failed to hear, firsthand, the story of Ben Lilly's last bear hunt in Arizona—which may have been the end of the Arizona grizzly.

The following anecdotal article, which appeared in *Arizona Highways*,[1] contains some interesting data on southwest bears and the reminiscences of several old-timers who can still remember Arizona's grizzly-bear days. It is reprinted here with the kind permission of the author.

SHOULD YOU HOPE to find a grizzly bear—wild and self-fed, that is—in Arizona today, your chances of doing it are about the same as meeting a four-armed bandit on the same range. There have been rumors of a few—but so far, they are only rumors. If you go hunting for grizzly bear *stories* in Arizona, you will have good hunting and fine results. There are many of those. Arizona had many grizzlies once upon a time.

[1] Vol. XXX, No. 6 (June, 1954), 12–13.

The best grizzly story I have heard—so far—was told to me by David Dickinson, Cottonwood, Sedona and Verde Valley's able and charming entrepreneur.

According to Dickinson, in the early days of Oak Creek Canyon, before there was an automobile road through that beautifully sculptured gorge, there lived in its upper reaches an old hunter named Kip Whaley. What money Kip needed for flour, sugar and coffee, he earned by hunting grizzly bears, and selling their hides in Flagstaff. Kip grew to be pretty good and built himself a reputation as a bear hunter.

One summer, a couple of "schoolmarms" from "down east" came out to Flag, the better to get acquainted with the west. They hired a local cowboy, at the moment foot-loose, to guide them about the country. The cowboy thought of Oak Creek as a good place to show off his region to best advantage, so guided his two patrons into its beauties. He was pleased at their "Oh's and Ah's!"

Once on the canyon floor they soon came to Whaley's ranch. As sometime luck will have it, Whaley was home. Kip made his appearance at the sound of the horses' hoofs—looking much like a grizzly bear himself.

Said the cowboy, "Ladies, I'd be proud to have ya meet up with Kip Whaley, the best dog-gone grizzly bear hunter in these-here parts."

"Oh," exclaimed one of the schoolmarms, "How thrilling. A real grizzly bear hunter! Mr. Whaley, won't you tell us of some of your narrow escapes?"

Whaley shifted his tobacco cud to the other cheek, ran his red tongue around his lips, looked up at the teacher and replied, "Hell, lady, I ain't never had no narrie escapes—but some a them grizzlies hev!"

Arizona had two species of grizzlies—*Ursus Horribilis Imperator,* the more common, often known as "Silver Tip," and *Ursus Horribilis Horriaeus,* or desert grizzly—sometimes called the Sonoran grizzly.

The desert grizzly was a little smaller, his skull a little higher at the eyes. He was often lighter in color and apt to be sunburned or bleached atop the back and head. Either one was plenty of bear in a fight!

As his Latin name, *Horribilis,* indicates, the grizzly was a horrible bear. Especially when roused. Stewart Edward White says, "When roused, the grizzly is the most dangerous animal in all North America." Always sly and crafty, the grizzly was also extremely fast on his feet for so big an animal. So fast, in fact, that a hunter had little chance to run away from him.

Unlike the American black bear, the grizzly was too heavy to climb trees very far—so, given enough time, a man could shinny up a tree and be safe.

The average male grizzly weighed about 600 pounds, but the White Mountains occasionally grew some to 800 pounds and two in Arizona have been estimated at 1000 pounds—which is *some* bear in anybody's language, in anybody's country!

Hugh O. Cassidy, Forester for the Apache National Forest for nearly 40 years, wrote this remembered incident.

It was in the Autumn of 1920. He said he had ridden into a sheep camp over near Baldy Peak, where he found the Mexican herder in a state of extreme excitement. This old Latin told Cassidy he had a mare and her colt running loose on the cienega in front of his camp and upon returning there from the sheep herd found a big grizzly near by trying to catch the colt. The shepherd said he charged this big grizzly on horseback, but the bear just stood up on its hind legs, waved its arms and looked fierce. "Then," said the Mexican, "I left! The mare and colt left, and I guess the bear left too."

Some days later Cassidy was again passing this sheep camp. There was a huge grizzly hide nailed to dry on the wall of the old log cabin. The Mexican herder had obtained a rifle from somewhere and killed the bear.

What did the Arizona grizzly eat? Well, they ate almost everything. Their diet included grass, roots, grubs, berries, nuts, insects, snakes, fish, frogs, bird's eggs, small and large animals, from mice to full-grown cattle—and, yes, carrion. Food the grizzly could not finish off immediately, he cached for three or four days by rooting up dirt and debris along its sides. Thus, he put his brand on it and woe to anyone, or anything, caught molesting it. He'd best be most fleet of foot!

A grizzly would range from 20 to 25 miles looking for food. If it were hard to come by, some experts say he would go as far as 60 miles. This bear liked the high, rolling uplands interspersed with rocky ridges densely thicketed. Their range was naturally at a higher altitude than the American black bear's, but often they dropped down into the black's natural range for food.

In picturesque Luna Valley, a little over the Arizona–New Mexico boundary in New Mexico, lives Vain G. Snyder. He hunted with the famed Ben Lilly many times. In fact, he was sort of Lilly's camp boss for a while. Mr. Snyder told me of some of Lilly's observations regarding grizzlies.

Lilly said the grizzly was king of the mountains—or anywhere else he chose to be. He said he never saw a grown grizzly of either sex turn off-trail for a mountain lion—no matter how large the lion —nor had he ever found tracks of a grown grizzly that had. He had found tracks where the lion had off-trailed for the grizzly— where the grizzly had actually taken the food right out of the lion's mouth! It was Lilly's opinion, also, that no grown Sonoran grizzly ever off-trailed for a jaguar—at least he'd never seen any tracks to indicate such.

The grizzly took what he wanted, when he wanted it, and asked no questions nor gave explanations. He gave no proof of ownership except his brute strength. That was sufficient. Only man's high-powered rifle gave him pause.

But wait a minute. Perhaps we are going a little fast right here. Yes, there was an animal for whom the grizzly would off-trail, and quick! That animal was the skunk—incense burner of the forest. Mr. Skunk went unchallenged—unmolested—by the grizzly.

Tracks show that the bear would make a wide detour around the skunk if possible. If not possible, the grizzly would get off the trail as fast as he could and lie down—pretend to be playing with something or tagging the low-hanging branches or leaves. Nobody believes he thought he was fooling the skunk much— much less the skunk.

And in this connection we find one of those strange circumstances of Nature. The mountain lion will off-trail for a grizzly. The grizzly will off-trail for the skunk. But the mountain lion

255

won't off-trail for the skunk. The mountain lion eats the skunk!....

No doubt you have often heard—perhaps seen in print—that a grizzly bear "hugged" his victim to death. Those who have watched them closely say the grizzly does *not* hug—but "slaps." Either way, the results are unpleasant.

In early times the grizzly bear's hide never had a very important place in the fur trade. A skin used to bring only five dollars! The Indians used them, among other things, as doors for their tepees. In 1920 a grizzly hide brought only $150. I wonder what such a hide, bagged in Arizona, would bring today?

Did men ever eat grizzly meat? Any sort of bear meat is supposed to be good to eat—if properly cooked. I guess most folks never have had any that was "properly cooked" then, for I have found no one who cares for it. No doubt, how hungry a person is makes some difference. One old grizzly hunter named Dave Brown knew what he thought about it. He said, "B'ar meat is the bestus in all the mountains. B'ar skins makes the bestus beds and thar grease, the bestus butter. Biscuits shortened with b'ar grease goes as fur as beans. Why, a man kin walk all day on one o' them thar kind o' biscuits!"

Little is known about the love life of the grizzly bear. They mate in midsummer, their cubs are born in hibernation, or, in Arizona and other warm winter climates, when the bears are not active. The Arizona grizzlies hibernated each winter but their sleep was not like that of their colder-climated cousins. Ben Lilly tells about one grizzly he watched all one winter up high on the side of Escudilla Peak, above Alpine. He said this bear made twelve trips in and out of its cave during its lay-up. He noted the bear drank while outside but took on no solid food.

Of course, there had to be a *last* grizzly bear killed in Arizona, but to find where that last one was killed, who killed it and when, has developed to be a task of no mean proportions. There is no *proof!* The *best* evidence is contradicted by other *good* evidence. There are even some who say there still are grizzlies in those fastnesses of Sycamore Canyon and the Apache Reservation parts of the White Mountains! A great array of excellent authorities, whose experience and training should carry much weight, say they do not believe there are any grizzlies left in Arizona—nor have there been for many, many years.

Arizona is a big state. It is full of wonders. It is full of remote areas where man's civilization has spread mighty thin. Arizona could have another wonder—a wonder it does not know it has— the wonder of a live, free, grizzly bear living within its borders. It could have a four-armed bandit, too!

LOS OSOS MEXICANOS

34

THE BEN LILLY LEGEND
J. Frank Dobie

J. Frank Dobie performed an inestimable service to the Southwest
and its inhabitants, present and future, by his diligent recording
of the folklore and legends of the country. The titles of his many
books reflect the customs and characteristics, the ideals and idio-
syncracies, the prattle and pranks of the men and women who
struggled to civilize the uncompromising deserts and mountains
of Texas, New Mexico, Coahuila, Chihuahua, and Sonora. In
his writing Dobie set down the living words of simple people and
the precise details of their everyday lives. His passing in 1964
marked the end of a literary and teaching career which made J.
Frank Dobie's name a household word among Southwesterners
and well known and respected everywhere.

Mention bear hunters in New Mexico, and old Ben Lilly is
instantly proclaimed the greatest. The following .passage, an
excellent portrayal of this now legendary hunter, is from *The
Ben Lilly Legend* (pages 110–16), by J. Frank Dobie, by permission of Little, Brown and Company, who published the book
in 1950. Copyright 1950, by The Curtis Publishing Company,
Copyright 1950, by J. Frank Dobie.

BEN LILLY WENT WEST TO the Texas border. He crossed the Rio
Grande at Eagle Pass, in July, 1908, and did not stop until he
was in the Santa Rosa Mountains of northern Coahuila. Bears were
thick in the "Santy Roses," as he called them, and for a few months
he killed venison for a mining camp. He sold jerked venison to a
Mexican store in Múzquiz, from which he also shipped hides. Here
Ernest F. Black, manager of the Mariposa Ranch, met him and
invited him to come to his range and hunt.

They rode out to the Mariposa together, and when they got

261

to the gate from which headquarters could be seen, about two miles away, Ben Lilly exclaimed, "You didn't tell me you had your womenfolks there."

"How do you know they are there?" Black asked.

"It takes womenfolks to grow flowers and vines."

He established camp at a spring, but occasionally ate at the house, and the "womenfolks" thought he smelled mighty "strong." He prepared hides and skulls to ship to the Smithsonian Institute at Washington. He killed so many deer that Manager Black saw that he would not have any left if the hunter remained much longer. He prepared to move on, northwest. He had acquired an old pack mare on which were packed his traps, corn meal and a bucket of wild honey. She took fright at a concrete water tank at Mariposa headquarters, stampeded and mixed honey, meal and traps all together on the ground.

To this day the high, rough and vast Sierra del Burro country, across the Rio Grande from the Big Bend National Park in Texas, is one of the most remote and thinly populated areas of the continent. Cerro del Carmen and adjacent mountains in the range are clad with pines; against them jut bleak foot hills; out from the foot hills sprawl wastes of alkali deserts supporting nothing bigger than greasewood. This desert land makes that horror of thirst and summer heat called the Bolsón de Mapimí.

In Ben Lilly's time the Fronteriza Mine, in the mountains about thirty miles from the Rio Grande, worked hundreds of peon Mexicans. Competing with the cheapest kind of labor, Lilly supplied them with antelope and deer meat. He hired burro drivers to pack goat skins of bear grease into the village of Boquillas on the Rio Grande. He could speak hardly a word of the country's language.

In the region was another remarkable man of the *campo*, who had, however, the perspective that comes from reading the classics. He had a small ranch and knew the lore about cattle, horses, rattlesnakes, deer, eagles, javelinos, jaguars and *vaquero* (Mexican cowboy) life much better than he knew the business of ranching. His real interest was collecting documents and writing a history of the Mexican frontier. A part of this history is a bulky manuscript entitled *Around the Camp Fire,* which he allowed me to copy. A few pages in it deal with Ben Lilly. In quoting from them I salute the memory of their author—Don Alberto Guajardo.

"El Senor Lilly spent his Sundays lying in the shade of a tree and reading the Bible. He was more interested in finding new species of animals than in just killing anything he saw. He often forgot his only camping utensils, a tin pan and an old tin cup, and left them at some water hole. When he found honey in a rock crevice or a hollow tree, he would gouge out handfuls of it and eat it from his hand, right there.

"One very cold evening he killed a large female bear and skinned it. He spread a cured deerskin under a rocky ledge, lay down on it and covered [himself] with the fresh bearskin. Like all hunters who sleep out in the wilds, he had his rifle, loaded and the trigger on the safety catch, beside him. He told me that he was sleeping very warm and sound when he felt something nuzzling the bearskin over him and heard a growl. Quickly he drew away, jabbed the muzzle into the intruder's breast and fired until he had emptied the magazine of his rifle. It was dark, but he felt the target with his muzzle when he started shooting. He showed me the perforated skin of the bear he killed. It was a male—mate to the female he had killed not long before he lay down to sleep."

Ben Lilly spent perhaps a year in this region. He worked on west into the state of Chihuahua and got down almost as far as Chihuahua City. He killed wild turkeys that he considered the largest in North America. "It is all such an enormous country," he wrote, "that a man has to be an expert to hunt successfully. Game may be plentiful in a certain locality one season and scarce the next. The hunter must do like the wild animals—travel and see where the food and water will be good. Year-olds do not incline to migrate like older animals."

On a mule trail—the *camino real,* "royal road," hundreds of years old—that corkscrews across western Chihuahua and down to the Yaqui River in Sonora, I once spread my bedroll at a location called La Quiparita. Here a fine spring of water flows out into a creek with low banks; "parks" between pine woods afford grass, and there is rich and strong grass on a mesa not far away. While we boiled daylight coffee we heard wild turkeys gobbling, and a little later saw a buck cross a glade. One may ride all day in that country and not meet another man on mule or burro and not see the smoke from a single habitation. A north-and-south trail crosses the Chihuahua-Sonora trail at La Quiparita. It is a very noted camp ground and the finest that I have ever camped at. I don't know whether Ben Lilly ever passed that way or not. I passed seventeen years after he had left Mexico. There was a legend among the few Pima Indians and Mexicans of the region that a grizzly with a white star on his breast claimed La Quiparita as his own, attacking all travelers who stopped there and surviving all attempts to kill him—until a bearded *Americano* came along.

This was, and is, one of the many bears of Mexican folklore—a half-brother perhaps to Juan Oso, the half-bear and half-man hero. He sounds like the bear that A. L. Inman remembers Mr. Lilly telling about. Most human beings may be divided into two classes: those who forget and those who have constructive memories. Inman is the kind of man who does not forget.

According to his memory, a grizzly of the Sierra Madre had formed the habit of killing and eating children. Mexicans bold enough to hunt it had never met anything but bad luck. Some families moved out of the bear's range. Then Ben Lilly came along. When authorities saw that he had no fear they offered him a thousand pesos to kill the grizzly—just as their ancestors had once paid gringos bounties on the scalps of Apaches.

Several days after he set a heavy trap, he found it gone. The tracks of the grizzly that had stepped into it were fresh, and as he followed them he expected to see him rise at any moment. He moved on the trail slowly, stealthily; but he moved. When he got his first view of the bear, the mighty animal was standing upright, across a gulch, watching intently. The bear's eyes had caught the motion of his pursuer maybe a second before the pursuer saw him. An instant later Lilly saw the monster gather trap and clog into a forearm and crash into the growth toward him. As he emerged, Lilly began shooting his .33 rifle, putting, he felt sure, a bullet into him at every shot. Still the grizzly came on. The last shot in the rifle magazine had been fired, Lilly had pulled his long knife, and then, only ten feet away, the bear dropped dead.

This bear story is not found in any of Ben Lilly's writings. I give it as an item in the Ben Lilly legend.

35

JUAN OSO: BEAR NIGHTS IN MEXICO

J. Frank Dobie

The grizzly bears of the Mexican Sierras were as ferocious as any others. When Coronado came north seeking the Seven Cities of Cibola, and when the Jesuit and Franciscan fathers rode their burros among the Yaquis, Pimas, and Papagos, the big bears undoubtedly gave them trouble just as they marauded the camps of northern explorers later on. Terse, fragmentary references to grizzly depredations appear in the translated journals of the Spanish missionaries, but the best tales are doubtless forgotten or still hidden in moldering manscripts.

The folklore of any land antecedes its conquerors and flows from the tongues of man long after parchment and paper have disintegrated. From a wondrous Mexican storyteller Frank Dobie has brought us the saga of Juan Oso, heroic half-bear and half-man, and other lore to substantiate the legend that bears sometimes stole young women for pleasure rather than for food.

One of the best-loved of Dobie's yarns, the Juan Oso story first appeared in *Southwest Review* (Vol. XIX, No. 1 [Autumn, 1933]), published at Dallas by the Southern Methodist University Press and Louisiana State University Press. The story later was included in *Tongues of the Monte*, published in Boston by Little, Brown and Company in 1957, © J. Frank Dobie, 1935, 1947. It is reprinted here with the kind permission of Little, Brown and Company.

DURING THE MORNING my horse grew tenderfooted from having cast a shoe the day before.

"We will get shoes at La Golondrina," Inocencio assured me, while I blamed myself for not having put some extra ones in a saddle pocket. "Don Santiago Blanco," he kept telling me, "is *gente de razón* and of good heart."

At last we got upon a high ridge, followed the mesa atop it for an hour, and then came to the brow of the descent. In the valley far below I saw a scanty, broken line of trees with leaves turning yellow, and knew they were cottonwoods—the desert's sign of water. Beyond one patch of trees, at the foot of a steep mountain mottled with timber, I saw a curl of smoke going up from a cluster of *jacales* that in the distance appeared no larger than dog-kennels.

When, late in the day, I drew rein in front of the house of Don Santiago Blanco, the swallows were skimming the ground and gathering home to their nests built along the poles and under the bear-grass thatched roof of the wide and open *enramada* against the cabin. From their loafing positions in this shed stepped forth three or four men, who had no doubt sighted us coming down the trail an hour before.

In the democratic manner of *rancheros* a shade too far down the ladder of property to be called *hacendados*, Don Santiago greeted my *mozo* as an old friend.

"And so you have been in the home of my *compadre* Don Alberto Guajardo," he exclaimed after we had talked a few minutes. "You must stay with me at least three days—longer if you will. The only shoes I have are for mules. Tomorrow I will despatch a man to Múzquiz to get horseshoes. The next day he will return. Come, my friend, into your house.—Pantaleón, see that Don Inocencio has help in caring for the beasts.—Felipe, get your machete and go at once to the field and cut grass.—Come, come, my Señor, into your house."

As soon as we were within, my host halted in front of me, stood up straight, and, looking me in the eye, spoke these words: "You are now in your house. My name is Don Santiago Blanco, at your orders. This is my wife."

And Doña María also placed herself at my orders.

The house so freely and with such formal, yet simple, sincerity offered to me was but a *jacal*, a little better built and somewhat more commodious than the four or five other huts clustered around it without plan and inhabited by dependent *parientes*, or kinsmen. No urgency compelled me to resort to rawhide shoes for the horse in order to keep pushing ahead. I regarded my situation and was pleased with the delay.

After drinking coffee, we went out under the shady *enramada* to sit. I was placed in the only chair that could be classed as furniture. Don Santiago sat on a kind of bench hewn out of a mesquite limb that had grown four prongs now serving as legs, crooked but stable. The animals had been led away. The impudent-looking red-headed man of around thirty whom Don Santiago had previously addressed as Pantaleón and two other *parientes* were standing about. All of them wore *guaraches*, the soles of which were made of old automobile tires and were held to their feet by rawhide thongs. It was but natural that they should take advantage of the break in the monotony of life afforded by my advent to gaze and listen.

"Pantaleón," said Don Santiago as soon as we were well settled, "you take Gregorio there and Anastacio, get the oxen, hitch them to the cart, and go at once to the mouth of the Cañon Centinela and bring in the carcasses of the seven deer I shot this morning. I hung them in the motte of oak trees at the place where the trail from La Mariposa turns up the canyon. If the meat is not brought in tonight, the bears will surely eat it."

There was silence for a minute. Then Pantaleón, more impudent in manner than in voice, asked, "How many deer, Don Santiago, did you say?"

"Seven, and horns so enormous on—"

"Seven at one blow!"

Pantaleón threw these words into the midst of Don Santiago's sentence as suddenly as a stone from the sling of any angry *pastor* knocks in the ribs of one of his goats that has left the herd to browse on a distant bush. At the same time Pantaleón and the two other *parientes* fairly doubled up with laughter, while Don Santiago arose from his mesquite *banco* with indignation. It seemed to me that I could not possibly restrain myself.—But to catch the humor of that "seven at one blow," one must remember a little story common in Mexico.

One time, a long time ago, the King of Spain set out in disguise to find the most valiant man in all his kingdom. He went from city to city, from town to town, looking, listening, spying, smelling out every where for the *valiente*. One evening after dark while he was walking down a miserable lane, he heard a commotion inside a house at his elbow and then in ringing tones the words, *"Siete con un golpe!"*

"Seven at one blow," softly echoed the king. "Ah, at last I have found the most valiant man in all Spain." And with great joy in his heart he burst into the house. There a little tailor stood exulting over seven flies he was huddling together.[1]

Looking at the louts who had insulted him, Don Santiago stood for a full minute. *"Sinvergüenzas,"*[2] he spoke deliberately "will you or will you not bring in the carcasses of the deer? Think how much dried meat seven—"

"Con un golpe," jumped in Pantaleón, and again the *parientes* doubled over with laughter.

I looked at Don Santiago, astounded at his calm.

"Well?" he queried.

"No, Don Santiago," answered Pantaleón. "We cannot move the cart."

"Not move the cart!" Now Don Santiago showed genuine agitation. "Why not?"

"Because," replied Pantaleón, "while you were gone today, killing the seven deer *con un golpe*, a rattlesnake bit the axle and it swelled up so that the wheel does not wish to turn on it."

Don Santiago stood in his majestic gravity a minute longer. "Then let the bears have your meat," he said with contempt, and sat down.

Now Doña María and a barefooted *criada* brought a snow-white cotton cloth to spread over the little table under the *enramada* and offered me a basin—the half of a large gourd—of water and a towel embroidered with red roosters.

---

[1] So, by derivation, a braggart is a *matasiete*, a "kill-seven."

[2] Like "bloody" in England, the term *sinvergüenza* carries a connotation that a literal translation, "shameless one," in nowise suggests. Men have been killed for calling others *sinvergüenzas*.

"It is but humble fare we have to offer," apologized Don Santiago as he and I sat down.

"I like the fare of your country," I replied truthfully, "and I am as hungry as a wolf."

"Then all is well," Don Santiago added, "for as the *dicho* has it, 'To hunger there is no hard bread and nothing lacks salt.'"

Course by course, the women served us: a thin soup made out of goat meat and onion; *sopa de arroz* (fried rice flavored with chile and onions); *huevos rancheros* (eggs fried and sauced with a strong concoction of chile and garlic, which would have been better with tomatoes added); *cabrita en su sangre* (kid cooked in its own blood); *frijoles fritos* (beans boiled and then fried); as dessert a slice of *queso de tuna* (a "cheese," or conserve, of the prickly-pear apples); and at the end *café ranchero* (coffee boiled in milk and water and sweetened in the pot with *piloncillo*, the native brown sugar). All the time we were eating, the *criada* and Doña María, carrying hot, freshly-cooked tortillas in their bare hands, replenished—ten times faster than we could consume them—the stack between us on the table.

"*Buen provecho!*" Don Santiago gravely said when we had finished.

"And may it benefit you also," I returned with thanks. Certainly I had no disposition to complain at the fare, although I did think my host might have improved it by bringing in at least one of the fourteen deer hams left hanging out for the bears to devour.

Before we finished eating, the long-lingering twilight had surrendered to darkness and the *criada* was hovering over us with a lighted *ocote*, which had, no doubt, been brought down from the mountains on a burro loaded with a month's supply of torch-pine.

It was my pleasure to offer cigarettes not only to Don Santiago but to Doña María and then to the *criada*. By the light of three *ocotes* left to burn on a well-smoked rock, I saw that the *parientes* had gathered, silent.

"If the bears are so plentiful in these parts," I said, "I will go out hunting tomorrow morning."

"Yes," responded Don Santiago, "they are so plentiful that

they are a barbarity. There is one in particular that I wish you would kill. He has damaged me much."

There was a pause of silence. Then Don Santiago shifted himself to look towards the northwest in the direction I was facing.

"See that bright star," he said, "—under the lead ox of the Big Cart."[3]

I looked at the star indicated.

"That star," Don Santiago went on, "almost has its spurs in the top of a bluff which in winter time breaks the cold *norte* trying to blow away this ranch. It is called La Sierra del Gruñidor."

"But why," I asked, "is it named the Growler?"

"Because," interposed Inocencio, who had heretofore been among the silent ones but who considered it his perogative to answer any general question I asked,— *"Porque es el nombre que le pusieron* (Because it is the name they gave it)."

"No," Pantaleón put in, "it is called Gruñidor because the wind up there makes a growling and a grumbling and a rumbling that would terrify Santa María herself. The pass up there is called the Pass of the Bad Overcoat, for no coat is enough when one comes through it against the wind. Yes, yes, the wind up there is three furies. One time when I was coming through the pass with a burro loaded with grass, the wind caught him and blew him over the bluff."

"Bueno," Don Santiago went on, a patient tone in his voice, "here under this very *enramada* where we sit a kinsman of mine named Tranquilino Molino [What a delightful name, the Tranquil Mill, for a musician!] used to play the accordion every evening and night and often also during the mornings. The accordion belonged to me, and if Tranquilino were playing it after I went to bed, he would leave it on the table here, where no dew could fall on it."

"Well, one morning he came over to play the accordion, and it was gone. We searched everywhere, but we could not find it.

---

[3] *La Carreta Grande* is of course Charles Wain, the "lead ox" being the extreme star in the handle of the dipper. Sometimes the constellation is simply "*El Carro.*"

The people here are all honest, and nobody could think what had become of the accordion."

"How *triste* it was without any music!" Pantaleón commented.

"Then about three nights later," Don Santiago continued, "I heard and all the other people of La Golondrina heard the music of an accordion coming down from the Sierra del Gruñidor. I could not think who might be playing it. In the morning we went up the mountain, but we could find no tracks of any Christian being, only of bears, deer, and other animals. And other nights the accordion sounded. It was very curious. Then the serenades stopped.

"About that time I went to Múzquiz. I had to sell some goat hides and buy provisions. A *mozo* carried the goat hides on a mule. First, however, I must tell you that I have a goat camp two leagues away behind the Sierra del Gruñidor. Sometimes I do not visit it for a week or ten days. It is called Majada Escondida because it is so well hidden. It is a good *majada*—a *jacalito* for the *pastor* to live in, pens made out of rock, and a well to supply water for the little animals."

"And what beautiful little animals!" Pantaleón exclaimed with an eagerness that seemed as fresh and spontaneous as it was diplomatic. "There are more pintos red-and-white and black-and-white, and more black goats, and more yellow goats, and more brindled goats, and blue goats and brown goats and tan goats and more billy goats with long, long beards than in anybody else's herd. How they can climb! What *cabritos* they are! And fight! *Por dios*, Don Santiago, tell how those black billy goats fought!"

"Oh, that is just a joke, *a cosa compuesta*—a thing put together." Don Santiago hesitated.

"Tell it, tell it anyhow," Pantaleón urged. "What a barbarity!"

Plainly not unpleased, Don Santiago told "the thing put together."

"Why," he said, "one time I went over to the *majada* and about a mile from it saw two black billy goats fighting on a knoll. When I found the *pastor*, I told him that he had lost two billy goats and that he should go get them. Five days later I went again to the *majada* and, passing the little hill where I had seen the black billy goats fighting, I looked and saw them still at it. But all that was left of them was their two tails just brushing through the air and going at each other. I rode up closer. The tails were plainly the tails of my billy goats. Not another thing was left of the animals. Their heads, their horns, their legs, their bodies—everything was worn away, vanished. When I asked the *pastor* why he had not separated the black billy goats and brought them to the herd, he declared he could not make them quit fighting. What fighters!"

"Bravos to the tail-end!"

"But I will come back to my *historia*," Don Santiago announced. "*Bueno*, the first man I saw when I got to Múzquiz was my *pastor*, my own *pastor*—the *pastor* I thought to be at Majada Escondida tending the flock."

" 'What,' I said to him, 'are you doing here?'

" 'I came to get from the old herb woman some bark of the wild cherry to cure a pneumonia that I felt approaching me,' he answered.

" 'But how long have you been here?'

" '*Patron*,' he answered, 'I came eight and one-half days ago.'

" '*Por Dios*,' I said, 'what did you do with the goats?'

" '*Pues*,' he said, 'I left them shut up in the pen so they could not stray off. I intended to return to them immediately, but God did not will for me to go back so soon.'

"There I was. There that *pastor pendejo* was. And—my goats? They must all be dead of thirst and hunger, I thought. I did not even take time to sell the goat hides or buy provisions. I told Don Ceferino of *Las Quince Letras*[4] to send coffee by the *mozo*. I almost killed my horse getting back to La Golondrina. There I caught a fresh one, and spurring him to the *majada* I melted his tallow.

"When I ascended the last hill, I looked to see if buzzards or crows were flying around over the pen. I saw none. I had a little hope. As I drew near enough to catch a vista over the top of the

[4] "The Fifteen Letters," a favorite name for shops throughout Mexico, the letters of the three words, in Spanish, numbering *quince* (fifteen).

walls, I thought I saw a goat standing on the trough. Perhaps, I thought, God has remembered me and I can draw water from the well and pour it in the trough and the goats will drink and then they will eat and grow fat again. The trail went down into a low place and I could no longer see over the wall. I rode now at a walk, for, as you know, it is well to let a horse cool slowly at the end of a hard ride. Riding slowly that way, I could hear. My ears were open for the bleat of a goat. I heard no bleat, but I heard the creak made by a rope pulling up water. *Por Dios,* I thought, who can have come to this tail-end of the world to water my goats? There is but one trail into Majada Escondida. I had seen no tracks on it.

"Then I came nearer, so near that I could see plainly inside the corral. The goats were alive and some of them were drinking water out of the trough. And, *por Dios* and all things most pure, the one who was drawing water was a bear!

"I sat frozen on my horse and watched him. The goats seemed well contented. They are such stupid animals! The bear kept on drawing water with his hands. He could manage the rope and bucket as well as you or I. Then, all at once, he smelled me. 'Wuh,' he said, dropped the rope, and ran through the gate and tore out into the sierras.

"I made an examination. By tracks and other signs all was clear. The bear had been herding the goats out of the pen every morning, bringing them in to water in the late afternoon, and then killing one or two for his supper. What other animal would know to fatten his meat? I went to the *jacalito,* where the *pastor* sleeps. There I found my accordion. I understood now who had played it up on the mountain. What a wretched bear! *Que barbaridad!*"

"What a barbarity!" echoed in chorus Inocencio, Pantaleón, and the *parientes.*

"Certainly in the morning I shall hunt this bear," I said.

"If God wills," Don Santiago reverently added.

"*Si Dios lo quiere,*" echoed Inocencio, Pantaleón, and the others.

I unrolled my bed on a cot which consisted of a bull hide stretched over a wooden frame. It was under the *enramada.* On the ground a little off old Inocencio prepared his bed with my saddle blanket to supplement his own serape. Before he had wrapped the serape about him to lie down, he came to me with the *novia* (bride, or sweetheart), as he called my .30-30 rifle. "They are all good people here," he whispered, "but it is well always for a caballero to have his *novia* by his side when he sleeps." And I fell asleep at once, *muy contento*.

By the time the first rays of the morning sun were beginning to take the sharp chill out of the high November air, every man of the little *ranchería* was standing against the east wall of his *jacal*, warming at "the stove of the poor," or, as some call the sun, with "the cloak of the poor," each wrapped in a blanket that draped the ground in front of his feet and enswathed his face up to the hat brim. Why the *peones* of the towns and cities have no fires—except to cook by—is explainable; but despite the customary protest that a warm house gives colds, coughs, and pneumonia, I have marveled now, as I often marveled, at the absence of some sort of fireplace in hovels in the mountains so close to wood that one has only to reach out a hand to get it.

While we were eating breakfast, the men of the *jacales* stood on an open mound near at hand looking into the vast world stretching away from them on all sides. They were near enough for me to note their silence and passive immobility. Too lax in figure for statues, they yet appeared a fixed part of the landscape, gazing they knew not for what purpose, waiting—for nothing. Thus watching, their ancestors stood. The ancestors had a purpose; custom requires none. And so, following the custom of "those who have passed before," the descendants will stand until something yet undreamed of comes out of the immensity and silence to break their vigil.

Don Santiago had already offered me a horse for the hunt, and I knew that during our absence mine would be well cared for. Inocencio was too familiar with all this country for me to need any other guide.

As Inocencio saddled and packed, Pantaleón approached me with a most tristful visage. "*Patron*," he said, "you see in what poverty we live here. Don Santiago is a good man, very, very good, but what can he pay us for our services? This morning he is despatching a man to bring the horseshoes you have ordered from Múzquiz. I have a wife so sick that she is dying. It shames me to ask you, but would you as an act of charity give me about *doce reales* with which to send for medicines?"

I gave the "twelve bits" without hesitation.

"May God repay you," Pantaleón returned, crossing himself.

At a gap near the mouth of Centinela Canyon, up which we proposed to camp, we encountered a vivacious old fellow who was a veritable Mexican edition of the Arkansas Traveler.

"Are there any bear in this country?" Inocencio asked him.

"I hope none will eat me," he replied.

"How about water at the spring?"

"It is wet."

"Which way are you going?"

"If I don't get lost, I may arrive at the Encantado."

And without a *con permiso* or any other expression of politeness, the old fellow spurred his rocinante off for the ranch called Enchanted.

I hunted all day without seeing a single fresh bear sign, and the one white-tailed deer that I got a shot at I missed. Inocencio had whetted his appetite for venison, and several times during the evening he referred to the escaped deer.

"Don Panchito," he said, after we had finished our *gordas* and dried beef roasted on the coals and he had replenished the fire, "I will tell you a story about a hunter of deer." He was squatting before the fire, turning alternately the palm and the back of his right hand to the blaze in a manner peculiar to himself, at the same time appearing to examine the hand with his eyes.

"You know well," I replied, "how I like stories, above all at night like this, told in the open air by the light of a fire."

"One time," Inocencio began without comment, "a hunter who had never been able to kill a deer, although he had hunted often in a good deer country, came upon a big buck asleep. This buck was standing under an open tree and the hunter was so close to him that he could see his quiet breathing. As the hunter looked at the big buck there so near and so still, he was very happy. At last he was sure of a deer. And as he drew up his gun, very slowly, to fire, his head filled with plans.

" 'I'll take all that meat home to my family,' the hunter said to himself, 'and I'll cure the hide and make moccasins out of it. I'll wear one pair of the *teguas*, and I'll trade two other pair off for a calf. The calf will grow to be a cow and she will have other calves. While we are all having plenty of cheese, one of these calves will grow to be a fine, strong ox. I'll trade him off for a mare. The mare will have a colt, and I'll trade him off for a jack. Then the jack and the mare will bring mules. I'll just raise mules —mules—mules. There'll be one mule at first, then two mules, then three mules, then four, then five, then six, seven, eight.'

"The string of mules filed by in front of the hunter's eyes so that he could not see the big buck asleep. He saw them all loaded with *cargas* and he saw himself as the *conductor* of a whole *recua* of pack mules, *arrieros* helping him. He saw the mules stringing out along the trail to Chihuahua. He could keep himself silent no longer. At the top of his voice he yelled out 'Hi-lo!'[5]

"The big buck awoke with a jump and was a half-mile away in the brush before the hunter could shoot."

I was far from being sure that Inocencio had related this story merely for the sake of entertainment. Perhaps that was why the next afternoon the pack mule carried venison to contribute to the kitchen of La Golondrina.

As, near sundown, I rode into the corral, Pantaleón staggered up to my stirrup as drunk as a top. I divined at once that the money I had given him was somehow connected with the mescal he had so patently been drinking, and, remembering his sick family, I rated him in downright language.

He drew himself up proudly, removed his thatched sombrero, and solemnly announced: "*Patron,* to you he lacks not nor will lack respect, but so long as there is a distillery Pantaleón Maldonado y Orantes will drink mescal."

Leaving Pantaleón Maldonado y Orantes thus resolved, I turned to meet Don Santiago, whom I saw coming hurriedly from

[5] The cry used by *arrieros* driving mules or burros, and also by vaqueros driving cattle. It means, "String out!"

the house. He protested that he was undone. He had been disgraced by having his honored guest touched for money under his very roof. How he had learned about the paltry *reales* I did not learn. It was true, he went on, that Pantaleón was a kinsman —on his wife's side. He had come of a good family, but for all that he was nothing but a *sinvergüenza*, a *pordiosero*[6] no better than the *léperos* of the city. He was a living example of the proverbial genealogy: "Grandfather *arriero*—father *caballero*—and son *pordiosero*."

But philosophies, humiliations, and explanations were soon forgotten in the company I found gathered under the *enramada*. First there was a goat and fat-cow buyer from Saltillo, presented as Don Anastacio García. More conspicuous, but lower down in caste, was a gigantic vaquero named Esmilo from the Piedra Blanca ranch to the northwest. At the supper table only the buyer joined Don Santiago and me, although later, as I shall relate, the vaquero Esmilo took the floor.

Naturally there were allusions to my bear hunt and questions concerning my former experiences—or lack of experiences—with that animal. The talk took the direction of bears in general.

"Yes," commented Don Santiago, "the bear is a very curious animal, very smart."

Now that a fresh audience was provided, I prepared myself to listen again to the story of the bear and the accordion.

"My father," continued Don Santiago, "was a very famous hunter of bears. He lived in the Sierra Madre in Chihuahua, and hunted there and in Durango. One time he was going alone into the sierras to hunt. When night came he made a little camp down in a *bajada* and turned his mule loose. This mule was a true mule of the *campo*. She could be turned loose anywhere and she would never go far away. She was little but very strong. Her name was Tabaco, because one time she pitched a sack of Lobo Negro tobacco out of the pocket of her rider. Ah, what a mule she was! Well, my father turned her loose, ate some little *gordas*

[6] A beggar; literally a "for-God's-saker," the name being coined from the whining cry, "*Por Dios*" (in God's name), with which beggars prefix their plea. *Lépero* also means beggar but connotes rascality and the rabble.

that he warmed on a little fire, and went to sleep. He had yet a long way to ride, and so, very early, before the Guía had led El Lucero[7] into the sky, he got up.

"He took his reata in hand and stood listening in order to locate the mule. He heard a little sound in the grass and brush and went towards it. When he was near, he bent over to the ground to skylight the animal. He saw a black shape and whirled the reata to lasso it. He started to lead it towards his saddle, but the beast would not lead. He wondered what was the matter with the mule, for usually she led very easily. He walked towards her to put a *bosal* over her nose; the creature snorted and tried to pull away. One can never tell what a mule will do. Finally he got up to the animal's head. Then he found that he had roped a bear. Because he had left both his machete and his gun at the camp and because the bear was becoming very restless, he had to let it go."

"*Caramba!*" exclaimed Esmilo, "but one time—"

Esmilo got no further.

"So even a good hunter, like our friend here who went out today," continued Don Santiago gracefully, "may not always get a bear. Another time my father was chasing a bear and shot it while it was running. He saw it stop, seize some grass, and stuff it into the hole made by the bullet. He was taking careful aim to shoot again when all of a sudden the bear seized a rock and hurled it at my father. It missed him but it hit the horn of his saddle and tore the rawhide off it. The bear picked up another rock and my father retreated.

"The best way my father had to hunt bears was with a machete. He would find a bear and make him angry. The bear would come towards him and he would get behind a tree. The bear would try to reach around the tree after him. Then my father would chop off its hands with the machete. The Tarahumare Indians taught him this *modo*."

Here Esmilo managed to get in a word.

"I have never hunted bears with a machete," he said, "I used

___

[7] Lucero, called also *Estrella del Pastor* (Shepherd's Star), is the Morning Star. Preceding it is a dimmer star, always fixed with relation to Lucero, that is called *La Guía*—the Guide.

to have a wonderful dog that would smell a bear out and keep him in a tree, barking, barking, barking until I came. He was named Tres Orejas—because one time a bear split his right ear in two from his head to the tip and then he had three ears. One morning I was going up into the Piedra Blanca mountain to help kill some wild cows that could not be either driven or led down. We were drying the meat and bringing it down on mules to sell. Tres Orejas went along with us.

"Just as we got up on the mesa I heard him bark. I started after him, but a minute later we struck five wild cows and a *toro orejano*.[8] There was nothing to do but to go after the cattle. We got them and we got some more and that afternoon I could not find Tres Orejas. He did not come to camp. When we got back to the Piedra Blanca ranch four days later, Tres Orejas was not there. *Bueno*, about six months later I was again on top of the mountain, and right in a canyon that cuts through it I found Tres Orejas. He was sitting on his hind legs with his tongue sticking out and his nose pointing into a pine tree. I looked up in the tree and there was a bear. The bear and the dog were both dead. They were just dried up skeletons! No buzzard, no crow, nothing had bothered their skins, and they were both as natural as life."

Utterly ignoring the interruption, Don Santiago resumed his narration: "At La—" but the fat-cow buyer was ahead of him. He had a most unvarying tone of voice and was altogether *muy serio*.

"There are," he announced, "many instances of the dog's faithfulness." At this point a cur happened to be smelling about his feet in quest of a crumb, and the fat-cow buyer gave it a kick. "A very noble animal indeed, and—"

"Also he is sometimes very greedy, as you, Don Santiago, have no doubt observed," Inocencio interposed, at the same time glancing toward Esmilo and the fat-cow buyer. "One time a dog with a bone in its mouth was walking across a river. When he was half-way over, he met another dog also carrying a bone in his mouth. He jumped on this other dog and as a result he not only lost his

8 A maverick bull.

own bone but was knocked over into the swift current below and drowned."

It would never have occurred to Inocencio that his interruption might afford a target for his own fable.

"You, Don Santiago," he concluded, "were on the trail of a bear until the dogs went to barking."

"They were not my dogs," Don Santiago answered. "As I was saying, at La Quiparita, there was a very famous bear. He had a white star on his breast and so he was called Lucero. The trail from Chihuahua to Sonora crosses La Quiparita, and here this bear used to catch people and eat them."

"Certainly he would not kill a woman and eat her," Esmilo remarked.

"*Pues*, the meat of a heifer is more tender, more savory than that of a bull." The cow buyer spoke authoritatively. "And if a nice Christian heifer came along with just enough fat on her to make her bones round and soft and not too much to shake loosely on her *nalgitas*, why would not the bear eat her."

"Don't make me think of such a thing," Esmilo almost exploded. "The bear always has a better purpose for Christian heifers."

"Yes, the purpose of a vaquero from Piedra Blanca." Inocencio settled the matter, probably not intending that his remark should be taken in the altogether complimentary manner in which Esmilo accepted it.

Don Santiago went on. "No bullet ever seemed to hurt this bear—not even a bullet with a cross cut on it. Then after Lucero had molested travelers for many years, my father went out to kill him with the machete. He found the bear without trouble, jumped behind a pine tree, and the bear came on. But this Lucero bear was so quick that his arm dodged the machete stroke. Then he slapped my father down and bit him cruelly. At the slap my father lost his machete. He knew nothing else to do now but appear dead, like a coyote that has been caught. Only God knows why, but after the bear considered my father dead, instead of eating him, he started off. My father raised up ever so little; the bear saw him, wheeled, and came back to cuff him some more. There was no great distance between the life left in my father and death, but for five hours he played dead. Every once in a while the bear would smell at his mouth and nose. At last he left."

"*Pues,* Don Santiago," roared out Esmilo, "you have not told the most wonderful thing of all about the bear."

"What is that?"

"It is his way of stealing young women and keeping them."

"I am not telling lies," answered Don Santiago.

Esmilo was on his feet, laughing, the pine torches laid on the rock lighting up his tousled black mane, his thick black lips, and his gnarled, burly frame. He had the floor, and now for more than an hour he stood, sat, leaped, crept, whirled, poised motionless, now casting his sombrero to the floor, now hanging it on the back of his head, now with legs spread wide apart running his hands through his hair, his voice as coarse and stout and sensual as the features of his pock-marked face. After the tale that he thus poured out is forgotten, I shall remember him as the most brutally fierce talker I have ever listened to. He began with one of the ancient rimes that story-tellers in his land so often start with:

> The drunkard drinks wine
> And the boy eats bread.
> If this tale's a lie,
> It's not out of my head.

And this is the tale that he told.

One time a young women named Consuela belonging to a family who lived alone in the sierras went to the spring to get an *olla* of water. After she had filled the *olla* and was raising it, she felt her waist embraced. She tried to break away but was powerless. She was strong. She had strong clean legs and hips. She had strong arms and neck. Her back was straight and her chest was wide with firm breasts. She looked to see what strength held her. It was a bear.

He took her to his cave. They were more than two days reaching it, the bear sometimes carrying her in his arms, sometimes on his back, sometimes letting her walk by his side. When he could, he traveled in water, so as to hide his tracks. But even if people had followed him and caught up with him, they could have killed this bear only with a blade of Toledo or Oaxaca. Such a bear is *embrujado, encantado*;[9] bullets cannot harm him. Only the best steel can reach his vitals.

The cave was away up in a canyon, distant from any trail but the trail of deer, and down in the canyon under it trickled the waters from a *chupadera*, or seep-spring, in a place too rough for any cow or horse or man ever to visit it. About the *chupadera* and down the moist canyon bed grew wild cherries, *tejocotes*, *capulines* and other fruit-bearing trees. It was late summer, when berries are ripe, but after having spent a night in the cave with the bear, Consuela needed more than berries to satisfy her hunger. The bear watched her pick for a while; then he took her back into the cave, rolled up into the entrance a great boulder that for all her strength and desperation she could not budge, and went away. When he came back hours later, he brought a freshly killed fawn. She understood that it was for her to eat. As her people were little better than barbarians, more Indian than Castellano, she had no trouble in eating the liver raw. She pulled off the skin and hung pieces of meat to dry and be cooked in the sun.

Thus the bear and the young woman lived together. Sometimes the bear would shut her up in the cave and go a long distance off and bring back ears of corn from the fields down under the mountains. In time he allowed her to go with him to gather food. He well knew where the rich scarlet berries of the *madroña* grew, he took her to the best patches of black *brazil* berries and the orange-colored *granjeno* berries. He delivered to her pieces of dripping honeycomb clawed from crevices in the rocks. The bear is more like a man than any other animal. He can walk upright; he has hands to use; he eats the same food that *cristianos* eat; his brain is quick to understand. No, it is not impossible that a bear and a *cristiana* could live together.

Consuela became used to the bear. Whenever he went away from her, he always left her in the cave with the boulder to guard

[9] Bewitched, enchanted.

it. She made bags of deerskin and brought in fruits to dry; she dried meat to keep. She ground up corn on rocks, and though for a long time she had no fire to make tortillas, the dry powdered corn mixed with powdered meat and dried berries made a food that kept her strong and well.

The late winter months and the spring months were the hardest for Consuela, and for the bear too, for then the earth yields little food, except game and a few roots and the early flowers of the yuccas. Sometimes the bear was sluggish for days at a time, but in this country the animal does not sleep all winter as it does in the north. Bears do not understand fire, but when Consuela, after she had been a prisoner for many months, started a flame by friction of sotol stalks, her master forced her to make the fire inside the cave. Perhaps he understood the signal that smoke makes. She cooked the blooms of dagger and palm by placing them in water in a bag of deerskin and putting hot rocks in the water to make it boil. One can even boil coffee that way. With a knife made of flint and the help of the strong arms and claws of the bear, she cut the meaty parts of sotol and maguey and brought them in to roast.

So about a year passed and Consuela began to suffer violent pains. She had the bear take her down into a flat, and there she gathered the potato-like roots of the broad-leafed *mula* weed, which looks so much like a beet. She boiled these roots in the water heated with rocks and drank tea. One morning after she had drunk a great deal of the *te de mula* a child was suckling her breasts.

From his waist down this child was bear and from his waist up he was man. The old bear brought in more food than ever. The boy grew and the hair came out thick on his legs and hips. He had a good head and Consuela taught him to talk. He was very astute, very cunning, very much alive in the brain. While he was yet a toddling, his mother taught him to shoot a bow and arrow. No longer now did the bear keep her prisoner in the cave.

The years unrolled. When the boy was six, he was bigger than most boys are at sixteen. One day while the old bear was gone far

284

away on a hunting trip, the boy asked his mother where her home used to be before she came to live with the bear. She told him.

"Let's go see people," he said.

"Oh, I am afraid to leave," she answered.

"Do not be afraid," he said. "If the bear tries to stop us I will kill him. Besides, if we leave while he is gone, he can never find us."

Consuela was ashamed to go among people; yet she was eager. At last she consented. Before setting out, she took some skins and put them on her son and fastened them with thorns and sewed them with deer tendons so that he was dressed. She was particular to cover him well from the waist down. Her own dress was of skins, and both of them wore *guaraches* made of hide.

They had to travel a long time before they came to people. Some did not believe the story Consuela told of her life with the bear, but when they saw the boy they had to believe. Yet when he was clothed like a Christian and had shoes on his feet, nobody could see the hair on his legs or note his other features of a bear. Then his mother took him to the *cura* and had him christened. This priest named him Juan Oso—John Bear.

The *cura* was a very rich man, and when he perceived how astute and alive in the brain Juan Oso was, he took a great interest in him. He put him in a school to learn to read and write. Juan Oso learned as fast as a mare can trail her colt by smelling its tracks on the ground. But his mates found out about his hairy legs, and one day one of them, a big bully, jerked his pants down so as to expose him. Juan Oso was as strong as an ox. With one blow he struck his tormentor dead. There was no more school for Juan Oso.

More years passed, and now Juan Oso was bigger than any other man in the world. He stayed about the ranches, but sometimes he would go alone into the sierras and be away for weeks and months. He was very restless. One day he went to the *cura*, who was also his godfather, and said to him: "Padre, I wish to travel."

"Very well," replied the *curita*. "Tell me what you need for your travels and I will provide everything."

"I need but two things," Juan Oso answered: "a walking cane and a pair of burros loaded with money."

"I can have a *mozo* load the money on burros at once," said the *cura*, for he was very, very rich, "but it will take some time for me to have a fine cane inlaid with woods and bone and ornamented with a head of gold. For that is the kind of cane you shall go provided with."

"No, no," cried Juan Oso. "I do not want any fancy inlaid work and I do not want a cane with a gold head. All I want is a cane made out of pure iron, and I want it to weigh two tons."

"Very well," said the rich *curita*, and he gave orders to the blacksmiths to make the walking cane of iron and to make it exactly two tons in weight. It was finished and given to Juan Oso. Swinging it gaily, he set out, followed by two burros with sound backs tightly loaded with gold and silver.

At first Juan Oso visited the cities and there he made the coins flow in a regular stream. His fine *charro* suit and his *sombrero* were spangled with silver. He had a saddle inlaid with silver. He bought out saloons so that he could treat his friends, and gay girls swarmed around him as thick as horseflies. Within a year all the money was gone and Juan Oso had nothing left but his giant hands, his bear legs, and a good machete for which he had traded the iron walking cane.

Then Juan Oso went alone into the sierras. He would not starve. Like his father, he could rob bee trees. Like his mother, he could grind the mesquite beans into *mesquitemal*. As in his childhood, he could shoot arrows from a bow and kill meat. He wove rope out of the *ixtle* or fiber of *lechuguilla*, and with this rope he waylaid a mountain sheep, roped her, milked her, and made cheese of the milk.

One day while Juan Oso was out in the sierras he saw a lone man running as fast as an antelope. He stopped the man. "Why are you running so?" he asked.

"I am running," the man replied, "because God made me a *corredor*—a runner. I run from one mountain peak to another, down one slope, across a valley, and up to the next *cumbre* just for fun. I never tire. I am the fastest and most tireless *corredor* in the world.

"Why, then," said Juan Oso, "come with me. I can't pay you gold or silver, for my money is all gone, but I can provide you with food."

So the *corredor* went with Juan Oso. He often ran down deer, and so the two had plenty of meat.

After Juan Oso and the *corredor* had been together a number of days, they saw a man asleep down in a deep valley, a *carabina* by his side. The sleeper awoke as the two strangers neared him and grabbed his gun.

"Don't shoot," shouted Juan Oso. "My name is Juan Oso, a friend. Who are you?"

"I," replied the man, "am a *cazador*—a hunter. I can shoot the eagle in the air, the antelope racing across the prairies, the deer leaping over the brush. I can shoot farther away than other men can see. I kill game such a long distance off that I have no strength to run and get it."

Just then Juan Oso saw a buck deer running slantwise up a mountainside half a mile distant. "Look!" he cried. "Shoot it!"

The *cazador* shot, the buck fell, and the *corredor*, like a second bullet, sped away to bring in the game. A few minutes later he returned with the deer hanging over his shoulder.

"You and I would make a fine pair," said the *cazador*. "You could run about starting up the game, I could shoot it, and then you could bring it in."

"*Si, señor*," said Juan Oso. "Join us and we will all live together."

So the three went on. Fifteen days later they came to a man who was pulling up a tree.

"Who are you?" asked Juan Oso as he admired the strength of the man.

"I am an *arrancador* (one-who-pulls-up)," answered the man. "I can pull up only little trees now. My people are poor with nothing to eat. I have gone away from them to browse like a wild animal. I pull up only little trees and eat the insects at the roots. If I had stronger meat, I could pull up the biggest oaks that grow."

"Come with us," said Juan Oso. "We have a hunter who can bring down anything that flies or runs. We have a runner who can outrun the antelope and bring in game whether it falls in the bottom of the deepest *barranca* or is snagged on the highest mountain jag."

So the *arrancador* joined Juan Oso and they four ate all the meat they wanted. But after a while they came to a vast desert country spread out between barren mountains that grew only such bitter growth as the *gobernador* (greasewood) and that gave forth not one spring of water. The ground was white with alkali. Perhaps this country was what people now call the Bolsón de Mapimí. And Juan Oso and his followers were almost blind with thirst and they were almost blind from the glare of the hot, bleached ground. They were crossing a gravelly gully when Juan Oso stumbled upon a man stretched out on his stomach inhaling deep, deep breaths.

"Who are you?" asked Juan Oso. "And what are you doing?"

"I am one who sucks water out of springs and lakes and rivers and causes it to flow to me. I can change the course of a great river. I wish I could draw food to myself as I draw water, but I cannot."

"We have food for armies," Juan Oso answered, "but we are dying for a drink of water. *Por Dios*, go on sucking the air and bring water down this arroyo."

The man continued sucking air. Before long the thirsty ones heard a rumble. Then they saw a tide of water sweeping down. It was clear and not muddy as is water after a rain. They drank and drank and they filled their gourds. There was so much water and it was so delicious that they bathed in it, and they were very contented.

The man who could suck rivers of water went on then with Juan Oso and the *corredor* and the *cazador* and the *arrancador*. They went a long way and they came in sight of a city. It had now been a great while since Juan Oso had been in a city. He decided to enter this one in a royal manner. He went ahead. Behind him came the hunter, gun ready. Behind the hunter but often prancing out first on one side and then the other, came the *corredor* with a giant buck dangling from his shoulders. Behind him came the *arrancador*, who just at the edge of the city pulled up a mighty cottonwood tree and went along holding it as an umbrella. Last in the line came the man who could suck in rivers; he was not trying to suck in rivers now but he was breathing deep and making a rumbling sound, and his cheeks puffing out and sinking in looked more curious than the gills of a whale.[10]

Such a spectacle as Juan Oso and his procession made naturally aroused curiosity. The whole city stirred itself in wonder and alarm. A general and a regiment of soldiers galloped up and halted the parade, making Juan Oso and his men prisoners.

"Who are you?" asked the king of the city when Juan Oso was led before him.

"I am Juan Oso, a peaceable man."

"No you are not peaceable," roared the king. "Do not try to contradict me. You have alarmed my people and disturbed the peace more than an army of revolutionists would have done. You and your men must die."

"Is there no recourse?" Juan Oso asked.

"Yes, there is one recourse. Yonder is a great forest, the trees thick and high, the ground underneath them covered with brush. If you can clear this land for fields by this hour tomorrow, your lives are saved." The king laughed and turned away.

Closely guarded, Juan Oso and his men went to the forest. Immediately the *arrancador* began pulling up trees. Pines, cedars, oaks, he wrenched each tree out with one pull and cast it back over his shoulder. Juan Oso himself pitched the trees into great piles. The hunter, the runner, and the sucker-of-rivers burned them. That night the city was as bright as day from the light of the bonfires. The people were more alarmed than ever. By daylight the ground where the forest had been was as clean as a threshing floor.

Now this king was a tyrant, and he was afraid of such forces.

10 It is possible that the narrator, Esmilo of the Piedra Blanca, never saw a whale.

"I promised to save your lives," he said to Juan Oso. "I shall keep my word; at the same time I shall keep you prisoners."

"Is there no recourse?" asked Juan Oso.

"Yes, there is one recourse. On the other side of the mountain from here a bold river rushes down into a waste of lands. If you can change that river so that its waters will irrigate the new fields, you shall go free."

Then Juan Oso with his men, all heavily guarded, went out to a dry arroyo bordering the vast plain they had cleared. The man who could suck rivers lay down and began to inhale. He inhaled with such force that roofs were pulled off some of the *jacales* in the city. After a while the people heard a rumbling sound; then those who were not afraid to look saw a wonderful stream of water rushing down the creek.

The morning after this Juan Oso and his men again appeared before the king.

"I have saved your lives, I have promised you your freedom," said the king. "But before I give you a passport to go out of my kingdom, one other service you must do me. Among the crags of yonder high mountain lives an eagle that every day for a hundred years has swooped down, getting lambs, colts, and even now and then a child to carry to its nest. This nest is on a pinnacle so steep and lofty that no man can scale it. Whether at rest in its eyry or in flight, the eagle is safe from all marksmen. Bring this enemy to me dead or alive, and you shall go freely and safely where you will."

The hunter, who heard these words of the king, was already scanning the crag. At the very moment when he looked, the eagle, appearing no larger than a bat, began rising and circling above its nest. The hunter raised his gun. The eagle fell dead—on top of the peak. Now the *corredor* sped. A wonderful thing the people saw. This *corredor* could run up the perpendicular wall of a bluff as easily as on level ground. He was like a *pájaro carpintero*.[11] Within half an hour the giant wings of the eagle were spread above the doors of the king's palace.

The king was delighted. He had burros loaded with all kinds

11 The carpenter bird, woodpecker.

of wines and foods for Juan Oso and his men, gave them mozos
to serve them, and invited them to stay in his kingdom as long
as they wished. Juan Oso decided to go out into a range of sierras
west of the city, where water and game and timber were abundant, and camp.

The first day he went exploring he returned at noon to find
the camp all torn up and the *corredor* lying on the ground bruised
and bleeding.

"What has happened?" asked Juan Oso.

"While I was cooking the venison," the *corredor* answered,
"a black man, a regular giant, as ugly as the devil himself, seized
me and beat me. Then he tore up the camp."

Juan Oso had the thought that the black devil would come
back the next day. So he stayed in camp. Sure enough, at noon, just
at the time Juan Oso was turning some deer ribs on a stick over the
coals, the black devil sprang upon him. Juan Oso whirled, caught
his machete, and with one lick cut the devil's head in two and sliced
off his right ear. This ear he put in his pocket. Meantime the black
devil's body was flopping around like a chicken with its head
cut off, and directly it flopped over the rocks into a hole so
deep that the bottom could not be seen.

Immediately strange sounds, some hoarse, some soft, began to
be heard from the hole. The next morning before daylight Juan
Oso sent the *corredor* to the city to bring back the longest rope
made. The *corredor* brought two enormous coils. Juan Oso
spliced the two ropes. Then he tied one end around the *corredor*
and prepared to let him down. It was understood that one jerk
on the rope would mean to lower away and two jerks would
mean to haul up. Before the first coil of rope had been played out,
Juan Oso felt the signal to haul up. When the *corredor* appeared
at the brim of the hole, he admitted that he had not reached
bottom. He was just afraid to go any deeper. One by one Juan
Oso tried lowering his other men. The darkness, the strange noises,
and the awful depth made each one signal to be raised before
he came to the bottom.

Then in a great rage Juan Oso tied the rope around his own
heavy body and ordered all four of his followers to lower him.

Down, down he went, the lengths of the first rope, then past the splice, then down more and more of the second rope. The men above felt only signals to lower away. Finally the jerks ceased. Juan Oso was at the bottom.

Off to one side he distinguished the crying of soft voices. He went straight to the sounds. There he found four beautiful young women. They told how the black devil had stolen them and carried them to the bottom of the well. Juan Oso was happy to be the rescuer. He led the four beautiful young women to the end of the rope, tied one to it, and gave the signal to pull. Steadily the rope went up, and then after a long while it came down again. Thus each of the four was delivered from the black devil's den.

When the rope came down the last time, Juan Oso tied it around his own waist and signalled to pull. There was no answering haul. He jerked harder; he yelled, he roared. Only echoes came back to him. He did not know what could be wrong. As a matter of fact, the *corredor*, the *cazador*, the *arrancador*, and the man who could suck in rivers had each carried off one of the four beautiful young women without regard to the fate of Juan Oso. They had left the rope tied to a boulder.

Hours passed. Juan Oso ceased to yell and roar. Then he felt hunger. He took steel and flint and punk out of his pocket and struck a light. The cavern floor was strewn with all kinds of debris. Juan Oso built a fire. Then he pulled the black devil's ear out of his pocket and put it on the fire to roast. Just as it began to cook, he heard a hoarse voice groan out, "Don't burn me, don't burn me!"

Juan Oso had forgot all about the black devil. He lighted an *ocote*, ran about, and in a crevice found the groaning devil, his head cut open, his right ear cut off. Such a thing gave Juan Oso the *corajes*.[12] He grabbed the black devil and with a mighty swing hurled him up out of the well. But the black devil continued to moan, "Don't burn me, don't burn me!" The moan seemed to Juan Oso to come from miles away. The hideous sounds were unpleasant to him. He took the black devil's ear off the fire and put it back in his pocket.

[12] Something like "a fit of the spleen" but more serious.

Now an idea came to Juan Oso. He jerked the rope again. This time he did not expect any response. He was testing the rope to see if it were well tied. It appeared to be fast. Juan Oso began pulling himself up hand over hand. He pulled himself out of the hole.

He went straight to the city. He found the population in great rejoicing over the rescue of the four beautiful young women. Their marriages with Juan Oso's followers were already being celebrated. His own fortune was better than a dream. The king was so pleased that he gave Juan Oso the princess to marry.

At this point in the narrative, which I may not have quoted exactly in every instance, for it is hard to remember so many words, Esmilo explained that curiously enough Juan Oso had never been in love.

"Who knows why? Yet perhaps for this he was so strong. Now he made love to his betrothed, and he sang her a song that the *gente* on the frontier still sing. It goes thus."

At the first three notes a burro nearby set up a prolonged braying. I believe that nobody present, however, except myself regarded the harmony. It is impossible to put down the burro's song, but almost literally this is what Juan Oso, according to Esmilo, sang to his beloved:

> I was born in the womb of a mountain
> Listening to the lightning's crash.
> I was born in cavern darkness,
> And now I faint under passion's lash.

> "The son of thunder," they called me,
> Brought forth in that night of dread.
> Beasts of the mountain suckled me,
> And now with love I'm dead.

"And to live in, Juan Oso had a palace with chandeliers like a cathedral. He kept the black devil's ear in his pocket, for without it the black devil would be forever powerless.

"In time, children were born to Juan Oso and his wife, and not one of them had bear's feet or bear's hair or any other feature of the bear. And Juan Oso lived *muy contento* all the rest of his life."

As he finished this story, Esmilo of the Piedra Blanca showed his swart face and his white fangs in a laugh that would have fitted well either the black devil or Juan Oso. In the manner in which he had begun, he concluded with a rhymed convention out of antiquity:

> I went down one lane
> And came up the other.
> Basket full of holes—
> Now tell another.

But Don Santiago was in no mood for another. Before he went to bed he called me to one side.

"This man Esmilo," he said, "is a *sinvergüenza*. He has no regard for the truth. He is just a *hablador*.[18] Your route is the same as his, but I advise you to travel alone and to have absolutely nothing to do with him. He ruins everything I say."

In after times I had for a *mozo* in the Sierra Madre a civilized Yaqui Indian, Cruz by name, who told me a story about another giant half-bear and half-man named Policano; also of a young woman rescued by *arrieros* from a cave in which a bear had sealed her up. Later on at an abandoned mining camp in Chihuahua I met a native who had inherited from his forefathers the *historia* of a bear's kidnapping in that region a *senorita* on the eve of her wedding and keeping her for a week before the rich *hacendado* who was her father, the frantic lover, and other ranch people found her imprisoned at the end of a box canyon, where the bear had been bringing her roasting ears and stolen tortillas. Despite such a plethora of tales, I have never passed and never expect to pass another bear night such as I experienced at La Golondrina.

The next morning, taking care not to leave in company with the man who had ruined everything my host said, I shook hands

18 While *hablador* may be translated merely as "talker," the word carries the connotation, at times, not only of idle but of false speech.

with each individual of the ranch, the *parientes* one and all wished me a happy journey.

"May you go with God!" Doña María said.

"May God care for you!" Don Santiago said.

After I had ridden half an hour, I turned in the saddle for a last look at La Golondrina far below. The only life I could make out was a curl of smoke and four or five diminutive figures, motionless, standing on the bare mound, not so much watching as waiting, waiting, waiting.

THE BIG BEARS OF ALASKA

36

THE ALASKAN GRIZZLY
Harold McCracken

Few men have studied Alaskan bears at closer range than Harold McCracken. He began observing the world's largest bears while still in his twenties as a leader of a photo-scientific expedition to Alaska. Following this, he spent many years hunting Alaska brown bears[1] and other big game, and later he led an archaeological research expedition to the Aleutian Islands for the American Museum of Natural History. His interests have not been confined to grizzlies, however. While many readers will know him as a lecturer on Alaskan wildlife and a writer of hunting stories for popular magazines, others will be more familiar with his books on two famous western artists, Frederic Remington and Charles M. Russell.

The following selection from McCracken's magazine writings portrays the blood- and bone-chilling experiences of being shipwrecked in the Bering Sea country, where the writer and a companion planned to hunt caribou and brown bears. McCracken encountered almost more bears than he could handle on this trip, as the reader will discover. The story appeared in *Field & Stream*[2] and later was included in *Field & Stream Treasury*.[3] It is reprinted here through the generous consent of the author and the editor of *Field & Stream*.

THE GREAT ALASKAN GRIZZLY—the Kodiak brown bear (*Ursus middendorffi*) and its even larger Alaska Peninsula brother (*Ursus*

[1] The so-called brown bears and grizzly bears have been classified as the same species by recent taxonomic studies. (Letter from Albert W. Erickson, project leader, Bear Project, Alaska Department of Fish and Game, dated November 27, 1964.)

[2] (February, 1920), 903–907.

[3] *Field & Stream Treasury*, edited by Hugh Grey and Ross McCluskey. (New York, Holt, Rinehart and Winston, Inc., 1955), 137–45.

gyas)—is probably as far famed as either the African lion or the Bengal tiger. And yet, probably less is known of its life history than of any of the other larger mammals. He is, nevertheless, a sort of fictitious byword at the hearths of all those hunter-sportsmen who enjoy the savor of genuine hazard in their quest for sport and trophies. A beast whom most prefer to "talk" about hunting, rather than face in mortal combat. And his 1,000 to 2,000 pounds of brawn and power is unquestionably the embodiment of all that even the most adventurous care to seek. He is supreme in size, in brute power, as well as in physical dexterity, sagacity, and pernicious damnableness in the animal kingdom. And this, not in the mere belief of a casual observer, but weighed and tried on the scales of science. To go into details regarding the life history, the "whys" and "whens" and "hows" of his life career, would entail a goodly volume, which, though immensely interesting in every detail, would be far too cumbersome in such a place as this.

His home is that long, slightly curved arm that reaches out from the southwestern corner of Alaska, separating the North Pacific Ocean from the Bering Sea, and dabbling off in the spattered Aleutian Islands. The Alaska Peninsula is today one of the most wild, least visited and less known of all the districts on this continent.

But in reality, the Alaska Peninsula is, for the most part, a terribly wild Garden of Eden. Its waterways boast more fine fish than any other similar sized section of the globe; on its rounded undulating hills and tundra lands are great herds of caribou, the finest of edible flesh; it is carpeted with berry bushes; there are fine furred animals in abundance; millions of wildfowl, duck, geese, eiders, seals, sea lions; big bears—everything necessary for the welfare and happiness of primitive man. It is a truly primitive land.

While the great Alaska Peninsula bear is a carnivore, or flesh eater—and what applies to this bear also applies in many respects to his brothers the sub- and sub-sub-species of other districts of Alaska—yet he has frequently and correctly been called "the great grass-eating bear" and also "the great fish-eating bear." All animals subsist in the manner and on the foods that demand the least effort, hazard and inconvenience to their life and comforts. Thus the bears of the Alaska Peninsula have chosen fish and grass and berries as their main diet of food, varied with an occasional caribou, a seal, or meal from the carcass of a dead whale or walrus washed up on the beach. During most of the months of the year, the streams are choked with salmon, affording him an inexhaustible supply until well into the middle of the winter. And as hibernation is for the most part only an alternative for existing under winter conditions, when it is hard or sometimes impossible to get food, and as the Alaskan Peninsula is in winter moderated by the warming Japan Current, making it a quite mild and livable heath for old Gyas, he is forced to spend but a relatively short period in the "long sleep." This increased activity, together with the abundance of fine food, accounts for the unusual size to which the bears of that district grow.

And he is very much aware of his size and strength; and the fact that he has had no outside natural enemy through the line of his ancestors has made him aggressive, haughty and overbearing, fearing nothing and crushing all that impedes his way.

Thus the Alaska Peninsula grizzly is to be found a most unscrupulous fighter, and his acquaintance with man and his high-powered rifles is as yet too short and limited to have impressed upon his brute mind that here is a most powerful mortal enemy. He usually charges when wounded, more than frequently when a female with very young cubs is suddenly surprised or attacked, and occasionally when watching a fresh "kill" or "cache," and surprised. And, if old Gyas decides to fight, woe betide our bold Nimrod unless he is a good shot and nonexcitable, or accompanied by someone who possesses these valuable facilities. For a wounded grizzly will not stop for one to reload his gun, nor pause to be shot at until the vital spot is struck. He means blood! Fifty bullets that are not placed in the proper spot will not stop him; and you can't back out once he accepts your challenge. Not that one is certain of being charged by every Alaskan grizzly that he fells; I have had even females retreat until knocked down. But these cases are really the exception, and the experiences of practically all the old bear hunters of that district—I have known most of them—will bear me out in the statement that these Alaskan grizzlies almost invariably charge under the three circumstances I have cited. The natives of Alaska do not often go to look for these big bears. They have a great deal of respect for them—as all others who know them have.

We are at King Cove, a native village near the site of the once famous village of Belkovski, center of the sea otter hunting grounds of old. We are about 600 miles southwest of Kodiak, the nearest town of over fifteen white inhabitants; and very near the extreme western end of the Alaskan Peninsula, and almost due north of Honolulu by location. And here, where the traveler is almost never seen, we will start out to hunt for the biggest of carnivora—start it by incidentally being shipwrecked, almost drowned and getting a foot severely frozen.

It was on the morning of Wednesday, November 1, 1916, that I left King Cove in a 28-foot covered-over powerboat with Captain Charlie Madsen. We headed for the Isanotski Straits, at the end of the peninsula, and the Bering Sea country, where I intended hunting Grant's Barren Ground caribou and the big grizzlies at several desirable localities near the end of the peninsula.

It was cloudy; looked like another snowstorm; but the wind being from the north, rave it might and the low hills of the mainland would protect us until we reached the end of the peninsula, where we could hunt bear and wait for more favorable winds. But the winds of the North are most fickle!

It was a most magnetic sight as we plied out towards the cape at the entrance of the bay, sending flock after flock of salt-water ducks flopping off over the swelling surface of the blue-green sea. An occasional seal could be seen plunging headlong into the water from the jut of a reef or an outcrop of the rocky shoreline. The hills were gray, dappled with the first settling snows of winter, and the clouds were heavy and leaden looking.

As we rounded the cape the swells became more pronounced, carrying a deep, rolling, green-sided trough. But our boat plied steadily on, plunging its nose fearlessly into the rising waves.

Breasting some five miles of rocky coastline, we rounded the second cape at the entrance to Cold (Morofski) Bay, which protrudes some twenty-five miles back into the peninsula, almost making what is to the west an island and what is to the east the end of the peninsula. As we had expected, the wind was raging out of the bay to seaward. But heading the boat's nose towards Thin Point, about ten miles distant, we started fighting our way to the protection of the opposite cape.

Madsen had been watching the sky with misgiving and shortly announced that the wind was changing to the southwest.

I naturally inquired what would be the best course to pursue, knowing that it undoubtedly meant more storm and that we would soon be in the thick of it.

"Cap" decided we would take a chance on reaching Thin Point before the wind had swung to the southwest and thrown the storm in our faces. Once behind the cape we would be safe.

But we were not halfway across when the wind, swinging out past the protection of the peninsula and clashing against the tide, was soon lashing the sea into a stormy havoc. Diving into one great swell, the wind toppled its crest over the boat, washing overboard the hatch-cover and pouring a volume of water into the hold upon our supplies and outfit. I got on deck and endeavored to get a piece of canvas nailed over the open hatchway before another big one should pour its volume into the boat, at the same time clinging as best I could to the pitching vessel.

In the midst of all this, and as if to impress more forcibly upon us our insignificance in this big affair, our engine stopped. Gas engines are hellish things anyhow, and always buck in just the wrong place. But one must act quickly in a case such as this, and almost before I knew it the boat's sail was up and we were racing back before the wind, toward the entrance of the bay we had not long left.

I took the rope and wheel, while Madsen endeavored to get the engine running again, though vainly.

But the wind was now coming in such gusts that each one nigh turned our boat onto its nose. It was also snowing and sleeting, almost hiding the outline of the coast.

A gust hit our sail, turning the boat clear on its side, taking water over the rail, and we narrowly escaped finding ourselves in the arms of Neptune himself. Madsen left the engine and decided we would run before the wind and tack into King Cove Bay.

We crossed the entrance to the bay, driven at top speed towards the opposite cape and line of rocky reefs.

Going as close to as safe, the sail was drawn in with an endeavor to throw it to the opposite side, thus turning the boat. But the wind was too strong and the sea too rough, and try as we might, we would only be driven helplessly on towards the reef where the waves were dashing their foam and spray high in the air. Then a big wave took the flopping sail, pulling the boat over onto its side until the canvas was torn from end to end. As a last resort the anchor was thrown out; this failed to catch sufficiently to hold us and was regained at great difficulty when we saw that hitting the reef was inevitable.

The first rock of the reef that the boat hit, jammed its head through the bottom of the hull and we clambered out into the big dory we were towing and started for shore through the narrow, raging channels in the reef. But this being an open boat, it soon swamped in the breakers and we were forced to take to the water and make shore as best we could. Swimming was impossible, but keeping our heads above the water as best we could, and riding the waves, we were soon washed up on the rocky shore, like half-drowned rats.

To build a fire was impossible for lack of material; we must wait until the boat washed over the reef and was driven ashore. So, wet and cold, and facing a biting snow and sleet and rain-pelleted wind, we walked back and forth over the rocks and waited.

Through all this, while we had been battling with the elements for our very lives, I had noticed with no small interest how very little the storming and havoc had inconvenienced the little creatures that made their homes in or on the sea. The ducks swam about, quacking, and apparently thoroughly enjoying their buoyant existence. So even storms at sea, it seemed, were a mere matter of relativity and part of the everyday life of those that made their home thereon.

Eventually the boat came ashore—it was fortunately a high

tide—and getting aboard we got out block and tackle, sunk our anchor as a dead-man, and pulled the boat up as best we could. Supplies and everything were drenched and several planks in the hull were smashed.

When we had done all that we could we started for the village —a hard hike. It was well after dark when we reached the squatty barrabaras, or native dirt huts, of King Cove, and we were wet and tired and miserable—ready for a meal and the blankets.

As I began to thaw out, however, I found that part of my right foot had frozen—the leather boots I had been wearing having shrunk and stopped the circulation of blood, causing the freezing. I was laid up for over a week with my foot, though it took Madsen, with the assistance of several natives somewhat longer to get the boat repaired and back to the village.

Such are but a bit of the "pleasures" that often come with hunting big bear at the western end of the Alaskan Peninsula.

I was especially fortunate in making a one-day bag of four of these Alaska Peninsula bears, a big female and her three yearling cubs, the latter being as large as quite mature Southern brown bears I have gotten.

Deciding to spend a day alone in the hills after caribou, I took the .30-40 Winchester—in consideration of the bear—and followed the beach of a lagoon or bay to its head about two and a half miles from the village. From the head of the lagoon a valley rose at an easy pitch for about two miles to a low divide on the opposite side of which was a large valley extending out into the Pacific. This was a very good place for caribou.

At the head of the lagoon I stopped to shoot some salt water ducks with a .22 Colt revolver, but had fired but a few shots when I was attracted by the bawling of a bear. Glancing in the direction of the sound, I saw a brown bear making a speedy, somewhat noisy, getaway up through the alders from where he had been no doubt eating salmon in the creek a few hundred yards up-valley from me. He was then a good five hundred yards distant and in the alders. I fired, hoping at least to turn him back down the hillside, but he made the top of the ridge and went over it out of sight. I started a speedy climb up through the alders

toward the top, not far from where he went over. By the time
I reached this, Mr. Ursus had gone down the other side and was
making a "hiyu clattewa"[4] along the opposite side of the valley.
I started up the ridge toward an open space in the alders with
the intent of hurrying down to the creek and descending it with
the hopes of heading the bear off or getting a shot at him while
crossing a wide rock slide a few hundred yards below. But I had
not gone a dozen steps when I saw three other bears coming along
at a good pace on quite the same course that Number One had
taken. This was somewhat more of a "bear party" than I had
really anticipated inviting myself to!

I felt quite certain that they would cross a small saddle through
which the previous one had passed, and I decided to wait until
they had come out of this and were somewhat below me before
chancing a shot. I was alone, I remembered.

Squatting down in the alders, I waited with gun ready and,
I must say, nerves tense. The first one to come through the saddle
was the old female, a big, high-shouldered brute that strode in a
manner indicating it was looking for me every bit as much as I
was waiting for it. She was followed by her other two yearlings—
big fellows almost as tall and as broad as they were long. Being
alone, and feeling that the female would undoubtedly fight, I
deemed it most wise to play doubly safe. Conditions were fortunately in my favor. The wind was from seaward, and the
alders were heavy enough to conceal me from her none too good
eyesight, and it would be difficult for her to determine from just
what direction the report of my rifle came. The dispatching of
the old one was of course my first move. The rest would be
comparatively easy. I did not have an opportunity of a good
shot, however, until the three had reached the creek bed and
crossed and started up along the other side. I slipped into a
heavy clump of alders and waited. She was not then, I was
quite sure, aware of my whereabouts at least. She lumbered
slowly along, yet ever watchful, I could see. Coming out in a
little open space she stopped and made an apparent survey of
the surrounding vicinity. I took a coarse bead and let drive at

[4] Chinook jargon for quick getaway.

her shoulder. I could fairly hear the bullet slap into her. With a nasal bellow she wheeled and made a vicious swipe at the nearest yearling. I fired again, at which she wheeled and charged madly along the hillside opposite me. She went into a small ravine and in a moment came up into sight on one side and stopped, snout swaying high in the air to catch a scent of the danger. I steadied myself, took aim and at the report she went down in a heap and rolled out of sight. "A bull's eye!" I thought, and breathed a sigh of relief.

The two cubs had made off in the opposite direction, stopping occasionally to look about. I knocked down one of these at the second shot breaking his back, though he raised on his forelegs and bawled for all he was worth. I was about to let him have another, when out of the ravine came Mrs. Ursus, mad and apparently as much alive as ever, although dragging her right foreleg. She scrambled through the alders straight to the bawling cub. Greatly surprised, and a little uneasy, I again let drive at her. She threw her head to one side, at the same time letting forth another nasal cry. At my next shot she wheeled completely around and charged along the mountainside for a short distance with head held high and every nerve strained to its utmost to locate the cause of her molestation—snarling and bawling in a manner that made me perspire uncomfortably. She was desperate and no doubt calling upon the souls of all her past ancestors to assist her in locating the peculiar new enemy. Then she charged back to the cub. Finally she made a dash almost straight in my direction.

One does not fully appreciate the thrills of real bear hunting until he has experienced just such circumstances as this. To be alone in such a case is a quite different matter from being in company—poor though it may be.

She at last came to a standstill, standing half sidelong to me, and I clamped the gold bead square on her neck and let drive. She went down, got up, and tearing a few alders up by the roots, unwillingly sank in a heap. She had finished her career as a big brown bear on the Alaska Peninsula.

The rest was quite easy and uneventful.

With the assistance of three natives I skinned the four, took the necessary measurements for mounting, and brought the pelts in by boat. The natives, however, made a second trip, bringing in every bit of the meat of all four, salting it down for winter use. The pelts were in fine condition and beautiful specimens, the large one measuring a full ten feet. They are now in the Ohio State Museum.

It was on Sunday, November 19, 1916, that I bagged the original "bearcat"—one of the largest bears ever killed on the continent.

We were hunting around the eastern side of Frosty Peak, a high volcanic mountain towering between Morzhovi and Morofski Bays and about ten miles from the Pacific. This is about twenty miles from King Cove, near the end of the peninsula, and a very good place for big bears. It was a *big* one that I wanted now; and though numerous tracks and one medium-sized bear were seen, none were bothered until the original "bearcat" was found. That took two days under Old Frosty.

I had previously been hunting Grant's Barren Ground caribou on the Bering Sea side of the peninsula and before we landed at the foot of Frosty Peak on our return there was a good twelve inches of snow on the ground. In places it had already drifted to a depth of five feet. Bear hunting was quite an easy matter—though a little unpleasant on account of the snow and cold—as it was a small matter to track the animals. As the streams were still open and full of salmon, but a small percentage of the bruins had sought their winter quarters, the pads of their big clawed feet having beaten paths along the iced shores of the stream where they came periodically to gorge themselves.

It was late afternoon of the second day under Frosty Peak that we found the fresh trail of our longed-for quarry. We had been investigating the broad alder-patched table of one of the valleys that cut up toward the pinnacle of Old Frosty. There were numerous tracks along the creek where the brownies had been feasting on the silver salmon, though no fresh ones of a really large bear. But as we came well up to the head of the valley we saw the well-distinguished trail of an unquestionably large bear where it had made its way up through the snow on the mountainside into a heavy growth of alders. This was at the very foot of the peak and in the highest growth of alders. Upon reaching the tracks we were well satisfied that they could have been made only by the paw and claw of just the bear that we were seeking. Although it was evident that he had been in no special hurry in making the climb, yet it was all that a six-foot man could possibly do to step from one track to the next.

To the left of the alder patch was a comparatively open track of rocky ground with only a sparse patch of brush here and there. It was certain that he could not, if still in the thicket, escape in that direction without being noticed. But on the right there was a low ridge, the opposite side of which dipped down into a deep wide ravine. The alders extended to within a few yards of this ridge, and to see the other side it was necessary to mount to the top of it. Also, it was quite probable that the bear had already gone over this ridge and might then be high up in the canyon near to its hibernation quarters.

Being unable to locate the bear with my glasses, I decided to make a complete detour around the patch, to be assured whether or not he was still in there.

So leaving Charlie on the flat below, I took the two natives and started up through the alders on the trail of old Ursus. As soon as possible we mounted the ridge at the right and went along the extent of it to assure ourselves that the bear had not crossed. This he had not. But to make doubly sure that he was still in the alder patch, we went above and around it to complete the circle about the place. He was without question lying somewhere in that thicket.

Upon reaching the flat, and as a last resource, we fired several volleys up through the alders. Then one of the natives spotted him standing in a thick growth of the alders, where he had gotten up and was looking inquiringly down at us. We moved down opposite to him and I fired from the shoulder. He started off along the mountainside, like an animal that had just broken from its cage. Then I fired again. Mounting a little knoll in the open he peered dubiously down at us—in unmistakable defiance. I held on him full in the chest for my next shot, at which he let out a bellow and came for us. My shots had hit, though he had not so much as bit or clawed at the wound on either occasion—merely jumped slightly. He was then about 200 yards distant, though I was well aware of the short time it would take him to cover that distance. And he was a big fellow—looked literally more like a load of hay than a bear, coming down the mountainside.

I had previously told the others not to shoot until I called for help, as I was anxious to fell this big brute single-handed. But on he came, and though try as I might, I could not stop him. My shots seemed to be taking no effect whatever. And then, when he had come about half the distance, I yelled "Shoot!" And I'd like to have done so long before. The four guns spoke simultaneously, but old Gyas still kept coming.

I squatted down in the snow, and resting my elbows on my knees, decided to take the long chance—a shot for the head. I was confident that Madsen could stop him before he reached us, and determined to take a chance shot of dropping him in a heap. The two natives, however, were not so confident and began to move backward, shooting as they went.

He turned an angle to cross a small ravine, and while he was mounting the opposite side at a decreased pace I held just forward of the snout. The first shot missed, as I saw a flit of snow where it hit just in front of him. But at the second shot he dropped in a heap, falling on his belly with his nose run into the snow. After waiting for some moments to make certain he was beyond the trouble point, we climbed up through the alders to where he lay. The others stood by with guns ready while I went up and poked him with the end of my own gun. He was dead.

This had all taken but a few minutes, though relatively it seemed a great deal longer.

He was indeed a big fellow—genuine bearcat. We gutted him, and as it was getting late, hit for camp. The next morning we went back to skin the animal—and no small task it was!

He had been hit twelve times, we found. Nine of the shots had entered the neck and shoulder and two in the head and one in the abdomen. One bullet had hit him squarely in the mouth, shattering the tops of his lower teeth on one side, piercing the tongue and lodging in the back of his throat. Four of the .30 caliber leads were retrieved from the shoulder, where they had not so much as reached the bone. The shot that stopped him struck him well up on the brain box, but squarely enough to break the casing of the bone and penetrate the skull, though only a part of the lead entered the brain, the most of it spattering off in the fleshy part of the head. It was lucky shot on an even more lucky day!

We estimated his live weight at from 1,600 to 1,800 pounds, and the skin at twelve feet in length. The actual measurements of the tanned skin, however, as made by Chas. A. Siege, noted taxidermist of Spokane, Wash., are: eleven feet four inches maximum length, by ten feet six inches spread of fore legs. The skull, measured one year after killing, eighteen and one-quarter inches, or one-half inches under the world record, according to Washington, D.C. authorities.

37

THE FEAST OF IVAN[1]
Harold McCracken

No animal is more photogenic than the smoothly contoured, sur-
prisingly dexterous bear. But to photograph him in his native habitat, particularly when that habitat is situated in the Far North,
is a hazardous and extremely uncomfortable undertaking. Any
reader planning to take pictures of Alaskan grizzly bears in the
rough can learn much from the following chronicle of Harold
McCracken's riskish rendezvous with the big brown bears of
Alaska. (You do not have to be a photographer to enjoy this
thrilling story, however.)

WHEN THE SALMON start coming into the fresh-water streams,
they come like tidal waves. Within a few hours every estuary
on the bay may be chocked to the surface, as the "silver horde"
begins the last short part of its long journey to spawn and die.
Not one of the millions that come in will ever return to the salty
sea. And here the feast of the bears begins.

After the first run of salmon comes in, the Alaska brown bear
eats little else, and a full-grown bear will devour a hundred
pounds or more from dusk to dawn, day after day and week after
week. As the fish move upstream, the bears move with them,
picking out their own favorite fishing spot, to remain close by
and come out of the alders regularly every afternoon to renew
the abundant repast and eventully move on to a convenient source
of supply that is nearest to the winter den.

Once the bears had settled to their fishing, my problem of

[1] From *The Beast That Walks Like Man* by Harold McCracken, Copyright
© 1955 by Harold McCracken. Reprinted by permision of Doubleday & Company, Inc. (pp. 229-37).

getting pictures was considerably simplified, and we soon found a successful formula. Before going near a good fishing section of a stream we would carefully observe the daily movements of the bears through our binoculars, from some elevated lookout position as far away as possible. We would watch through the afternoon to find out where each bear came down to the stream and again in the morning to make sure where they went to bed down for the day. We might spend two evenings and two mornings on the lookout. Where the bears had not been disturbed, they would often have their day beds only a couple of hundred yards from where they fished; and they would regularly follow the same routine day after day.

When we were certain where the big hairy fishermen were quietly snoozing, and where they would probably amble down the well-trodden trail to the stream, we would slip out during midday to improvise a blind and await their return. It was not just as simple as that, for the direction of the wind and the sunlight and a position of photographic advantage were important factors. There was also a little matter of weather. Time after time all the circumstances seemed to be in our favor, only to have a dense fog and cold rain keep drifting in from Bering Sea. There were occasions when we built a blind in the pleasant warmth of sunshine and the dirty weather closed in just before the bears came out. And, once the bears were made aware of our presence, there was nothing to do but move on to a new location.

We were soon capable of telling a good fishing place as far away as we could see it with binoculars. The bears always picked the "riffles," where the water was shallow and ran over a wide rocky bottom. In these places the water might be only a couple inches deep and the salmon would almost have to crawl upstream through the rocky obstructions. Every minute of the day there would be fish going past these riffles; sometimes they were literally alive with squirming, splashing fish of up to fifteen or more pounds in weight, and it was no problem whatever for a bear to walk out and pick them up, one after another, until his voracious appetite was satisfied. And the bears invariably came down to dinner so regularly each afternoon that we could almost set our watches by their appearance. They kept right on feeding until morning.

It has long been a popular belief that grizzly bears hook the salmon out onto the shore with a swipe of their long-clawed paws. That they are capable of this sort of fishing, and occasionally do so, is beyond doubt; but the more normal method is just to walk out onto a shallow place and pick up the salmon in their teeth. Carrying it out onto the shore, they will strip off the flesh as dexterously as an Eskimo woman using an *oolo* knife. Laying the salmon on its side, the bear will hold it securely with the claws of one paw while he cleverly tears off the whole fillet with his teeth; then, turning it over, he will repeat the procedure—leaving little more than the head, tail, and bony skeleton. Often they will crouch down on their broad brown bellies and take it quite leisurely, nibbling and using the back of a big paw much in the fashion of a plate to catch the crumbs before they fall into the sand.

The feast of the bears was also a feast for the sea gulls. There was generally a flock of the noisy sea birds around the bears' fishing places, awaiting their return. They would hop about from rock to rock, trying to peck out the eyes of the salmon as they swam by. But they were really waiting for the bears. Often these gulls would become impatient and fly, squawking, over the spots where the hairy fishermen were still snoozing in their day beds in the alders, raucously urging them to get started at catching salmon. They would follow a bear down the stream, flying noisily around him and hovering close until the skeleton of a salmon was left on the shore. Then the birds would swoop in and fight over the remains. The gulls were like bird dogs in keeping us informed as to where the bears were and when they were coming down out of the alders.

Andy and I would stay in our blind until it got too late to make pictures. Even in the fog and rain we would wait just to watch the bears, and there was hardly a time we were not rewarded with some new experience of excitement, amusement, or revelation about these fascinating creatures. When we saw one whom we recognized from previous observations, it was like seeing an old

friend, and we talked about them in much the same manner. We learned that they were the most cautious when they first came out and their boldness increased as it became darker. Very frequently we had them less than seventy-five feet away, sometimes more than one at a time. There were occasions, however, when we suddenly realized it was almost dark and there were far too many grizzlies prowling around entirely too close, and we made a hasty retreat. Wet, cold, and miserable, we would make our way wearily but happily back to the meager shelter of an over-turned little canvas canoe, with only the wet moss to lie on to get some rest, or maybe just eat a little cold food (we never built a fire when in good country) and eke out the endless night by sitting huddled in the rain and periodically prancing up and down to get warm. It was in the middle of the days that we got our best rest—just as the bears did.

One evening, as we made our way through the rain to a place of retreat, we ran onto a big bear who gave us a bit of excitement. It was almost dark, due to the heavy, low-hanging clouds, dense fog, and rain. We were traveling along the bank of a stream and saw this old fellow leisurely eating a salmon directly ahead on our course.

"Aw, he'll break and run when we get closer. . . ." assured Andy, as we trudged wearily on our way. We had been traveling for a mile or more through marshy country, where there wasn't a place to sit down or rest our heavy packs; and we were in no mood to go six steps out of the way. But this big grizzly showed no signs of budging as we got closer and closer. Finally, at about thirty yards, we stopped and Andy yelled at the old fellow and waved his hat in the air, to try to scare him away. Instead of running the bear got to his feet, and the hair went up on his back as he stared defiantly at us. The wind was blowing at right angles, so he was unable to get our scent. What his weak little eyes told him we were I do not know; but he certainly showed unmistakable signs of aggressive intentions. Andy slipped a cartridge into the chamber of his 280 Ross as the bear made a couple of suspicious movements in our direction.

316

"That bear's apt to charge," warned Andy, although shooting any bear was the last thing we had any desire to do.

We both shouted and waved our hats. But all this didn't seem to mean a thing to Mr. Grizzly. He didn't seem to like our looks or the sounds of our voices and made another couple of menacing steps toward us.

"Maybe if I circle out around him, into the wind until he can get my scent . . . he may stop all this foolishness. . . ." suggested Andy. "Maybe he's never seen a man with a gun before."

The bear stood defiantly watching my companion as he walked slowly out around this arrogant critter to where the wind would carry the human scent to him. His big head occasionally swung back toward me, as he appeared to be trying to figure out just what it was all about. We had already gone so close there was serious doubt that he could be stopped before he got one of us, if he suddenly decided to do so. One of the fundamental rules in dealing with these big grizzlies, among those who know them, is never to let one get closer than you can conveniently and accurately put at least three shots from a high-powered rifle into them where it will do the most good. Andy was so tired, and, with a fifty-pound pack on his back, quick and accurate shooting would be severely handicapped. It was a dangerous situation.

Then, very suddenly, the bear sprang into action, as though a powerful spring had been released. The instant he got the scent he made a wild leap and went splashing across the stream and continued racing away through the tall grass of the marshland, as though a dozen devils were right at his heels. He had not associated what he saw with man, the only thing on earth that is feared by these creatures; but, once he got that human scent, he realized what a cardinal mistake he had made and took off with all the speed of which he was capable.

How different bears are from humans in this respect. They do not depend on their weak little eyes as they do on their much more highly educated noses. It is just the opposite with humans. If we had smelled that bear, for example, we would never have been convinced of his presence until we actually saw the animal; for man depends on his eyesight to the same proportionate degree that bears depend on their sense of smell.

We covered a considerable area of the country, transporting the camera and canvas canoe from one stream to another, carrying everything over the alder-covered ridges, across wide areas of mossy tundra, where walking became an ordeal, or through big marshes, where there was often the hazard of breaking through the floating vegetation into bottomless depths of muddy mire that was as bad as quicksand. Sometimes we just dragged the canoe over the tall, wet grass. We saw the bears practically every day, except when we went back to the little base camp to catch up on rest in a sleeping bag and a couple of big meals of hot food for our neglected stomachs. According to entries made in my diary, the numbers of these grizzlies seen on the following consecutive days were: 6—7—9—6—12—none—18 and 10 bears. Our lives became increasingly adapted to the daily routines of the hairy fishermen, with whom we became more and more familiar.

When we were traveling along a stream we never walked on the shore but in the water, where tracks leave no telltale scent. When we carried the canoe and camera ashore, to make a temporary camp or take off overland, we would wash out our tracks from the water's edge to as far back from the shore as we could, using a light tin bucket that was carried as part of the equipment. We also had a special method of camouflaging the overturned canoe if the grass was not tall enough to hide it. I had improvised a net of codfish line, which fitted over the canoe much like a woman's hair net. Into this it was easy to tuck tufts of grass, which gave our shelter the appearance of a hump on the tundra.

One dreary, drizzly early morning we had a visitor, as we lay huddled, shivering, underneath the canoe, half awake and wondering if sunshine would ever come again—and convinced that no human being in his right mind should subject himself to such a personal ordeal, just to watch some grizzly bears all doing what comes naturally to them. Several times during the night we heard bears sloshing along the shore or splashing in the stream, about seventy-five feet away.

As approaching daylight filtered through the fog and drizzle, the great shaggy head of a bear appeared looking down through the grass, not more than ten feet away. Seen through sleepy, half-open eyes, it set off something in the nature of a chain reaction of impulses that was much like a mental explosion. We almost kicked through the canvas bottom of the canoe in a wild scramble to get out. The overly inquisitive bear made an equally sudden and undignified effort to get somewhere else. He almost fell over backward in getting started. By the time we were wide awake enough to know what was actually going on, the big grizzly was trying to cross the seventy-foot stream in a single leap; and he kept right on across the tundra, sending up a spray from the wet grass like the wake of a speeding motorboat.

We later found, from his tracks, that this bear had been walking along the bank of the stream and, seeing the unfamiliar hump on the tundra, had ventured over to investigate. About half way he had stopped and walked back and forth, suspiciously standing on his hind legs to get a better look. Then, curiosity getting the best of his better judgment, the old fellow had ventured to within about ten feet before finding out the mistake he had made. Why this bear had not taken the usual and simple precaution of circling to get the benefit of an explanation via scent on wind I cannot understand. Maybe he was just a dumb bear. He could have smelled us all right, for I hadn't had a bath for three months!

Time after time we watched these creatures in the normal course of their unmolested daily lives. Several times we saw them put their noses to work as they crossed our invisible tracks across the moss-carpeted tundra. They always seemed to show the same attitude toward man. It is doing these creatures an injustice to call this fear, for there was always a haughty aspect to their sudden alarm; and there was invariably an indication of cautious curiosity. One big fellow was more bold, or more inquisitive, than the others. After that first suspicious investigation he slowly followed the trail until it led him to one of the blinds we had improvised with alders stuck into the ground. Every little way he would stand up on his big, flat hind feet and sway his long snout to carefully sniff the air. As he approached the old blind, he became quite excited in his boldness, prancing about nervously as he stood up and stared at the man-made contraption, and a couple of times jumping back, as if fighting a strong impulse to make a wiser retreat. We couldn't help laughing as we watched his antics through our binoculars. Finally, to our surprise, this bear mustered enough brazenness to venture right up to where he could stick his nose inside where we had lain hidden for several hours. The scent must have been strong there. But he did not stay long after this. Apparently satisfying his curiosity and finding out all he wanted to know, he suddenly wheeled about and went racing away.

The most memorable of all these experiences was one evening when Andy and I lay in a drizzling rain on a lookout and watched twelve Alaska brown bears come out of the alders and wander down to fish in a short stretch of the same rather small stream. For about an hour and a half, until it got too dark to see them clearly, they were all in sight at the same time. This was on July 28. They were all big bears, and it was one of the most wonderful experiences I have ever been privileged to witness in all the time I have spent in game country, as well as one of the most informative of my observations of grizzly bears.

I had long realized how definitely and how strongly each grizzly was invested with his own individual character and temperament. We became increasingly aware of this from watching the many bears we saw day after day, and it was this realization that often prompted us to give some of them their nicknames. This particular occasion, however, provided the best evidence we had observed. I do not remember the exact procedure of events, for only remarks of a general nature were ever entered in the notes of my diary; and the recollections which stand out so vividly are important because of their implications rather than the order in which the happenings took place. For instance, one bear would amble leisurely down a trail out of the broad expanse of alders on the low hillside that rose a short distance beyond the stream. Walking out into the shallow water of the long stretch of riffles, he would pick up a salmon in his teeth, like a dog might carry it out onto the bank, would crouch down on his belly and begin methodically stripping off the fillets. As the next one came down the same trail through the grass and approached the first bear already enjoying supper, the second arrival would make a detour out around the first one, avoiding too close a meeting. It was plainly evident that these two were not on friendly terms, and there was no doubt as to which one held the other in unmistakable respect. When the third one arrived, however, the situation was completely reversed, and the first one got up and moved out of the way, standing off to one side while his obvious superior padded along on his way with haughty arrogance. When the next one came along, he might walk directly up to his neighbors; they would touch noses in a most friendly manner and stand eye to eye for a few moments of chummy greetings; then the late arrival would hurry out to get a salmon and rejoin his friend at a table for two. This is not exactly as it happened, but it is a faithful indication of the attitude of these bears toward one another. Throughout all the time that we watched them, moving back and forth at their fishing along that short stretch of stream and frequently meeting, there was no doubt that each individual and his temperament was a matter of full understanding to each of the others.

38

THE BEAR WHO WANTED IN
Martha Martin

In the following selection the reader glimpses a rich and reward-
ing life in the Alaskan wilderness, where marauding bears are but
an incident in a somewhat perilous existence. Martha Martin
writes of the experiences she and her husband Don and their
children encountered on a frontier where most of the necessities
have to be wrested from the country by force and strategy.
Following the loss of their baby daughter, the Martins adopted
two Yugoslavian children who had to be taught to speak English,
schooled at home in the three R's and shown how to protect themselves in the wilds.

    Home On the Bear's Domain, by Martha Martin, is the second
of two books telling of the Martin family's life in the upland
prospecting country of the forty-ninth state. It was published in
New York in 1954. The excerpt chosen for publication here is
reprinted with the permission of The MacMillan Company.
Copyright 1954 by The MacMillan Company.

THE MEN, after puttering around at chores for a few days,
decided to do some hand mining in the upper level. . . . They
wanted to get right at mining, but I reminded them that if we
were going to eat meat that winter they'd better go hunting first.
They decided they could both mine and hunt if they lived in the
log cabin near the upper tunnel, for that was a good hunting area.
They took their bedrolls and some grub and went off.

    Their first stay was for three nights, and they got one deer.
They left a quarter of it in the cabin for themselves and brought
the rest of it down to us. Since they now had their work pretty
well lined up, they felt they could give some attention to the chil-

dren, and suggested that the boys take turns going up to the cabin with them. The boys, delighted at the thought of hunting and "working in the mine," agreed to wash dishes, pack the wood and water, and to perform generally in an angelic manner. Because Little Billy was ahead with his lessons, he had the first turn.

When they got to the cabin, they saw that the door was open. Everything in the cabin was a mess. The leg of deer was missing, and it was plain to see which way it had gone, for there was only a hole where a window had been. Worse yet, bear droppings smeared the floor. The men wasted some time accusing each other of leaving the door open and thus inviting a bear in. Then Sam came down to the house to get another window sash while Don cleaned up the bear dumplings.

They stayed up there three more nights, and killed three deer. One deer was put into the salt barrel there, and the other two were brought down for me to can. This time both men made sure the door was closed. But they weren't really worried about the bear's returning, for it was already November and time all bears were in their winter dens. Very likely this old bear had been on the way to his den when he passed the cabin, saw the door open, and a quarter of a deer lying on the table. . . .

The next day the men left early for the Hill. This time Burt went with them. Again the cabin door was open. The barrel of salt meat was gone—and so was another window. The men were pretty mad, and they said they would hunt the bear down and kill it. But they had Burt with them, and they didn't want to take him on any long bear hunt. They looked around, trying to find where the bear had hidden the meat, but they couldn't.

Because that was the last spare window sash we had, they nailed boards over the hole and went on about their business, always keeping a sharp lookout for the bear. They stayed three nights, killed one deer, and brought it down with them.

The men stayed with us overnight, skinned and butchered the deer, packed some food, and went back up the hill. Because of the bear problem none of the boys went with them. In a couple of hours they were back, and in such a wrath it's a wonder they didn't bite themselves. The old bear had been in the cabin again and had wrecked the place for sure. The table was upset and the dishes were smashed. The stove was knocked down and the stove-pipe had been tromped on. The handle was broken off the iron frying pan. The bear had eaten the butter and the rolled oats and the bacon and raisins and a lot of other stuff. Coffee and beans and macaroni were spilled. Flour was all over the place. And the bear had gone out the other window.

The men took windows from the bunkhouse to put in the cabin, and gathered another outfit of everything they needed to live on the Hill. Both made two trips that day, and then Don left Sam at the cabin. Don said he would pack up the last load the next morning and be prepared to stay at the cabin until they got that bear if it took all winter. He meant it. The bear must have planned to spend the winter there too, for it had dug a hole at the side of the cabin and gone through it down under the floor, where it had gathered moss and grass to make a winter bed.

The bear came again that night, came in the rain and the dark when Sam couldn't see to shoot, and came right up onto the porch! Sam thought the bear might open the door, come in, and find him the only available fresh meat. So he pounded on the dishpan to scare it away. When he heard it go off the porch, he opened the door a tiny crack, poked the gun barrel out, and fired a shot just to let it know he was holding down his claim on the bear's domain.

As soon as Don got up there the next morning, they went bear hunting and had no luck at all. The weather was foul and threatened to become worse. They didn't even see a deer, and all the deer tracks pointed downhill, a sure indication of a bad storm. They quit hunting early, went back to the cabin, and plugged the hole down under it with heavy poles and logs. Then they sat and discussed ways and means of getting the bear.

Soon after dark the bear came again, went directly to its hole, and did a lot of growling when it found it plugged. For a while it tried digging new places, then gave up and went around front to find something to eat. They heard the cracking of deer bones and a lot more growling. The animal knew the men were in the cabin and was pretty mad about it. They fired a couple of shots out the door and it went away, but I don't think the men slept very well that night.

The next day, because the weather was too stormy for hunting, Sam reinforced the base of the cabin to keep the bear from digging another hole and Don picked up every single scrap that a bear might think of eating. He collected some of the bigger bones and a skin, tied them together with a wire, fastened some tin cans to the bundle, and wired the works to a stump. He ran a string from the tin cans into the cabin, took out a window sash, got his gun, tied the string to his foot so that he could make the cans rattle, and then shut his eyes and practiced shooting at the noise. Since he wouldn't get a chance to shoot by sight, he figured that he might do it by sound. The men did their chores, got ready, and waited.

It was a wild black night. Rain poured down and wind whipped through the trees. Sam got tired of waiting and went to bed. He said no bear would be foolish enough to go prowling around in such foul weather, but Don kept watch. Toward midnight he heard it coming. He poked Sam. Together they listened. Sure enough, there it was. Above the howl of the wind and the pounding of rain on the shake roof they heard its heavy steps. Don went to the fire to get his hands warm and flexible.

Three times the bear stomped around the cabin. Then it went out front and looked for something to eat. Don got to the window quickly, felt the frame and the wall, and held his gun ready. There came a big rattle, and before the first clanking had stopped Don shot at the sound.

He heard the bullet thud and knew he had hit something, but he didn't know whether it was the bear or the stump. There was no growl, no sound at all, but sometimes a bear just clears out on tiptoe. Bears don't say anything if they are killed, either. The men knew they had either killed the animal or missed it entirely. They talked about it until they could muster enough courage to peep out the door. They lit their lamps, opened the door a crack, and took a quick look.

Nothing nabbed them. Though they opened the door wider, they still saw nothing and heard nothing. Then they got real

325

brave, opened the door completely, held their lamps high, and took a good look around. They saw the tin cans but not the bear. They weren't going to do any more looking that stormy night, so they went to bed.

They found her next morning, dead as a doornail, lying about fifty feet away, down the trail. The bullet had gone in behind the shoulder and come out at the throat. She was a middle-sized female grizzly with a fine prime skin. Don decided to skin her and send the hide to a cousin in California who valued such things as bear rugs and had been asking us to get him one for his den.

The worst of the storm was over, but it still rained. Don thought the children shouldn't miss seeing the bear just because of a little rain, so he came down after us.

How excited the children were! How they talked and talked about the bear! They examined it thoroughly, asked many questions, and made lots of guesses. We figured out how the bear had opened the cabin door. Her fangs were on the wooden knob to help us.

The cabin porch is only an extension of the peaked roof; being high, it makes a handy place to hang deer out of the rain. We always hung the deer there, and we butchered some of them on the porch. The scraps and the skin and the useless parts were just tossed to the ground in front of the porch and left where they fell. Because, while the butchering was going on, the men carried the good parts into the cabin, the wooden knob on the door was often turned by a bloody hand. Some of the blood, and possibly even small scraps of meat, stuck to the door handle and dried there. That old bear must have come along licking up tidbits from the porch floor, smelled around and, happening to find a good smell on the doorknob, licked it hard enough to turn it, so that the door swung open and there lay the quarter of deer right before her. Being a smart bear, she remembered, did the same thing next time, and got a whole salted deer. Then she did it again and was again rewarded for her efforts. One of those times she must have bitten the knob, for her teeth marks are there; but she didn't bite it hard, since it wasn't splintered. The children thought her a pretty smart bear.

As soon as we got to the log cabin, Uncle Sam announced that he was cook for the day. Since we had appreciated his pumpkin pies, he would make us some more pies, but he wanted the little children to help him. I was on to Sam: he didn't want to smell an old bear, and quickly grabbed another job, the kind of job he couldn't be expected to leave even to help turn the bear over. But we were all having fun, and nobody cared whether he helped with the bear or not. Anyway, it didn't smell too bad. . . . And besides, Uncle Sam did cook us a good lunch.

GRIZZLIES IN FOLKLORE AND LEGEND

39

A GRIZZLY'S SLY LITTLE JOKE

Joaquin Miller

Do grizzly bears possess a sense of humor? The following short tale by Joaquin Miller offers evidence that such may be the case. But, on the other hand, perhaps the old Indian who related the story of the joking bear told it with tongue in cheek; the redman has a knack of concealing his enjoyment of drollery behind a stolid-faced façade. Miller lived among the Digger Indians of California for two years, however, and should have known who was playing tricks.

Joaquin Miller is best known for his books of verse depicting the Northwest frontier. "The Grizzly's Sly Little Joke" is taken from his book *True Bear Stories*, published in Chicago and New York by Rand, McNally and Company in 1900, pages 110–11. The book, written for children and dedicated to Miller's daughter (but enjoyable adult reading nevertheless), is presently available in an edition published in 1949 by Binfords and Mort, Publishers, at Portland, Oregon.

I KNOW AN OLD INDIAN who was terribly frightened by an old monster grizzly and her half-grown cub, one autumn, while out gathering manzanita berries. But, badly as he was frightened, he was not even scratched.

It seems that while he had his head raised, and was busy gathering and eating berries, he almost stumbled over an old bear and her cub. They had eaten their fill and fallen asleep in the trail on the wooded hillside. The old Indian had only time to turn on his heel and throw himself headlong in the large end of a hollow log, which luckily lay at hand. This, however, was only a temporary refuge. He saw, to his delight, that the log was open at the other end, and corkscrewing his way along toward the further end, he was about to emerge, when, to his dismay, he saw the old mother sitting down quietly waiting for him!

After recovering his breath as best he could in this hot contracted quarters, he elbowed and corkscrewed himself back to the place by which he first entered. But lo! the bear was there, sitting down, half smiling, and waiting to receive him warmly. This, the old Indian said, was repeated time after time, till he had no longer strength left to struggle further, and turned on his face to die, when she put her head in, touched the top of his head gently with her nose and then drew back, took her cub with her and shuffled on.

I went to the spot with the Indian a day or two afterward, and am convinced that his story was exactly as narrated. And when you consider that the bear could easily have entered the hollow log and killed him at any time, you will see that she had at least a faint sense of fun in that "cat and mouse" amusement with the frightened Indian.

40

BEGGING THE BEAR'S PARDON
Charles Fletcher Lummis

Charles Fletcher Lummis first became interested in the Indians of Western America when he was sent by the *Los Angeles Times* to cover the Apache disturbances led by Geronimo in 1886. After suffering a stroke in 1888 he went to live among the Tiguas at Pueblo Isleta. Here he became inextricably involved in researching and recording Indian history and mythology. In the 1890's he became editor of *The Land of Sunshine*, a popular magazine of its day published in Los Angeles, where he gained for himself a place among that company of American editors irrevocably linked with their media and its locale.

The Navaho legend reprinted here is taken from Lummis' *Mesa, Cañon and Pueblo*, published in New York and London by the Century Company in 1925, pages 162–63. Permission for the use of this excerpt was generously granted by Appleton-Century, Book Publishers.

WITH THE PUEBLOS, the mountain lion or cougar is the king of beasts—following our civilized idea very closely; but with the Navajos the bear holds first rank. He is not only the greatest, wisest, and most powerful of brutes, but even surpasses man! The Navajo is a brave and skilled warrior and would not fear the bear for its deadly teeth and claws, but of its supposed supernatural powers he is in mortal dread. I have offered a Navajo shepherd, who had accidentally discovered a bear's cave, twenty dollars to show it to me, or even to tell me in what cañon it lay; but he refused, in a manner and with words which showed me that if I found the cave I would be in danger from more than the bear. The Indian was a very good friend of mine, too; but he was sure that if he were even the indirect cause of any harm to the bear, the bear would know it and kill him and all his family. And so even my princely offer was no inducement to a man who was working hard for five dollars a month.

There is only one case in which the Navajos will meddle with a bear. That is when he has killed a Navajo, and the Indians know exactly which bear is the murderer. Then a strong armed party, headed by the proper religious officers (medicine-men), proceed to the cave of the bear. Halting a short distance in front of the den, they go through a strange service of apology, which to us would seem entirely grotesque, but which to them is unutterably solemn. The praises of the bear, commander of beasts, are loudly sung, and his pardon is humbly invoked for the unpleasant deed to which they are now driven. Having duly apologized beforehand, they proceed as best they may to kill the bear, and then go home to fast and purify themselves. This aboriginal greeting, "I beg your pardon, and hope you will bear no resentment against me, but I have come to kill you," is quite as funny as the old farmer I used to know in New Hampshire who was none too polite to his wife, but always addressed his oxen thus: "Now, if you please, whoa haish, Bary! Also Bonny! There! Thank you!"

41

SKINNING A BEAR
Author Unknown

The following morsels of whimsy, taken from a collection with a title quite as amusing as the stories themselves, go back into American backwoods folklore so far that their originators are long forgotten. They were published in *Twenty-five Cents Worth of Nonsense; or, the Treasury Box of Unconsidered Trifles*, Philadelphia, New York, and Boston, Fisher & Brothers, 184?, and were reprinted in *A Treasury of American Folk Lore, Stories, Ballads, and Traditions of the People*, edited by B. A. Botkin and published in New York by Crown Publishers, in 1944. "Skinning a Bear" appears on page 24 of the *Treasury of American Folk Lore*, "The Tame Bear" on page 26.

ONE DAY when Oak Wing's sister war going to a baptizing, and had her feed in a bag under her arm, she seed a big bear that had come out from a holler tree, and he looked first at her, then at the feed, as if he didn't know which to eat fust. He kinder poked out his nose, and smelt of the dinner which war sassengers maid of bear's meat and crocodile's liver. She stood a minute and looked at him, in hopes he would feel ashamed of himself and go off; but he then cum up and smelt of her, and then she thort twar time to be stirring. So she threw the dinner down before him, and when he put his nose to it, to take a bite, she threw herself on him, an caught the scuff of his neck in her teeth; and the bear shot ahead, for it felt beautiful, as her teeth war as long an as sharp as nales. He tried to run, an she held on with her teeth, an it stript the skin clear off of him, and left him as naked as he was born, she held on with her teeth till it cum clear off the tale. The bear was seen a week afterwards up in Muskrat Hollow, running without his skin. She made herself a good warm petticoat out of the pesky varmint's hide.

THE TAME BEAR
Author Unknown

THE CRETURS OF THE FOREST is of different kinds, like humans. Some is stupid and some is easy to larn. The most knowing cretur that I ever seed war a barr that my darter Pinetta picked up in the woods. It used to follow her to church, and at last it got so tame, it would cum into the house, and set down in one corner of the fireplace to warm itself. I larned it to smoke a pipe and while it sot in one corner smoking, I sot in the other with my pipe. We couldn't talk to one another; but we would look, and I knowed by the shine of his eye what he wanted to say, though he didn't speak a word. The cretur would set up o'nights when I war out late, and open the door for me. But it war the greatest in churning butter. It did all that business for the family. As last it got so civilized that it caught the whooping cough and died. My wife went to the minister and tried to get him to give the barr a christian burial; but the skunk war so bigoted that he wouldn't do it, and I telled him the barr war a better christian than he ever war.

A BEAR FOR WORK
Author Unknown

This ludicrous tidbit of logging-camp memorabilia is taken from
Idaho Lore, of the American Guide Series, published in Lewiston
in 1939 by Caxton Press, and is used here with the permission of
George H. Curtis, secretary of state for the state of Idaho. Bears
are pretty ludicrous themselves, being large and clumsy looking
(and lovable, too, when so young that they have not realized they
are supposed to be ferocious). So they have just naturally made
a place for themselves in the hearts of humans and in the pages
of folklore.

PAUL PEAVY WAS IN TOWN from his logging camp buying supplies when Ted Chelde asked: "What in darnation you feedun
so much honey to lumberjacks for? Ain't that pretty fancy feed
for them?"

"This honey ain't for them. It's an investment."

"How come?" propounded Ted.

"Well, I make lumberjacks leave their coats in camp and in
freezun weather I get more out of them. But it ain't enough. So
I got the idea to make my silvertip cub work too. He's crazy
about honey and will climb a rainbow to get it. So I strap a pair
of broadaxes on his feet and give him a sniff at a can and then
shin up a tree with it. Up comes Annabel, the axes scoring the
tree on two sides. Then I lower the can and down he goes, and
raise it and up he shins, just hewing the tree as smooth as a whistle.
Then to make railroad ties all I gotta do is chop it over and whack
it into lengths.

PEEPING TOM
Beth Day

Beth Day takes the reader into British Columbia's grizzly-bear country, where Jim and Laurette Stanton exchanged civilization for one of the most remote regions of North America in 1919 and found contentment. The Stantons had no money, but Jim scraped a living by hand-logging—until the price of lumber hit rock bottom—and running a trap line. To the Stantons, the grizzlies were neighbors; living in a rugged land of giant glaciers, inaccessible forests and 13,000-foot mountain peaks never lost its charm. That grizzlies can be funny was no news to the Stantons after nearly half a century of contact with them.

Beth Day has written half a dozen books for adults, on a variety of subjects, and a number of children's books mostly about cowboys and cowgirls. She met Jim and diminutive Laurette Stanton through her father Ralph Feagles, who hunted grizzlies with Jim as his guide. "Peeping Tom" is taken from the book Beth Day's father suggested that she write about the Stanton's, *Grizzlies in Their Back Yard,* published in New York by Julian Messner, Inc. (© Beth Day, 1956), and is reprinted by permission of the publishers. The story appears on pages 147–49.

Scout was a natural-born hunter. He seemed to know exactly what his master wanted. If Jim took down his shotgun, Scout was ready to retrieve ducks, but if Jim reached for his rifle, Scout was set for deer, and he wouldn't have looked at a duck if it had sat on his nose. . . .

At home Scout stayed close to the cabin and made no effort to tangle with the grizzlies that grazed in the nearby flats. So long as they kept their peace, it was a live-and-let-live arrangement. Except for Peeping Tom.

Peeping Tom was too curious to keep his distance. A four-year-old red-coated male grizzly, he became fascinated with the sight of Jim working on his gas-boat. Jim had loaned his boat to a man who let it beat on the beach until the ribs were cracked, and Jim's first spring job was to caulk it. As soon as it was warm enough to work outside, he put the gas-boat up on ways built at the top of the high-tide mark and crawled under to work. He was lying on his back, pounding oakum into the boat seams, when he suddenly had the odd sensation that he was being watched. He rolled over—and looked directly into the face of a big red grizzly, peering under the boat at him from a distance of eight feet. He stared curiously at Jim for a few minutes, then, apparently satisfied as to what Jim was doing, lumbered off a few feet and lay on the grass, with his head down so that he could see under the boat and watch the work.

This was too much for Scout. He made a furious barking charge and succeeded in running the bear off. But fifteen minutes later the big red grizzly was back again, peering under the boat, his face as friendly and interested as before.

Next morning he was back. Once again Scout ran him off. Fifteen minutes later he reappeared. This went on for several mornings, and finally Scout got tired of running him. The bear lay on his side of the boat, watching Jim work, and Scout lay on the other, his worried eyes on the grizzly to make sure he didn't start trouble.

He didn't. Each morning during the two weeks that Jim worked on his boat the bear walked over, got down where he could stick his huge head under, "smiled" at Jim, then settled down a few feet off where he could watch. In the afternoon, when hunger finally overcame his curiosity, Peeping Tom would wander over into the flats to dig some roots for his dinner. But next morning he was back—on the dot. He never made trouble—he simply liked to kibitz.

45

COYOTE AND GRIZZLY
Katharine Berry Judson

A native of New York State, Katharine Berry Judson came "out West" in 1905 to work as librarian at Kalispell, Montana. The next year she became head of the periodical department in Seattle Public Library, a position she held for five years. After taking her master's degree at the University of Washington in 1911, she became an instructor in the researching of Northwest history at the university. It was during this period that Miss Judson's published works appeared. These included a number of books on the Pacific Northwest, particularly early Oregon history, and half a dozen small volumes of Indian legends taken from tribes of the Mississippi Valley, Plains States, the Southwest, Pacific Northwest, and Alaska.

The two grizzly-bear legends appearing here from the Nez Percés of Washington and Idaho and the Tlingits of British Columbia and Alaska were taken, respectively, from *Myths and Legends of the Pacific Northwest, and especially of Washington and Oregon*,[1] and *Myths and Legends of Alaska*.[2] They both indicate the great respect with which the grizzly was regarded by the Indians of the Pacific Northwest.

ONCE THERE WAS A GRIZZLY who was always angry. One day when traveling through the woods she came upon a band of Indians. She ate them all. In the evening, when she had reached home, she had a bad headache and in the night she became very sick because she had eaten so many Indians. She was sick for a

[1] *Myths and Legends of the Pacific Northwest, and especially of Washington and Oregon*, selected by Katharine Berry Judson (Chicago, A. C. McClurg & Company, 1910), 114–15.
[2] Katharine Berry Judson, *Myths and Legends of Alaska* (Chicago, A. C. McClarg & Company, 1911).

week and almost died. She sent for Coyote to come as a medicine man. But Coyote said to his friends, "I do not care if she dies. It would not hurt me or anybody else. Everybody would be glad of it." But as his wife told him to go in company with others, he finally went up to see Old Grizzly.

After a while he came to Old Grizzly's house and made medicine. Then she got well. He told her she was sick from eating too many choke cherries, because he thought all the people would run away if he told the truth and said it was from eating too many Indians. But when the people were gone and he himself was ready to run he told her she had eaten too many Indians.

Old Grizzly jumped up and chased Coyote. He ran up the hills; he ran down the valleys; he ran through the woods. At last he changed himself into a buffalo eating grass by the trail. Now Grizzly Bear thought she would catch Coyote, no matter into what form he changed himself. So when she saw the buffalo, she started to kill it, but then she saw Coyote's trail running past it. So she followed the trail. When she had gone some ways, Coyote changed himself into his own form again. He called after Grizzly Bear and said, "You are only a foolish old bear. You can never catch me."

When Grizzly Bear heard Coyote's voice, she started after him again. After a while Coyote changed himself into an old man who had smallpox. He was in a tepee by the trail. His clothes were old and worn. When Grizzly came up, she looked into the house. She asked the man if any one had passed. He told her a man had crossed the river. She saw a bridge with tracks on it. The bridge was made of willows. Now she thought she could get across on that bridge, so she walked on it. The bridge broke, she fell into the water, and was drowned.

Then Coyote turned himself into his own form and went back to his people. He told them he had killed Grizzly Bear.

46

WHY THE TLINGITS USE
THE GRIZZLY BEAR CREST

Katharine Berry Judson

A LONG TIME AGO when some of the Kagwantan clan were catching herring at Town-at-Mouth-of-Lake, a bear came to the place where they were fishing. The bear reached through the smoke hole and stole the herring they were drying. Then the people said; "Who is this thief that is stealing our fish?"

Because they said that, the grizzly bear killed all of them.

Then the Kagwantan seized their spears and set out to kill the bears nearby. When they found them the bears were lying in holes they had dug out for themselves. The people said to them, "Come out here. We will fight it out." So the bears came out and the people killed them. They took the skins from the heads of the bears and preserved them. That is how the Kagwantan came to use the grizzly bear crest.

YELLOWSTONE PARK GRIZZLY BEARS

47

THE HUNGRY GRIZZLIES
OF YELLOWSTONE PARK

M. P. Skinner

Since this book was conceived in Yellowstone Park it is only fitting that it should end there. In all fairness, the bruins of Yellowstone cannot be ignored. The Park is the one place where they are still plentiful. In General Hiram M. Chittenden's book, *The Yellowstone National Park*, published in 1895,[1] this early explorer of Geyser Land wrote, "Bruin generally accommodates him [the tourist]. The fine instincts of that intelligent brute have shown him that it is much easier to get a living from the refuse about the hotels than to forage for it in the wilds of parsimonious nature. Nightfall, therefore, always brings him about to the great delight of the game-seeking tourists. The incidents of each season to which these bears unwittingly give rise are among the amusing features of tourist life in that region." (Unfortunately, not all incidents with bears, either black or grizzled, are "amusing." Many visitors to Yellowstone and other western parks are injured each year while feeding or photographing bears.)

M. P. Skinner, who studied Yellowstone bears for thirty years, wrote *Bears in the Yellowstone* (published in Chicago by A. C. McClurg and Company in 1925) especially for Park visitors who wanted to learn more about the bears. Although many of Yellowstone's silvertips have, in recent years, been drugged with tranquilizers, measured, tattooed, tagged and "wired" for radio tracking[2] they still behave much as they did when Chittenden observed them. The following excerpt from Skinner's book (pages 45–50

[1] General Hiram Martin Chittenden, *The Yellowstone National Park*, 3rd ed. (Cincinnati, The Robert Clarke Company, 1899), 184; also available in a 1964 edition, edited by Richard A. Bartlett and published by the University of Oklahoma Press.

[2] Craighead and Craighead, "Knocking Out Grizzlies for Their Own Good," *National Geographic Magazine*, Vol. 118, No. 2 (August, 1960), 276–91.

and 65–68) offers proof that bruin has not changed his habits much. Any tourist who has visited Yellowstone Park recently knows the bears are still hungry.

IN SUCH A PLACE as the Yellowstone, where practically all the bears are seen about kitchen-scrap piles, and foraging about camps, it seems very natural to assume that this is the bears' food, or at least the main part. . . . Of course, it is fortunate for us all that bruin *does* like these man-made foods, otherwise most of us would not see so much of him as we do. On the other hand, we would not have so much trouble with camp-foraging bears and we would not have to guard our supplies so closely. Still it was these scraps that originally brought the Yellowstone bears to our notice and made them so famous that now it has become an established custom to pour out these supplies for them at certain well-known places.

These bears did not take to garbage suddenly and at once. Still less did they come in a body and suddenly become a main attraction of the Park. They had to learn the way, had to learn they would be safe, and even had to learn to like man-made food. When they started to show themselves away back in the early nineties, they came at dusk and only one or two at a time. As they learned they were safe and the food rich and easy to get, they came oftener, earlier in the day, and in increased numbers. Of course, a female bear, who had learned to like scraps, brought her cubs to get some of the good things. And soon practically the whole population at least knew where it was to be had. Still there have always been several bears who never come to the feasting grounds.

Strange to say, early each season, the bears are chary of coming to these garbage piles, and come only at night and then furtively. It is as if they were fearful that the previous year's protection and friendliness had been withdrawn, and need reassurance each season. But it does not take them long to acquire it, and soon they get bolder and within ten days come out in daytime, and a few days later they are feeding on the garbage at all hours of the day. In a way they seem to know about when the truck is due with fresh supplies, for they often begin to congregate about that time.

Most of the scraps are eaten upon the spot and very little is carried away by the black bears. The only exceptions being the more highly prized and delectable bacon rinds and ham skins, especially from boiled hams, which are almost always carried off to a safe place where the bear can enjoy them in peace. The grizzlies are much more apt to carry food away. Indeed there are a number of bones distributed along the trails leading away from the feast, although this may have been done by coyotes or other animals. . . .

There are a number of well-worn bear paths radiating from each "bear-pile" like spokes from the hub of a wheel. And the bears seem finicky in their choice of which one to use. They may approach by one path and depart by the same, or by any other. Although some days they favor one path and some days another, they seldom arrive or leave together. The bears, always unsociable, live and travel, each one by himself and seem to look upon their fellow eaters as undesirable acquaintances forced upon them. . . .

At each hotel and camp in Yellowstone National Park, the remains from the tables are collected once, and sometimes twice, a day and carried a short distance away and thrown out. At Mammoth Hot Springs the number of bears is not large and all are black bears—the brown bear being only a colored black bear is included in the latter term. . . . At Old Faithful the bears are rather more numerous, although most of them are black bears, occasionally a true grizzly or silvertip will make his appearance. At West Thumb there are usually a few black bears about. At both Lake Outlet and the Grand Canyon, black bears are very common—sometimes as high as twenty or thirty being seen at once—grizzlies are common enough so that ten or a dozen are often seen in the evening. . . . Bears are more likely to be in the forested areas, but they are sometimes seen out in the open also. Somehow the idea is prevalent that the grizzly is more wedded to the forest than the black bear; but this is not so now, and never was. True, the black bear always has been a forest-ranging bear;

but in the old days, the grizzly often was found far out on the plains and a long way from trees of any kind.

Three-fourths of the bears we ordinarily see in the Park are near scrap piles, yet it is evident that this is not their principal food, or even any considerable part. Bears are hungry folk and eating most of the time, after dark as well as by daylight. With a population of two hundred bears, eating garbage even half the time would mean a hundred bears so engaged *all* the time. Whereas there are many hours during each twenty-four when not one bear is to be seen and there are seldom more than ten bears in sight at once at any point. To satisfy myself I watched and timed closely sixty-nine bears and found they ate from five to forty-five minutes at each visit, the average meal requiring twenty-four minutes. . . .

In the fall of the year, just before the bears enter their long winter sleep, they are intensely hungry and will go to extremes to get food. In October of 1920 I was at the Basin Ranger Station. While peacefully sleeping during the night of the twenty-second, I suddenly awakened to find myself sitting bolt upright on my cot listening to faint cracklings and bumps that seemed to come from the rear. Stopping only to catch up a handy axe I rushed out to see what was the matter. I did not see the bear but his tracks in the snow showed who the marauder was. It was too dark and cold to see just what damage he had done, but in the morning I had a better chance. From his tracks I found this bear had come up behind the Station and circled it three or four times, each time stopping to try the kitchen door. But that door was barred and resisted his efforts. Then he had turned his attention to the woodshed. This was merely a shell of a building with its siding nailed to the outside of the studding. As is usually the case, each board of this siding overlapped the next lower board and so afforded a hold for the bear's claws. By hooking his claws under the edge of the lower board and heaving upward he had torn off three boards and opened up the whole inside of the shed. Apparently he had entered the shed and was preparing to break open an old refrigerator box when my sudden jump from bed scared him away. So he got nothing. But he came back again on the night of the twenty-fourth and again on the twenty-seventh. Each time the noise I made scared him off so promptly that I neither saw him nor surprised him at his work. Yet he was so strong and dexterous that each time he got from three to five of those boards off before I could get out although I had nailed them fast as securely as I could each time.

... In May of 1915 I visited a faraway cabin where a young chap was spending a lonely time caring for horses at a stage relay station. He told me he had been visited a few nights previously by four grizzlies bent on breaking into his meat house, and showed me the battle ground inside, and the holes in the sod roof. It was in the spring and the bears, only just recently from their winter's sleep, were ravenously hungry. During the early evening, they were heard shuffling about the station, but as they made no overt attack and bears were a common occurrence, they were not molested. They became so quiet that my friend concluded they had gone away and went to bed at his usual hour. Some time during the dead of night he heard a thump-thump on the roof and soon located it over the meatshed that adjoined his bunkroom. He had a rifle, but had used up all his cartridges during the winter on coyotes and had neglected to get any more. But as the sounds increased in volume he caught up his lantern and a handy pitchfork and dashed into the meatroom. This was a stout log lean-to with no other opening than the door into the bunkroom. It needed only an instant to show that the bears were on the roof and *digging through!* The roof was of clay and sod and was still frozen, for there had been no fire under it, although the sun had melted the winter snow from the top. Still more fortunately the split poles supporting the earth were heavy and stronger than usual and overlaid with thin sheet iron, so that the bears had much more trouble than they would have had ordinarily. It was a difficult job but in time they got through the clay, bent back the sheet iron and began to spring the poles apart. Then began a long, hard fight. Whenever a crack showed, the pitchfork was jabbed up through, and whenever it struck a paw or the bears' underparts it brought snarls and "woofs." The paws were so tough, very little damage was done to them, but once in a while a fortunate jab brought blood from nose, breast, or belly. Occasionally a nose or a paw came down through a crack, but a steady clubbing on them caused their withdrawal and more howls. The bears would not give up the contest, but now that the strong odor of the ham, bacon and fresh meat came direct to their nostrils they redoubled their efforts. The poles were strong and the sheet iron protected the roof, but still it is likely they would have succeeded if they could have held out long enough, for George's violent efforts to keep all four bears busy in different parts of the roof were fast tiring him. There were many times during the long night when it seemed as if he must give up, but finally dawn began to break. At first the bears hardly noticed it, but after a time they became less active and shortly after sunrise they jumped down and retired, growling, to the woods. But the roof was a wreck. The frozen clay was scattered in chunks all about the building, the sheet iron bent, twisted and torn by tooth and claw into a tangle of metal shreds, and the stout roof poles were twisted, clawed and sprung apart until I wondered the bears had not tumbled through. George had not fully recovered when I saw him and he told me he was so exhausted that he doubted if he could have held out for another hour.

SPECIAL INCIDENT REPORT
E. L. Robinson

The following previously unpublished report from the files of Yellowstone Park's Old Faithful Sub-District is so congruent with an experience the authors had at Old Faithful Campground that we were delighted when we received it from Chief Park Ranger Wayne R. Howe for inclusion in this anthology.

In the autumn of 1963 we were camped in the older section of Old Faithful campground. Kept awake most of the night by a tentful of poker-playing collegians, we walked to the restrooms before dawn, Edgar accompanying me because my compass is nonoperative and the distance considerable. As we neared our destination we heard a horrible clatter—as if a horse were trying to kick its way out of a trailer. On our return the noise had not diminished, but when Edgar turned his flashlight toward the group of trailers and tents dimly visible under the pines we could see nothing amiss.

In the morning, in a nearby campsite occupied by a group of boys traveling in a golden hearse with a Pennsylvania license, we found that the bears had been busy. As I went for a morning walk along the same path taken before daylight, I found a number of excited people gathered at the place where we heard the commotion. I heard enough to put two and two together and get "bears" for an answer. Sure enough there had been several; at least one slamming a foot-locker around in a metal U-haul trailer in an attempt to rob the larder. One had been up a tree; all had left "when a man walking his wife to the john flashed his light this way." Could those bears have followed us in the dark and stayed to rob the boys in the golden chariot? Perhaps it was Sylvia, the mamma grizzly concerned in Ranger Robinson's report, with a new set of cubs.

Subject: Female Grizzly and three cubs episode.

A LARGE FEMALE GRIZZLY was first seen on May 15, 1961, in the Old Faithful area. She had three small cubs and did not seem to be in any hurry to leave and showed no fear of people. She stayed in the Old Faithful area; was observed on the 16th in the meadow behind Old Faithful Inn and the small Yellowstone Park Company Cabins that are referred to as "Skid Row." She has a green tag in each ear indicating that she has been tranquilized and is one of the group that Dr. Craighead is studying.

The next time that the grizzly (hereinafter called "Sylvia") was observed was on May 27 when she was reported at Midway Geyser Basin between the road and Firehole River. This was a wonderful opportunity for visitors to view nature in the raw. Cars were lined on both sides of the road as long as she was in the vicinity. A ranger watched the bear, (actually, watched people to keep them away from Sylvia and her three cubs), as reports were coming in to the ranger station that visitors were getting very close and were in real danger of being killed or badly mauled. It was then decided to leave a ranger watching at all times during daylight hours. The trap was set at Midway on May 31 but Sylvia moved out that afternoon. So the trap was returned to Old Faithful and reset in the campground.

On June 1, the rangers were preparing for another day of "baby sitting" Sylvia and her family at Midway but she was not to be found. At 11:30 A.M. a visitor reported seeing her and the cubs at Riverside Geyser. She finally stopped in the open meadow in front of Lower Hamilton Store and "grubbed" and grazed within fifty yards of the road. On the 2nd of June, rangers "baby sat" Sylvia all day. On June 3, she was not in sight and we thought our troubles were over but again this proved to be wishful thinking. At 8:00 P.M. she and her family leisurely strolled across Old Faithful Cone in plain view of approximately 250 visitors who were waiting for an eruption. One lady was apprehended for throwing bread to the bear, and was severely reprimanded.

At 6:45 A.M. on the 4th, Sub-District Ranger Robinson was awakened by G. H. Ogburn (the alarm was ready to go anyway), who stated that Sylvia was in the meadow by Lower Hamilton Store and visitors were approaching too close. Again we "baby sat" all day. She moved into the meadow behind "Skid Row" again and stayed until 4:15 P.M. when she moved to Lower Hamilton Store within twenty-five feet of the entrance. Visitors were within fifteen feet of her when rangers arrived. She was only interested in showing off her babies and grazing on the lush green grass. She grazed in the open meadow the remainder of the afternoon. Apparently, during the night she moved to the meadow behind "Skid Row" where she spent the day. On the 6th, she moved into the old part of the campground where she made a general nuisance of herself, by strewing garbage, frightening campers, etc. It was necessary to be with her and watch constantly to see that she did not harm anyone. At 6:30 P.M. all hands were on duty to try and discourage her from staying in the campground. She was finally driven away by throwing rocks, keeping her out of the campground. It was decided to patrol all night. She was not sighted in the campground until 4:20 A.M. and was last seen at 7:20 A.M.

A constant patrol continued all morning, to try and locate her, as Dr. Craighead was due in the area in the afternoon. She could not be located and was not seen until 3:20 P.M. about one mile from Old Faithful toward West Thumb. We all attempted to locate her and at 6:30 P.M. she was spotted in the Deer Tracks picnic area. We patrolled the Old Faithful campground until she was again spotted at 8:30 in the old section. It was too late for an accurate shot. It was then decided to wait until the following morning to attempt any shot.

At 6:00 A.M. on June 8, a visitor knocked on the door of Ranger Robinson's quarters and advised him that Sylvia and family were in Loop "B" of the campground. When Ranger Robinson arrived she was in the act of destroying visitor's ice chest valued at $15.00. The visitor wanted her driven away, but Ranger Robinson showed no interest whatsoever in chasing her.

Instead he contacted Dr. Craighead,[1] Maurice Hornocker,[2] Ken Miller, Jim Valder, and Darrell Coe, who all proceeded to find her. Dr. Craighead located her and with a cap-chur gun immobilized Sylvia,[3] also all of the cubs. They were loaded in the trap. Sylvia and one cub in one trap and two cubs in the other. Dr. Craighead stated her weight was 225 pounds.

During the time that she was in the area, thousands of people had the opportunity of seeing their first grizzly. We are still amazed that no one was injured. Sylvia seemed interested only in showing off her cubs. It is certainly a relief to have her away from the area and if she never comes back that will be soon enough.

[1] Frank Craighead and his brother, John, were engaged in a project to investigate important aspects of grizzly-bear ecology in Yellowstone Park, initiated in 1959 and supported by a five-year grant from the National Science Foundation and by annual grants from the Research and Exploration Committee of the National Geographic Society, the Wildlife Management Institute, the Boone and Crockett Club, and the National Park Service.

[2] Maurice Hornocker, of the Montana Co-operative Wildlife Research Unit, Montana State University, was also working on the project described in footnote 1 above. The Montana Fish and Game Commission also participated in this work.

[3] Craighead and Craighead, "Knocking Out Grizzlies for Their Own Good," *National Geographic Magazine*, Vol. 118, No. 2 (August, 1960), 276–91.

Alter, J. Cecil. *Jim Bridger*. Norman, University of Oklahoma Press, 1962.

Bell, Charles Napier, ed. *The Journal of Henry Kelsey, 1691–92*. Winnipeg, Dawson Richardson Publications, Limited, 1928.

Bell, Horace. *On the Old West Coast. Being Further Reminiscences of a Ranger*. New York, William Morrow & Company, 1930.

———. *Reminiscences of a Ranger; or, Early Times in Southern California*. Santa Barbara, Wallace Hebbard, 1927.

Bidwell, General John. *Echoes of the Past, an Account of the First Emigrant Train to California, Frémont in the Conquest of California, the Discovery of Gold and Early Reminiscences*. Chico, *Chico Advertiser*, no date.

Borthwick, J. D. *Three Years in California, 1851–54*. Edinburgh, Blackford & Sons, 1857.

Botkin, B. A., ed. *A Treasury of American Folk Lore, Stories, Ballads, and Traditions of the People*. New York, Crown Publishers, 1944.

Chittenden, General Hiram M. *The Yellowstone National Park*. Cincinnati, The Robert Clarke Company, 1899.

Clark, Frank. "The Killing of Old Ephraim," *Utah Fish and Game Bulletin*, Vol. 9, No. 8 (September, 1952).

Cooper, Courtney Ryley. *High Country: The Rockies Yesterday and Today*. Boston, Little, Brown & Company, 1926.

Craighead, Frank, and John Craighead. "Knocking Out Grizzlies for Their Own Good," *National Geographic Magazine*, Vol. 118, No. 2 (August, 1960).

Dana, Rocky, and Marie Harrington. *The Blond Ranchero: Memories of Juan Francisco Dana.* Los Angeles, Dawson's Book Shop, 1960.

Day, Beth. *Grizzlies in Their Back Yard.* New York, Julian Messner, Inc., 1956.

Dobie, J. Frank. *The Ben Lilly Legend.* Boston, Little, Brown & Company, 1950.

————. *A Guide to Life and Literature of the Southwest.* Dallas, Southern Methodist University Press, 1952.

————. "Juan Oso: My Mexican Bear Nights," *Southwest Review,* Vol. XIX, No. 1 (Autumn, 1933).

————. *Tongues of the Monte.* Boston, Little, Brown & Company, 1957.

Dodge, Col. Richard Irving. *The Plains of the Great West and Their Inhabitants, Being a Description of the Plains, Game, Indians, &c. of the Great North American Desert.* New York, G. P. Putnam's Sons, 1876. New York, Archer House, Inc., 1959.

Ellis, Edward S. *Kit Carson.* Chicago and New York, M. A. Donahue Company, 1889.

Estergreen, M. Morgan. *Kit Carson: A Portrait in Courage.* Norman, University of Oklahoma Press. 1962.

Godman, John Davidson, M.D. *American Natural History to which is Added the Ramblings of a Naturalist.* Philadelphia, R. W. Pomeroy, 1842.

Grey, Hugh, and Ross McCluskey, eds. *Field & Stream Treasury.* New York, Holt, Rinehart and Winston, 1955.

Harte, Bret. *Tales of the Argonauts and Other Sketches.* Boston, The Regent Press, 1875.

Hibben, Frank C. *Hunting American Bears.* Philadelphia and New York, J. B. Lippincott Company, 1950.

Hittell, Theodore H. *The Adventures of James C. Adams, Mountaineer and Grizzly Bear Hunter of California.* San Francisco, Town & Bacon, 1860.

Hornaday, William T. *Campfires In the Rockies.* New York, Charles Scribner's Sons, 1906.

Horzworth, John M. *The Wild Grizzlies of Alaska: A Story*

of the Grizzly and Big Brown Bears of Alaska, Their Habits, Manners, and Characteristics, together with Notes on Mountain Sheep and Caribou. Collected by the author for the United States Biological Survey. New York and London, G. P. Putnam's Sons, 1930.

Irving, Washington. *Astoria.* Ed. and with an introduction by Edgeley W. Todd. Norman, University of Oklahoma Press, 1964.

Judson, Katharine Berry. *Myths and Legends of Alaska.* Chicago, A. C. McClurg & Company, 1911.

———. *Myths and Legends of the Pacific Northwest.* Chicago, A. C. McClurg & Company, 1910.

Kelsey, Henry. *The Kelsey Papers.* Introduction by Arthur G. Doughty and Chester Martin. Ottawa, The Public Archives of Canada and the Public Record Office of Northern Ireland, 1929.

Lummis, Charles Fletcher. *Mesa, Cañon and Pueblo, Our Wonderland of the Southwest, Its Marvels of Nature, Its Pageant of the Earth Building, Its Strange Peoples; Its Centuried Romance.* New York and London, The Century Company, 1925.

McCracken, Harold. "The Alaska Grizzly," *Field & Stream* (February, 1920).

———. *The Beast That Walks Like Man.* New York, Doubleday & Company, Inc., 1955.

Martin, Martha. *Home On the Bear's Domain.* New York, Macmillan Company, 1954.

Miller, Joaquin. *True Bear Stories.* Chicago and New York, Rand, McNally & Company, 1900; Portland, Binfords & Mort, 1949.

Miller, Joseph. *Arizona: The Last Frontier.* New York, Hastings House, 1956.

Mills, Enos Abija. *The Grizzly: Our Greatest Wild Animal.* New York, Houghton Mifflin Company, 1919.

———. *The Rocky Mountain Wonderland.* Boston and New York, Houghton Mifflin Company, 1915.

———. *Wild Life On the Rockies.* Boston and New York, Houghton Mifflin Company, 1909.

Muir, John. *Our National Parks.* Boston and New York, Houghton Mifflin Company, 1901.

Nunis, Doyce B. Jr. *Andrew Sublette, Mountain Prince.* Los Angeles, Dawson's Book Store, 1960.

Roosevelt, Theodore. *Hunting Tales of the West.* New York, Current Literature Publishing Company, 1907.

————. *Hunting the Grisly and Other Sketches.* New York, G. P. Putnam's Sons, 1900.

————. *Hunting Trips of a Ranchman, Sketches of the Northern Cattle Plains.* New York and London, G. P. Putnam's Sons, 1885.

————. *The Works of Theodore Roosevelt.* Elkhorn Edition. New York, G. P. Putnam's Sons, 1893.

Ross, Alexander. *The Fur Hunters of the Far West.* Ed. by Kennith A. Spaulding. Norman, University of Oklahoma Press, 1956.

Russell, Charles M. *Trails Plowed Under.* New York, Doubleday & Company, Inc., 1927.

Ruxton, George Frederick. *Ruxton of the Rockies.* Ed. by LeRoy R. Hafen. Norman, University of Oklahoma Press, 1950.

Sabin, Edwin L. *Kit Carson Days.* Chicago, A. C. McClurg & Company, 1914.

Seton, Ernest Thompson. *The Biography of a Grizzly.* New York, The Century Company, 1900.

————. *Wild Animals at Home.* New York, Grosset & Dunlop, 1913.

Skinner, M. P. *Bears In the Yellowstone.* Chicago, A. C. McClurg & Company, 1925.

Stevens, Montague. *Meet Mr. Grizzly: A Saga on the Passing of the Grizzly.* Albuquerque, University of New Mexico Press, 1944.

Thompson, David. *David Thompson's Narrative.* Ed. by Richard Glover. Toronto, The Champlain Society, 1962.

Thwaites, Reuben Gold. *Original Journals of the Lewis and Clarke Expedition, 1804-6.* New York, Dodd, Mead & Company, 1904.

Vestal, Stanley. *Kit Carson, the Happy Warrior of the Old West:*

A Biography. Boston and New York, Houghton Mifflin Company, 1928.

Victor, Frances Fuller. *The River of the West. Life and Adventures in the Rocky Mountains and Oregon; Embracing the Events in the Life-time of a Mountain-Man and Pioneer: with the Early History of the North-Western Slope including an Account of the Fur Traders, the Indian Tribes, the Overland Immigration, the Oregon Missions, and the Tragic Fate of Rev. Dr. Whitman and Family. Also, a description of the Country, Its Condition, Prospects and Resources; Its Soil, Climate, and Scenery; Its Mountains, Rivers, Valleys, Deserts, and Plains; Its Inland Waters, and Natural Resources*. Hartford, Conn., and Toledo, Ohio, R. W. Bliss & Company; Newark, Bliss & Company; San Francisco, R. J. Trumbull & Company, 1870.

Winther, Oscar Osburn. *The Great Northwest: A History*. New York, Alfred A. Knopf, 1952.

Wright, William H. *The Grizzly Bear: The Narrative of a Hunter-Naturalist. Historical, Scientific and Adventurous*. New York, Charles Scribner's Sons, 1910.

Cap-shur-gun (used to tranquilize bears): 357
Caribou: hunted by McCracken, 299ff; killed by grizzlies, 301
Carillo, Don Carlos Antonio: 64
Carillo, Maria Josefa Petra del Carmen: 64
Carreta (Spanish cart) described: 64–66
Carrot River (Canada): 3n.
Carson, Kit: 41, 45–49
Cascade Mountains (Oregon and Washington): 92, 132n.
Cassidy, Hugh: 254
Cattlemen: 122; of North Dakota, 155ff.; of Arizona, hunt grizzlies, 210–14
Cave Landing (Santa Barbara County, Calif.): 64ff.
Centinela Canyon (Chihuahua, Mexico): 276
Central City, Colo.: 130–31
Central Park Menagerie (New York City): 174
Cerro del Carmen (Coahuila, Mexico): 262
Chaparral: 71, 76, 93, 96ff.; deer-brush, 141, 174
Chapman, Charles: 211
Chaquaqua Cañon: 128
Chelde, Ted: 338
Chico Valley: 59
Chihuahua, State of (Mexico): 263ff., 277ff.
Chihuahua City, Mexico: 262
Chinook jargon: 306
Chittenden, General Hiram M.: 347, 347n.
Chokecherries: 219, 342; eaten by grizzlies, 142
Churchill River (Canada): 5n.
Clark, Frank: 215–18
Clark, Captain William: 6ff., 21, 22
Claymore, Antoine: 39
Cleveland Museum of Natural History: 230
Clifton, Ariz.: 212ff.
Clifton *Copper Era*: 209–14
Clinton, De Witt: 20 & n.
Coahuila, State of (Mexico): 261
Coe, Darrell: 357
Coeur d'Alene, Idaho: 163
Cold (Morofski) Bay (Alaska Peninsula): 302

Colorado: Ruxton in, 50; Mills in, 182–92
Colorado River: 36
Columbia River: 30ff.; fur trade on, 25n.; Thompson explores, 13; mentioned by Adams, 92
Continental Divide: 130, 182ff.
Cooper, Courtney Ryley: 129 & n.
Cooper, Mrs. Courtney Ryley: 129
Cosper, J. H. T. (Toll): 210ff.
Cottonwood, Ariz.: 253
Cottonwood trees: 10, 38, 41, 70, 157; in Mexico, 267, 289
Cougars: 132n., 137, 160, 333; *see also* mountain lion
Coya Canyon (New Mexico): 235ff.
Coyotes: 71, feed on bear carcass, 198; in New Mexico, 233; in Nez Percé Indian legend, 342
Craighead, Frank, Jr.: 357n.
Craighead, John: 354ff., 357n.
Crescent Lake (California): 146
Crockett, David: 133
Cross Creeks of the Yellowstone River: 43
Curtis, George H.: 338

Dana, Juan Francisco: 64
Dana, Maria Josepha Petra del Carmen: 64
Dana, Ramon: 68
Dana, Rocky: 64
Dana, William Goodwin: 64
Day, Beth: 339
Day, John (fur trapper): 28–29
Dead Indian country (Oregon): 132n., 133ff.
Dead Indian Creek (Oregon): 134–35
Deer: 16–17, 60, 76, 105, 147, 178, 198, 221ff., 261ff., 276; hunted, 31–32; in Oregon, 132n., 134ff.; in Yosemite National Park, 147; blacktail in Montana, 219; seven "killed" by Don Santiago Blanco, 268–69; in Alaska, 322–25
Deering, Sir Edward: 4
Deering's Point (Canada): 3 & n., 4, 5n.
"Desert glass": 232
Dickinson, David: 253
Digger Indians: 331–32
Dobie, J. Frank: 182n., 221n., 261, 266ff.

Tuolme Indians: 2n., 92–106
Turkeys, wild: 128

Utah: 215–18

Vaca, Manuel: 60
Vacaville, Calif.: 60
Valder, Jim: 357
Verde Valley (Arizona): 253
Victor, Frances Fuller: 35 & n.

"Wahb" (orphaned grizzly cub): 193–97
Walker, General William: 72
Washington, grizzly bears in: 35 & n., 93, 163, 311
Wawona, Calif.: 146
Webster, Reese: 214
West, Ray B.: 215n.
West Thumb (Yellowstone National Park): 349ff.
Whaley, Kip: 253
White, Stewart Edward, quoted: 254
White Mountains (Arizona): 214, 252, 254, 256

Wild Basin (Colorado): 182
Wild cats: 70, 132n.
Wildlife Management Institute: 357n.
Willamette Valley (Oregon): 35
Willows: 9, 62, 189, 217, 342
Wolves: 97; mentioned by Lewis, 9; hunted by Ross, 32; tamed by Adams, 101, 105; prey on grizzlies, 160
Wright, William H.: 91, 163–74, 175–81

Yankee Doodle Lake (Colorado): 129
Yaqui Indians: 266, 294
Yaqui River (Mexico): 263
Yellowstone country: 36; fur trappers in, 42
Yellowstone National Park: 35, 347–57
Yellowstone Park Company: 354
Yellowstone River: 36ff.; fur trappers on, 40–41; Cross Creeks of, 43
York Fort (Canada): 3 & n.
Yosemite National Park, grizzly bears in: 141–51
Yosemite Valley (California): 143
Yucca: 284

www.ingramcontent.com/pod-product-compliance
Lightning Source LLC
Chambersburg PA
CBHW020523270326
41927CB00006B/421